# VENTURE CAPITAL

# Small Business Management Series
### Rick Stephan Hayes, Editor

*Simplified Accounting for Non-Accountants*
 by Rick Stephan Hayes and C. Richard Baker

*Accounting for Small Manufacturers*
 by C. Richard Baker and Rick Stephan Hayes

*Simplified Accounting for Engineering and Technical Consultants*
 by Rick Stephan Hayes and C. Richard Baker

*Simplified Accounting for the Computer Industry*
 by Rick Stephan Hayes and C. Richard Baker

*The Complete Legal Guide for Your Small Business*
 by Paul Adams

*Running Your Own Show: Mastering Basics of Small Business*
 by Richard T. Curtin

*Up Front Financing: The Entrepreneur's Guide*
 by A. David Silver

*How to Finance Your Small Business with Government Money:
SBA and Other Loans, Second Edition*
 by Rick Stephan Hayes and John Cotton Howell

*The Entrepreneurial Life: How to Go For It and Get It*
 by A. David Silver

*The Complete Guide to Buying and Selling a Business*
 by Arnold S. Goldstein

*Getting Paid: A Step-by-Step Credit & Collection Program that Shows
You How to Get Them to Pay and What to Do
If They Don't*
 by Arnold S. Goldstein

*Choosing Your Sources of Venture Capital*
 by A. David Silver

*Starting on a Shoestring*
 by Arnold S. Goldstein

*The Fundamentals of the Business Plan:
A Step by Step Approach*
 by Harold McLaughlin

*Venture Capital: The Complete Guide for Investors*
 by A. David Silver

# VENTURE CAPITAL

## The Complete Guide
## for Investors

A. David Silver

A Ronald Press Publication

**JOHN WILEY & SONS**

New York   Chichester   Brisbane   Toronto   Singapore

*Library of Congress Cataloging in Publication Data:*

Silver, A. David (Aaron David), 1941–
    Venture capital.

    (Small business management series, ISSN 0737-7290)
    Includes index.
    1. Venture capital–Handbooks, manuals, etc.
I. Title.  II. Series.

HG4751.S55   1985        332.6'6        84-19479
ISBN 0-471-88029-9

Printed in the United States of America

10   9   8   7   6   5   4   3   2   1

*To*

*Louis Werner*

# PREFACE

Venture capitalists are perceived by entrepreneurs, I believe with some validity, as enigmatic individuals. We show appreciation for an entrepreneur's carefully and creatively formulated business plan by demanding to own more of it. That frequently leads to a declining enthusiasm on the part of the entrepreneur, until after further negotiation, a deal is struck. The entrepreneur and the venture capitalist "live together" for 3 to 5 years, toward the mutual goal of a public offering or sale of the entrepreneur's business at a higher price than management or the venture capitalist paid. Occasionally, the process works smoothly.

The objective of this book is to provide information about the various steps in the venture capital investment process. Venture capitalism is an active rather than a passive profession. Venture capitalists act rather than react. They respond to bad news from a portfolio company manager by visiting the company, listening to the problems, and making changes. They add value to a portfolio company by showing its principals how to do certain things, making introductions where needed, and facilitating the rapid growth and development of the company. No other class of lender or investor takes as active a role in his portfolio companies as does the venture capitalist. It must be one of the more personally satisfying professions, because none of its players has ever left the field willingly. (Some, however, were forced to leave when they ran out of money.) The founders of the modern venture capital industry who have not died are still at it, even though they are in their seventies and eighties.

Success in venture capital investing requires the mastery of a complex set of skills, knowledge of people and markets, the matu-

rity to handle large sums of other people's money, and the enthusiasm and drive of an entrepreneur. Venture capitalists are the
principal facilitators of innovation and change in the world. They
are the angels to entrepreneurs, who solve problems for large
numbers of people, and create change, value, and wealth. To
achieve success in venture capital investing is to facilitate the
entrepreneurial process.

This book attempts to describe the fundamentals necessary to
launch a venture capital fund and the process for successful venture capital investing. The critical ingredients of maturity, verbal
skills, enthusiasm, and drive must come from many other sources.
Chapter 1 describes the methods of forming a venture capital
fund. There are optimal formations, such as the limited partnership, and sub-optimal formations, such as the corporate venture
capital subsidiary, as well as a variety of workable forms in between. It is important that the venture capitalist operate with a
certain amount of capital, that his goals and objectives are perfectly synchronous with those of his sponsors, and that the
boundaries of the relationship between sponsors and venture capitalist are clearly defined. To attempt to operate in a sub-optimal
environment can lead to a loss of both capital and mutual
satisfaction.

The selection of personnel to make investment decisions for the
venture capital fund is addressed in Chapter 1 as well. The objective is to assemble a group of individuals with the experience to do
effective pre-investment due diligence and post-investment monitoring of all investments, to add value to the portfolio companies,
to bring in other sources of capital, to rescue the companies when
they enter a troubled period, and to assist in liquidifying the investments when they reach maturity. The ideal management team
is not usually assembled, because it is rare to locate these technical, operational, and financial skills in one or two people. Even if
this team could be found and assembled, it may be difficult to
compensate people at this experience level within the constraints
of the 2% management fee that a fund manager typically can
charge investors. However, there are satisfactory methods for
compensating highly skilled personnel without having to charge
the investors a proportionately higher management fee. It requires

a knowledge of leveraging one's experience and one's talent. Chapter 1 also addresses the issue of how a venture capitalist assembles capital to begin a fund and provides a handbook for raising a venture capital fund. There are a number of traditional sponsors of venture capital funds and the reasons for their enthusiasm is discussed in this chapter as well.

Successful venture capital funds employ several unique means of attracting a large flow of investment opportunities (referred to as "deals") and attracting or creating deals of high quality. Chapter 2 discusses the most effective deal generation plans, which combine the following interwoven features: (1) *Public relations:* creating an image of the venture capital fund as a financial partner—one that adds value beyond capital—that highly qualified entrepreneurs would most like to deal with; (2) *Locating the best opportunities:* there exist certain ferreting techniques designed to locate attractive deals in the newest breakthrough industries and to create an entrepreneurial team capable of developing solutions to problems thus identified; and (3) *Extensive networking:* the financial communities of New York, San Francisco, Chicago, Dallas, and other major money-market centers frequently generate a higher-quality deal flow, because it is pre-sifted by people experienced in selling money to deals or deals to money.

Venture capital funds that rely on other funds to invite them into syndicates will obtain a reputation for slothfulness in investigating deals. If a passive investor begins to reject deals, it will lose its flow of deals from other funds. Thus, it must accept a high percentage of the deals offered to it, which leads to slothful investigation procedures.

The due diligence process is the subject of Chapter 3. When things go wrong in a venture capital investment, they do so for one or more of five basic reasons:

1. Faulty business plan.
2. Incompetent management.
3. The market failed to develop.
4. Bad luck.
5. Overpayment for the investment.

Because most of these problems can be avoided by a thorough due diligence process, before the investment is made, the venture capital fund's process is exhaustive. No fewer than 20 references on the entrepreneurs and senior managers and six references on middle management must be checked and key documents such as college and graduate school transcripts must be collected and reviewed prior to investing. The venture capital funds must conduct five exhaustive audits prior to investing:

1. Business plan audit.
2. Market size audit.
3. People audit.
4. Financial audit.
5. Legal audit.

The results of the five audits must be maintained in the fund's files to be reviewed by potentially interested co-investors and to serve as a master source of information for monitoring purposes.

Large venture capital funds that must invest substantial sums in individual companies obviate the need to invest with others. Known as Megafunds because of their enormous sums of money, they are likely to achieve lower rates of return than if they had fewer dollars to husband carefully. Syndicate formation and co-investing with sophisticated investors is a critical aspect of venture capital investing. How else can a venture capitalist test the *price* he is paying for a deal, unless that price is tested with other buyers? The choice of venture capital co-investors should be based on several factors. These include:

1. Monitoring abilities.
2. Networking abilities.
3. Size of fund and amounts available.
4. Geography.
5. Age of fund.
6. Experience of personnel.

One venture capital fund is not able to monitor every investment that it makes as closely as it would like to, unless it makes investments on a syndicated basis with hardworking, experienced venture capital funds. Chapter 4 discusses the principles and methodology of syndicate formation.

The methodology and basis for evaluating and selecting the terms of investment are also subjects of Chapter 4. Valuation is a dynamic rather than a static discipline. It changes with supply of venture capital and the demand for entrepreneurial opportunities. Yet it lends itself to fundamental systems and equations which experienced venture capitalists fasten onto. The terms and conditions of investment are also based on fundamentals that have worked well over the past 15 years. There is a network among venture capitalists in which terms and conditions that have been used successfully are discussed. Although this subject can be dealt with at great length by attorneys skilled in structuring venture capital investments, Chapter 4 covers the primary terms and conditions and explains why they are important. A good term sheet never made a good investment, but it has saved bad investments from becoming total losses. Terms and conditions of investing relate in an important way to monitoring.

A venture capitalist should attempt to be apprised of and to participate in all major decisions of each investment, at least until the companies are cash-flow positive, through board involvement (and by being vocal at board meetings) and through the terms of the investment agreements. The objective of close monitoring and carefully drafted, fairly restrictive documents, is to set up early warning signals that indicate when an investment is in trouble. The venture capitalist can take the necessary steps to protect the investment before it gets into more serious difficulty if he is a close monitor.

One general partner of the fund and, when possible, an experienced manager from a related field known to the venture capital fund, should go onto every board of directors or obtain a right of attendance at board meetings of every portfolio company. Actual monthly results should be compared with budgets and material differences should be explored at board meetings. If there are major differences, the investment agreement and associated documents will permit the fund to act quickly to protect its investment. Monitoring is discussed in Chapter 5.

The general partners of the fund, in many cases, will have considerably more experience launching start-up and early-stage companies than the entrepreneurs whom they invest in. Further, many entrepreneurs do not understand how to network in industry, how to leverage suppliers, customers, and banks, and how to accomplish difficult tasks quickly. A venture capitalist should be able to help portfolio company managers locate, interview, and hire key personnel; obtain additional rounds of financing; make OEM sales; borrow money from banks; and obtain licenses, government contracts, joint-ventures, and other transactions that are frequently beyond the knowledge base, abilities, and time constraints of portfolio company managements. Methods of adding value are discussed in Chapter 5.

Venture capitalists are required to assist portfolio companies in finding qualified investment bankers for initial public offerings and subsequent rounds of long-term financing, and in arranging second-stage financings and buy-outs with large industrial corporations.

Venture capitalists should use their numerous contacts in the principal financial communities and introduce portfolio companies to a wide range of different underwriters. They should be able to assist portfolio companies in arranging R&D tax shelters, long-term debt, short-term debt, and various other financings.

Venture capitalists should maintain a data base of acquirors of small, rapidly growing, high technology companies. In the event that a portfolio company's management team is not demonstrating signs of maturity to assure long-term profitable growth, the venture capital fund should act quickly to arrange a sale of the company to an acquisitive corporation. Chapter 7 describes the methodology of selling and liquidifying.

Portfolio management is the final subject, and it means that a venture capital fund should have a business plan and a strategy and should attempt to follow it. It should diversify its investments over time, across different industries, and in several geographic regions.

If all of the investments are in start-ups, the investors would rely heavily on a good initial public offering market 2–3 years hence to achieve liquidity. If the nation is in a deep recession at that time, with very few new issues, the fund would be in jeopardy. Further, if most of the investments are in the computer industry, a sudden change in that industry's direction by IBM or another leader could seriously jeopardize the portfolio.

Thus, the venture capital funds should strive to diversify their portfolios among the three stages of venture capital investing: start-up, first stage, and second stage. Although the preponderance of investments should be in the fund's geographic region, the general partners should invest a meaningful amount of the fund's capital outside the region.

The material given above represents an introduction to and overview of the subjects covered in the textual material. Each of these disciplines is explored in depth in the chapters that follow.

A. DAVID SILVER

*Sante Fe, New Mexico*
*November 1984*

# ACKNOWLEDGMENTS

I have worked in banking and venture capital for nearly two decades. Certain lenders and investors with whom I have been associated in banking have provided priceless information by their actions as much as their words. Barry F. Sullivan, President of First National Bank of Chicago and my first boss, is among the most creative and energetic commercial bankers in the country. He has been instrumental in bringing banking out of the Dark Ages. Maynard S. Wishner, former President, Walter Heller & Co., Inc., would enter the conference room where a nervous applicant sat, roll up his sleeves and say, "Let's see how we can make this loan." Heller made loans at prime plus 5 that could have been bankable, but for the fact that Maynard Wishner knew how to sell money. Henry E. Singleton, Chairman of Teledyne Corp., is an exceptional entrepreneur and manager. Interfacing with him in his cramped offices behind his gun metal grey desk in Hawthorne, California in the late 1960's was a lesson in venture management. I spent many hours with the late Charles V. Tandy, founder of Tandy Corp., at the time he was introducing microcomputers to 6000 Radio Shack stores. His combination of intelligence, courage, and humor provided me with some additional insights.

Among the first entrepreneurs with whom I worked and from whom I learned were Henry Taub and Frank R. Lautenberg of Automatic Data Processing, Glen A. Robinson of Scientific Atlanta and Andre A. Blay of Magnetic Video Corp., four of the most successful entrepreneurs of the 1970's.

Among the venture capitalists with whom I have worked closely, my Hall of Fame would select for its first five inductees, Royal Little, Tommy J. Davis, Don A. Christensen, Robert G. Davidoff, and

Timothy A. G. Hay. I do not know, nor do I care, if these five have garnered the most success. But few are the entrepreneurs or venture capitalists who have not had a life-changing experience from having worked with them on a company launch or expansion.

The engineering, production, and marketing staff for this book have been with me on three others, and they get better with age. These talented people include Dorothy E. Moore, Michael J. Hamilton, my editor, Marilyn D. Dibbs, and Mary Daniello. Working with John Wiley & Sons is a pleasure from top to bottom.

A happy man's best investment is the time he spends with his family. Watching the joy on a child's face when he blows out the candles on his birthday cake or runs in a field with friends, or sharing a spouse's sense of fulfillment and accomplishment, is all the reward I have ever sought for the many hours spent in the company-launching business. My family has the form and rhythm that I so tenaciously seek in others because Jerilyn, Claude, and Caleb Silver have so richly provided it.

A. D. S.

# CONTENTS

1   Formation of a Venture Capital Fund                          1

2   Generating a Deal Flow                                       47

3   The Due Diligence Process                                    79

4   Valuation, Terms, and Conditions                            195

5   Monitoring and Adding Value                                 219

6   Selling, Liquidifying, and Portfolio Management             231

Appendix                                                        251

Index                                                           253

# VENTURE CAPITAL

# FORMATION OF A VENTURE CAPITAL FUND

The first step in the venture capital process is to raise a pool of capital. Sponsors of or investors in venture capital funds are usually "sophisticated" private individuals, financial institutions whose principal business is making loans and investments, and individual corporations that seek additional advantages from their sponsorship of a venture capital fund. The optimal sponsorship arrangement of a venture capital fund is a blind pool or limited partnership in which financial institutions place a portion of their capital under management with a group of experienced venture capitalists who charge a management fee plus a share of the capital gains that are generated. The general partners or managers have a fiduciary responsibility to protect the capital invested by the limited partners while investing it in companies that meet the criteria and objectives agreed to at the outset. The general partners' share in the partnership's capital gain is made available, as a rule, only after it has increased the partnership's assets by 100%. Typically, there are numerous restrictions placed on the general partner which might include a prohibition on starting a subsequent venture capital fund until certain thresholds are reached and a prohibition on investment activities of the members of the general partner.

## SKILLS OF MEMBERS OF THE GENERAL PARTNER

It is a requirement of the marketplace that venture capital funds be managed by a general partner whose members are experienced

venture capitalists. The greater the experience of the general partner, the more capital it will be able to raise from investors. The
word "experience" means having done each of the functional
steps in the venture capital process for at least 5 years. Although
investment bankers, former entrepreneurs, financial journalists,
and certain other categories of participants in the venture capital
industry may seek to raise money to launch venture capital funds,
they do not as a rule realize their objective, or if so, only after major
modifications in their original plans. Their experiences in the venture capital industry have addressed certain functional areas, but
not all. The key is direct experience, and a honing of the requisite
skills in the functional areas cited in Exhibit 1.

Although it is frequently not possible for all members of the general partner to have lengthy track records in each of the functional
areas of venture capital investing, the combination of skills among
the managers should equal at least eight. For example, an executive of a rapidly growing high technology company, an executive of
a bank-owned small business investment company and a management consultant experienced in fixing small, troubled companies
would be likely to have sharpened skills in the pertinent functional shown in Exhibit 2.

In this example, there is considerable positive overlap, particularly in the post-investment areas of Monitoring and Adding value.
The financial and analytical areas—Structuring the terms,
Syndicating and Portfolio management—are emphasized less in
comparison with the active, hands-on functional areas of Moni-

**EXHIBIT 1.   The Eight Functions of
Venture Capital Investing**

Deal generation
Due diligence process
Structuring the terms and conditions
Syndicating the investment
Monitoring
Adding value to portfolio companies
Selling and liquidifying
Portfolio management

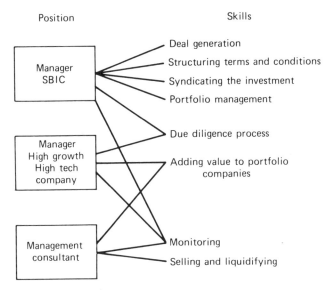

**EXHIBIT 2.** Combining Skills to Form a Venture Capital Management Company

toring and Adding value. The management team in Exhibit 2 is more likely to become very actively involved in its portfolio companies in management areas where the general partners can be helpful to the entrepreneurial team. These activities might include hiring, setting up production, designing a marketing plan, raising additional capital, and making acquisitions. The management team's perceived inadequacies in the financial and analytical areas could be strengthened at the staff level or through the use of consultants.

An alternative and quite acceptable management team would include two members of a small business investment company or venture capital subsidiary of a large corporation plus one former entrepreneur or manager of a rapidly growing company in a similar industry to the partnership's investment objectives. The skill areas of venture capital members of the management team should be broad without excessive duplication. For example, one of the two might have more contacts to enhance syndication and selling of mature investments to the public while the other might be experienced in deal generation. The growth company manager would shoulder more of the burden of monitoring and adding value to portfolio companies. Should the manager's duties become over-bearing, a staff person or consultants could be employed.

Three experienced venture capitalists, where each is a full-time, dedicated general partner, seems to be the optimal management team for managing a venture capital fund. In the earlier days of the venture capital industry, there were generally two general partners, but the funds were smaller. Kleiner & Perkins' first fund operated with $8.8 million. Davis & Rock had less than $5 million in capital. These two original venture capital funds, *circa* 1968, created legendary capital gains, yet none of the four individuals had experience in the venture capital industry. Other two-person teams of the 1968–1970 period that were successful include Hambrecht & Quist and Geiger & Fialkov. The skills that these individuals possessed were operating experience in rapidly emerging, usually high technology, companies and financial analysis. For example, Herman Fialkov had been a co-founder of General Instruments Corp. and Richard Geiger had been a securities analyst and portfolio manager. As the venture capital industry matured, the size of venture capital funds increased, which created the need for the third general partner. Indeed, the $350 million Warburg, Pincus & Co. venture capital fund formed in 1983 has an eight-person management team. The subject of the optimal capitalization for venture capital investing will be addressed shortly; but it remains to be proven that $350 million, or for that matter $150 million, can be invested and managed as carefully as $25 million or $50 million.

## INADEQUATE SUBSTITUTES FOR SKILL AND EXPERIENCE

Alternative management team structures have been created, with a high degree of success in raising capital, where the sponsorship and the endorsement of an experienced organization are substituted for skill and experience. For example, a venture capital fund in San Francisco with an excellent 10-year track record will become one of the members of a management team in another geographic region and will agree to assist the management of the regional fund in the areas of due diligence, structuring the terms, syndicating, and selling. Typically, the local managers are not experienced in venture capital investing, but perhaps have managed growth companies in the region, and are believed to be capable in deal generation, monitoring, and adding value.

Skill and experience at the local level cannot be substituted for a management contract with a distant skillful and experienced venture capital management company. The relationship of local ferrets and experienced operating personnel locating the deals, investigating them, and then discussing them with experienced venture capitalists in Silicon Valley or New York may sound good on paper. The plan may even work fairly well for a few years.

But what happens to the regional venture capital fund when its portfolio gets into trouble and the economy puts its foot on the neck of the fund's companies as well as the neck of the Silicon Valley advisor's companies? Can the distant fund staffed with experienced venture capitalists be responsive to the regional clone? It seems unlikely.

If 12 out of 15 portfolio companies in the smaller fund's investments simultaneously encounter serious business problems at a time when the economy enters a liquidity crisis and business downturn, the cloned regional fund will be inadequately staffed with skilled rescue personnel. Whereas the local staff could normally call upon the experienced venture capitalists for assistance in stabilizing its portfolio, calls for aid are not even answered because of fire-fighting back at Silicon Valley. The regional fund's portfolio shrinks in value or is written off for lack of managers experienced in work-outs and turn-arounds. Although joint-ventures may work effectively with products, when it comes to the services of a handful of skilled individuals, the probability of a joint-venture succeeding is slim.

The Silicon Valley venture capital industry has prospered mightily in the 7-year period beginning in 1976. The microchip, recombinant DNA, and the communications satellite have created hundreds of exceptional opportunities for venture capital investing. And the West Coast has had its fair share of the winners. In fact, difficult economic times have been rare in the portfolios of West Coast venture capital funds. Thus, experience in work-outs, reorganizations in bankruptcy, and turn-arounds is fairly uncommon among Silicon Valley venture capitalists. Therefore, if they sponsor a regional venture capital fund and advertise their monitoring skills, it is dubious that they could be effective at all in troubled times. People skills can be multiplied in the venture capital business if the time is available and the portfolio companies are not spread out geographically. The joint-ventured management company that relies on certain people skills imported from afar is not a suitable form during troubled economic times.

## CORPORATE-SPONSORED VENTURE CAPITAL FUNDS

A variation on the joint-ventured management company is the corporate-sponsored venture capital investment company. There is a short but interesting history of corporations forming venture capital investment companies or divisions. Corporations as large as Exxon and as small as Vulcan Engineering have entered the venture capital business for many reasons, most of them unrelated to the primary purpose of achieving maximum capital appreciation in the shortest period of time. The reasons range from windows onto innovation to cross-fertilizing entrepreneurs and corporate managers so that some of each might rub off on the other. Since 1972, the results have been negative in over 40 instances. There is nothing to suggest that if the source of capital for a new venture capital fund is a corporation, the fund would be a positive experience for investors and managers.

There are several reasons for this, the most important of which are the following: inability to adequately compensate the fund's management, unwillingness to fund the division in advance, lack of flexibility to accommodate changes in the status of portfolio companies, and changes in the corporation's senior management that could affect operations in the venture capital division.

### Compensation

Skilled venture capitalists typically earn equity interests in the portfolio companies in which they invest. It is this "piece of the action" shared by the entrepreneur, manager, and venture capitalist which more than any other factor, causes these three individuals to work closely toward a common goal. It is frequently the case that corporations lack the mechanism to enable certain employees to be able to participate in the common stock of the portfolio companies. Thus, the venture capitalists generally leave the corporation, causing temporary disruptions in the venture capital division and frequent indecision about agreements between portfolio company managements and the venture capital division. They leave under three conditions: (1) the corporation's portfolio does well and the venture capitalists leave to launch their own fund in which they can have ownership; (2) the corporation's portfolio has performed satisfactorily—50% winners, let us say—and other venture capital funds lure the corporate venture capitalists away and reward them with equity; and (3) the corporation's portfolio does poorly and the venture capitalists leave before blame can be attributed to them. In any event—success, average performance, or failure—the corporation is generally unable to properly compensate its in-house venture capitalists. They will leave to obtain an equity interest if they excel at the business. Although several corporations have attempted to create bastardized forms of compensation that include equity interests, the hierarchical structure of most large corporations prevents them from being competitive for the most skilled venture capitalists. Their inability to hold onto skilled venture capitalists while at the same time providing a training ground, has been a positive factor in the creation of numerous venture capital funds whose general partners at one time sang from the corporate choir book.

## Funding

Corporations will frequently create and staff their venture capital divisions, but require that the managers obtain funding on a deal by deal basis subject to the approval of a small executive committee within the organization. There are frequently excellent reasons for the corporation to behave in this manner, but it can delay the venture capital division from responding to funding deadlines at the portfolio company level. It may take a week or two to produce a signed check or bank wire transfer within a large corporation, that delay could be intolerable for a small company with payroll or critical ordering deadlines for which it did not adequately prepare.

Some of the stories of corporations forming venture capital subsidiaries and funding them in advance can make one's hair stand on end. In 1971, when President Nixon devalued the dollar, the Japanese conglomerate Mitsubishi was caught unaware with billions of dollars in U.S. banks. These dollars, if converted to yen, would have bought substantially fewer Japanese goods and services. Thus, Mitsubishi decided to invest the billions in U.S. goods and services. It retained the firms of McKinsey & Co. and Morgan, Stanley & Co. to locate suitable investments. One of their recommendations was to form a venture capital investment company. Mitsubishi thought that was an excellent idea, but only if the principal managers were of Japanese origin.

There were, at the time, no experienced Japanese-American venture capitalists in the handful of venture capital funds and small business investment companies. Undaunted, McKinsey & Co. and Mitsubishi located a Japanese psychiatrist and a Japanese aerospace engineer who collectively became the chief executive officers of Mitsubishi's venture capital subsidiary charged with investing $150 million in appropriate technologies. The opportunity exceeded their ability to seize it and within a year, with losses and shut-downs where once there was Mitsubishi's cash, the venture division was shut down.

One could say arguably that the $150 million would have been lost in the eventual conversion to yen anyway, and at least the money got a little exercise before it went down the sewer. Another argument is that Mitsubishi's timing was off; several funds that invested the bulk of their capital in 1970 to 1971 (if they did not have Federal Express in the portfolio—all three rounds of equity financing) did not perform all that well. There are other tales of woe in the anthology of corporate venture capital operations. It is remembered that Eaton Corp. surveyed the scene in 1971 as well and ventured into the business, staffing its division with two young staff members from corporate planning. Eaton's Chairman held onto the check-signing power. Their first investment of approximately $600,000 was in a company that was going to automate, by using some sort of blower, the manner in which stucco was affixed to buildings. It went out of business within a year. The second investment of about the same size had a quicker, less painful demise. Its entrepreneur cashed the check and skipped to South America. With that combined experience, Eaton reexamined its venture capital division under better lighting and exited poorer but wiser.

## Flexibility

Corporate venture capital subsidiaries, because they are such cumbersome, slow-moving creatures, are not the preferred syndicate partner of venture capital partnerships. Because of their responsibility to public stockholders, and the glare of the Securities & Exchange Commission, the press, respective congressmen, and other regulatory agencies, corporations are slow to react. Sometimes they get confused by a myriad of conflicting internal and external regulations. For instance, Exxon's once brightly-heralded venture capital subsidiary, Exxon Enterprises, Inc., was prohibited by internal regulations from owning a minority interest in publicly-held companies. Thus, it was disinclined to invest in enterprises that were public or to liquidify its successful investment via the new issue route. Its reasons dated back to the trust-busting era when the old Standard Oil was censured for aggressive investing. But why make that rule apply to Exxon Enterprises, which had a requirement to diversify, liquidify, and permit the entrepreneurs whom it backed to enjoy wealth if they did a good job? It became difficult for inflexible Exxon to find co-investors, because of the stiffness of its rule on minority positions in small, public companies. Syndicating is a means of letting others aid in the monitoring of portfolio companies and testing the prices paid. Suffice it to say that Exxon Enterprises acquired its successful information processing companies, created an operating company called Exxon Office Systems, and then destroyed everyone's incentive to work for it. Exxon's venture capitalists left to start partnerships and the entrepreneurs left to start new companies, in several instances obtaining launch capital from Exxon Enterprises alumni.

Time, Inc. had a venture capital activity for several years in the mid-1970's that shot itself in the foot because of its inflexibility. Time made some interesting investments that bore absolutely no relationship to one another. Three come to mind: a company with a proprietary process for making cotton yarn from yarn leavings gathered in the air and from the floor of cotton mills plus a stiffening fiber; a chain of racquetball clubs in Michigan which it renamed Sports Illustrated Racquetball Clubs, Inc. and offered free magazine subscriptions to new members; and Atari, Inc., the pioneer video game developer.

Mayfield Fund was the lead venture capital investor in Atari and it had its favorite Silicon Valley syndicate partners to whom it offered a piece of the Atari deal. But Time had its minions combing Sunnyvale and Cupertino for high technology start-ups and it knocked on Mayfield's door one day when the Atari investment was being put together. Time pleaded to be let into the deal and Tommy J. Davis, Mayfield's managing general partner, violating his wisdom of taking in inexperienced and distant partners, agreed that Time could have $500,000 of the financing.

At the closing 4 weeks later, Mayfield and Capital Management, another Silicon Valley fund, arrived with their signed documents and checks. Time arrived with several pages of questions from its counsel concerning the documents. Corporate counsel frequently is not aware of the conventional terms and conditions of investment agreements used in venture capital financings. Their world is much larger financings where they protect the borrower rather than the lender. Although not a priori inflexible, corporate counsel is not particularly suited to provide legal advice to a venture capital subsidiary.

A venture capitalist can locate a more responsive, less regulation-bound source of capital than a corporation. Even when the requirements of funding and flexibility are met, the corporate executives who chiselled the deal in stone with the venture capitalist may be replaced and the new executives may have a strong dislike for venture capital. Or, hard times can befall a corporation, forcing it to pull cash out of all areas. This happened to The Singer Co. in the mid-1970's, when drastic cuts were made across the board to save the parent. Its venture capital division was leveled, leaving the portfolio of entrepreneurial companies without financial backing or support.

## INVESTMENT BANKING SPONSORED FUNDS

Venture capital funds sponsored by investment banking firms have been popular since the democratizing of investment banks in the early 1970's. Note that the old line investment banking houses have remained essentially fiefdoms for their bright and well-heeled partners to become brighter and wealthier. For example, Morgan,

Stanley & Co., Goldman, Sachs & Co., and my former employer, Lehman Brothers, Kuhn Loeb, have not formed venture capital funds managed by their corporate finance departments. The partners in these firms and certain other old line houses act individually or collectively in the capacity of a venture capital fund. They are essentially passive investors and their venture capital investments do not constitute their primary activity. Thus, entrepreneurs are less well serviced by the old-time investment banking firms.

The democratized investment banks—those that began in the 1960's to offer partnerships to young people, women, and others based on their abilities—have enjoyed rapid growth and success in a number of ancillary service areas. To those more entrepreneurial investment banks, creating a venture capital fund within the corporate finance department was part of an overall plan to develop several new profit centers, such as a research or trading department in options, international securities, or launching a tax shelter or mergers and acquisitions activity within the corporate finance department.

Merrill Lynch Pierce Fenner & Smith perhaps typifies the expansion mode of the democratized investment banks. It offers a multitude of products one might normally associate with commercial banking. And Walter Wriston, the former Chairman of Citicorp said only partly in jest in a 1980 speech: "The most aggressive commercial bank in the country is Merrill Lynch." "The thundering herd," as it is known on Wall Street, formed a venture capital fund in 1981 and hired two skilled corporate venture capitalists to manage it: George Kokkinakis, formerly with Exxon Enterprises and Bruce Shewmaker, formerly with Time, Inc. The fund was capitalized at $60 million and Merrill Lynch placed the issue privately in units of $5000 each. It is too early to tell if Merrill Lynch Venture Capital Ltd. will succeed; that will depend to a great extent on the reward system for its management and the relations between Merrill Lynch and the venture capital fund. Certain conditions that could lead to conflict require discussion.

The primary objective of an investment bank is to generate fee income from arranging public and private financings and for providing other services for its corporate clients. When an investment bank forms a venture capital fund and becomes a part owner of its general partner, the investment bank's corporate clients could claim that they are now receiving less attention than before. Moreover, the investors in the fund could claim that the purpose of the fund is to incubate underwriting clients, and that they are less well served because of the need to fuel the underwriter with product from the fund. When the fledgling investment bank of Hambrecht & Quist attempted to launch its first venture capital fund in 1969, it was turned down repeatedly by institutional investors, primarily for just that reason. Several years later, Hambrecht & Quist successfully raised a $20 million venture capital fund, and it has established an excellent reputation in venture capital as well as investment banking in the late 1970's and early 1980's. At this point in time, H&Q, as it is known, is very actively multiplying itself by creating regional clones and spin-offs: H&Q-Arizona and H&Q-Larry Mohr. The former typifies the regional joint venture and the latter is a joint venture between a former senior officer in H&Q's venture capital fund and H&Q. Mr. Mohr doubtless wanted an opportunity to become the managing general partner of a venture capital fund and H&Q was willing to endorse him in exchange for part ownership in Mr. Mohr's management company.

H&Q has carried the conflict of interest problem on its back for very many miles and very successfully, in terms of raising capital. When an entrepreneur enters the doors at one of H&Q's many offices throughout the country, the entrepreneur could be calling on one or all of the following partnerships managed and owned in whole or in part by Hambrecht & Quist:

H&Q Ventures I

H&Q Ventures II

H&Q Ventures III

H&Q Ventures IV

H&Q–Arizona

H&Q–Mohr

H&Q Corporate Finance

Is this the hall of mirrors? Does the entrepreneur have a voice in which of the partnerships invests in his company? If, for example, H&Q IV makes the investment, will the entrepreneur receive as much attention from the H&Q person in H&Q IV who seems to know his company so well if that person is an employee of H&Q IV but owns some of the management company of H&Q–Mohr? The answer is that if the person has the time to assist the entrepreneur in H&Q IV's portfolio, he will probably do so, even though he cannot benefit personally. However, if time becomes a premium and the portfolio of H&Q–Mohr begins to take in water, the entrepreneur in the H&Q IV portfolio will become less well served. In fact, neglect could lead to financial difficulties and failure. If too many fail, who will be the first to point the finger? The investors.

The investors stand to suffer in two ways. First, assume an investor is in Fund No. 2, but not Fund No. 4. Further assume that Federal Express becomes a portfolio company of Fund No. 2 but not Fund No. 4. The gain of 50 times cost is not passed through to the investor in Fund No. 4. Since the personnel in the two funds are similar, why was the investor deprived of this particular gain? As the venture capital industry matures, it will have to deal more wisely with the issue of conflicts. As in other fields, it takes a legal action from a "damaged" party to call for all the cards to be turned face up. This has not yet occurred.

The opposite situation, where Fund No. 4 invests in Osborne Computer Corp., a loser, and Fund No. 2 does not, and the former takes a loss while the latter does not, suggests a conflict of interest situation as open to criticism as the former. These situations are not indigenous to investment bank-sponsored venture capital funds. However, it is just these kinds of funds that tend to multiply and create clones in order to generate more and larger fee income. In the next serious down-turn, when the venture capital funds bleed red ink from all orifices, those with conflicts of interest will attract investor vituperation and possibly litigation the way a hound dog attracts mosquitoes in an Alabama swamp.

The final area that causes concern for investment bank-sponsored venture capital funds is their tendency to put small amounts of capital into a large number of companies, thus diminishing their ability to provide quality monitoring and value adding services to all members of the portfolio. The tendency to spread their capital thinly is a means of claiming underwriting rights to the portfolio companies when they are ready for initial public offerings. The claim is either overt or covert. An investment bank with clout can block a portfolio company from selecting an under-writer on a price or merit basis. That may not serve the needs of the entrepreneur or the investors in the fund, but it generates fee income for the investment bank.

If an investment bank is able to operate with multiple conflicts of interest for a sustained period of time, then it owes its good fortune to intelligent and fair people. They should not be denied the opportunity to capitalize on their intelligence, financial skills, and track record. Notwithstanding the successes of investment banks in the venture capital business, their stock car race is not on an oval but on a figure eight. At some point, they will crash into one of their clients and there will be a need for some explanations.

## THE SPECIALTY SHOP VENTURE CAPITAL FUND

There is a natural tendency in the growth and development of any new industry for the newer members to advertise a specialty and attempt to attract a clientele that seeks a more tailor-made or specialized product or service. This is true of the venture capital industry as well. Of the venture capital funds that raised capital from institutional investors in 1983, for example, roughly one-half advertised a specialty of which the management teams had certain unique delivery skills. The other half, represented by existing funds with more experienced management teams raised newer and larger pools of capital without citing particular specialties.

Among the specialties most frequently listed by the new funds were the following:

1. Agriculture and extractive industries.
2. Cable television and communications.
3. Biotechnology.
4. Consumer goods and services.
5. Medical and life sciences products.

The specialty shop venture capital funds are managed by individuals with experience in the industries in which they intend to make investments.

They approach institutional investors that typically invest in a handful of venture capital funds, and they attract their capital based on industry diversification. In the same manner, venture capital funds that focus on a specific geographic region offer their investors regional diversification. Additional capital flows into specialty shop funds from corporations whose products can be made obsolete by technological innovation sponsored by portfolio companies of specialty shop venture capital funds. For example, Monsanto Co. derives a considerable percentage of its revenues from fertilizer sales. It is a frequent investor in biotechnology oriented funds. Monsanto's investments give it a window onto competitive technology. At the other extreme, consumer packaged goods companies are investors in consumer products oriented funds in order to see entrepreneurial innovations that might not otherwise be brought to their attention. Thus, there is sufficient investor demand for specialty shop venture capital funds and undoubtedly they will be popular until a saturation point is reached.

## THE FUND OF FUNDS INVESTMENT VEHICLE

Finally, for institutional investors that seek to own a diversified portfolio of venture capital funds, but lack the time or ability to properly select which funds to invest in, there has been devised an intermediary agency that provides diversification and other services to institutional investors. For a fee, usually equal to 1% per annum of the assets under management, these service organizations, referred to as Funds of Funds, will select and monitor a diversified portfolio of venture capital funds. Typical investors in Funds of Funds are very large pension funds, such as city and state employee retirement funds, that are relatively new to this form of investing, and pension funds located in remote areas not frequented by venture capitalists in search of capital.

The original Funds of Funds was launched by the Manufacturers Hanover Trust Co. in the late 1970's. The trust department of this large New York City bank had been investing its pension fund clients' capital in venture capital funds since the early 1970's. When the distributions of successful investments began pouring into the bank in 1978–1979, the need for a department to manage the distributions of marketable securities to the various pension funds became apparent. The department head, Raymond L. Held, initiated the idea of attracting new clients to Manufacturers Hanover's trust department by marketing diversified, hands free venture capital investing as a product. It has been successful, with Mr. Held's funds under management growing to more than $250 million. Five imitators raised that amount in 1983.

Funds of Funds will continue to proliferate because the profitability is attractive, especially to an investment manager employed by an institution who has become experienced in selecting and monitoring venture capital funds. For example, a $100 million Funds of Funds generates an annual fee of $1 million. Three managers could pay themselves $300,000 per annum and have enough left over for overhead expenses. Variations of Funds of Funds permit the managers to invest a portion of the capital directly into entrepreneurial companies. In this manner, the managers are able to generate capital gains over-rides in addition to handsome salaries.

Diversification is an attractive selling feature, along with managing the distributions of marketable securities. Further, it takes less training to select venture capital fund managers than to become a venture capitalist. Thus, an increasing number of Funds of Funds are likely to be created in the mid-1980's and probably marketed directly to individuals via insurance and mutual fund salesmen and stock brokers. Many investment vehicles once considered too risky for small investors are now as popular on Main Street as they are on Wall Street. It is only a matter of time until we see Sears, American Express, or Prudential marketing venture capital fund certificates for $1000 through storefronts and national sales forces. If one believes that the entrepreneurial process is a beneficial economic force, the additional capital and professionalism that layers of fiduciaries bring to the management of investments can only be construed as healthy. However, if inexperienced and unqualified organizations jump aboard the bandwagon, as they did with Real Estate Investment Trusts in the early 1970's, venture capital will become unpopular. It could conceivably become regulated, which would make becoming a venture capitalist about as much fun as working in the post office.

## SUMMARY OF THE GENRE


To recapitulate, the optimal venture capital management team is one that incorporates in two or three individuals all of the skills of the venture capital process: Deal Generation, Investment Structuring, Syndicating, Monitoring, Adding Value and Selling. The several hundred individuals who possess most or all of these skills are presently managing venture capital funds. The demand for venture capitalists by managers of pension funds and insurance companies exceeds the supply of experienced venture capitalists. As a result, variations of the traditional venture capital fund have been created. Although they are deficient in certain of the skills, they offer compensatory features such as regional or industry specialization of diversification through a creative variation of the mutual fund known as the Funds of Funds. The modern venture capital industry is in its second generation in this country. The founders—General Georges Doriot, Royal Little, Tommy Davis, Bill Hambrecht, and others—are grandfathers. These gentlemen and their peer group were fundamentalists, slow and careful, building-block type of men. Tommy Davis' first venture capital fund, called Mayfield I, had a mere $3 million to invest. General Doriot's American Research & Development Corp. invested the now legendary $70,000 in 1960 to launch Digital Equipment Corp. That investment grew to $500 million 20 years later. The students of Doriot, Little, Hambrecht, Davis, and other original venture capitalists are managing some 200 second generation venture capital funds. Their acquired wealth and the excitement that each day in the venture capital industry brings has attracted other, less qualified individuals who form a partnership with an investment banker or successful entrepreneur and the result is a specialty shop, or corporate sponsored or regional joint-ventured venture capital fund. Although these are in many respects inadequate substitutes for traditional venture capital funds, the improving quality of entrepreneurs, the strengths gained in syndicating, and the religious responsibility for accuracy and thoroughness laid at the feet of a fiduciary mitigate against disastrous losses for some of these mutant species.

## OPTIMAL SIZE OF A VENTURE CAPITAL FUND

Although it is possible to construe from the above remarks that anyone is a venture capitalist with $70,000 and a means of generating a deal flow sufficient to include the likes of a Digital Equipment Corp., that simply is not the case. Before Digital Equipment Corp. crossed breakeven point, General Doriot had to invest an additional $1 million. In 1984 dollars, that would be more like $3 million. Federal Express Corp. required three substantial rounds of venture capital. Multiple rounds of venture capital are required by virtually every entrepreneurial company, except those that go out of business in the development or production stage. In fact, every experienced venture capitalist invests one dollar with the knowledge that he probably will have to go another round with another dollar at a later date.

The optimal size of a venture capital fund is further determined by the necessary staffing requirements, the salary needs of the staff, and the direct and indirect expenses of maintaining a proper deal flow, due diligence operation, and monitoring function. The minimum acceptable staff size is two experienced venture capitalists as the fund begins operations and three to four venture capitalists as the portfolio begins to reach maturity. The management team will require one secretary-office manager initially and a second one when the portfolio begins to expand. The investigation expenses of a venture capital fund, particularly if they include payments for technical consultants, can be as much as $5000 per month. Then the management team will incur costs for marketing, printing, legal services, rent, telephone, postage, couriers, messengers, and utilities.

The salary level for experienced venture capitalists is approximately $120,000–$150,000 per annum, according to data gathered by Capital Publishing Corp. Assuming a venture capital fund is initiated with two senior people, one junior and one secretary and that indirect expenses are $70,000 per annum, the budget for a new venture capital fund would appear somewhat as illustrated in Exhibit 3.

There are several configurations for arriving at $400,000 per annum as the bare bones annual cash requirement of a management company. For example, three senior people at a salary level of

EXHIBIT 3.   Annual Budget for a
Management Company

| Salaries: | |
| --- | ---: |
| Managing general partner | $135,000 |
| General partner | 100,000 |
| Associate | 40,000 |
| Secretary-office manager | 25,000 |
| Insurance, benefits | 30,000 |
| Total salaries and benefits | $330,000 |
| Direct and indirect expenses | 70,000 |
| Total budget | $400,000 |

$85,000 each, plus two secretaries at $25,000 each produces approximately the same result as the Total Salaries and Benefits line in Exhibit 3.

Venture capital managers charge their funds annual fees based on committed or contributed capital. The management fee of a sampling of 15 management companies is approximately 2% per annum, on average as shown in Exhibit 4.

The means of charging fees for the 15 venture capital management companies in Exhibit 4 varies slightly depending on the experience of the management team and the relative ease or difficulty of raising the capital to invest. For example, in 1971, when Messrs. Kleiner and Perkins raised their first fund of $8.8 million, venture capital was not a respected trade and the fee they charged their investors was a paltry $300,000 per annum. By 1980, when gentlemen openly discussed their venture capital investments, Messrs. Kleiner and Perkins, plus the addition of two junior partners, charged their investors a flat 2.5% of $50 million, or $1,250,000 per annum. In 1983, Kleiner, Perkins, Caulfield & Byers III were to set new highs in management compensation, about which more later.

With the exception of Kleiner, Perkins, Oak, Sprout IV and Warburg, Pincus Capital Corp. which charge flat fees, the majority of venture capital management companies charge sliding scale fees, and the mid-point of the sliding scale is approximately 2% per annum. It is possible to make a case for an arithmetic mean

**EXHIBIT 4.  Management Fees Charged-Venture Capital Funds**

| Name of Fund | Month/Year Formed | Management Fees |
|---|---|---|
| 1. Kleiner, Perkins | 12/71 | $300,000 p.a. |
| 2. Kleiner, Perkins, Caulfield & Byers | 5/78 | $500,000 p.a. plus CPI |
| 3. Kleiner, Perkins, Caulfield & Byers II | 6/80 | $2.5% of net asset value |
| 4. Hambrecht & Quist II | 4/80 | 1% of net asset value |
| 5. Hambrecht & Quist III | 4/81 | 2% of committed capital plus 1.5% over committed capital |
| 6. Associated Venture Investors | 4/82 | 2.5% of net assets up to $15 million; 1.5% of next $15 million; 1% over $30 million |
| 7. Warburg, Pincus Capital Corp. | 10/80 | 2.5% of net assets under management |
| 8. Charles River IV | 6/82 | 2.5% of net assets up to $20 million; 1.5% over $20 million |
| 9 Oak Investment Partners | 10/78 | 1.5% of net assets; minimum of $300,000 p.a. |
| 10. Oak Investment Partners II | 8/81 | 2% of greater of net assets or committed capital |
| 11. Matrix Partners | 1/82 | 2.5% of committed capital for first 2 years; 3% next 2; 3.5% thereafter |
| 12. Robertson, Coleman II | 10/82 | 2.5% of capital; plus annual increases of .1% up to 3% |
| 13. Sprout III | 8/76 | 2% of assets up to $40 million; 3.3% over $40 million |
| 14. Sprout IV | 12/78 | 2.5% of assets under management |
| 15. Venad II | 7/80 | 2.5% of net assets up to $7.5 million; 2% up to $15 million; 1.75% above $15 million |

somewhat greater than 2% per annum, but new venture capital funds customarily charge smaller management fees until they become more well-known.

Assuming that 2% of committed capital or net asset value is the average annual management fee, then the minimum acceptable fund size is $20 million in committed capital. This is arrived at of course by dividing $400,000 by $20 million, which produces 2%. A venture capital fund could begin operations with $15 million and as the portfolio companies develop and increase in valuation, the $15 million would grow to a larger number against which the 2% management fee would be charged. An alternative is to set a floor expressed as a fixed dollar amount and a percentage of assets fee.

The business plan of the management company will dictate the annual operating expenses or budget. The budget will in turn determine the size of the fund. The greater the skill level of the general partners, the larger the budget and the larger the fund. In order to address the required skills of a management company, the minimum optimal size of a venture capital fund is $15–$20 million. There is some argument as to the practical upper limit of a venture capital fund.

## MEGAFUNDS

In 1983, a new kind of venture capital fund was created primarily in response to large amounts of pension fund dollars seeking to be managed by the most experienced venture capital fund management companies. These venture capital funds have raised in excess of $100 million, and thus have come to be known as megafunds. They include the following:

| | |
|---|---|
| Warburg, Pincus Capital Partners, New York | $340 million |
| Advent V, Boston | 163 million |
| Brentwood Associates III, Los Angeles | 160 million |
| Kleiner, Perkins, Caulfield, Byers III, San Francisco | 150 million |
| Oak Investment Partners III, Westport, Conn. | 150 million |

The investors in these huge venture capital funds were among the most sophisticated institutions in the country. In fact, the management companies generated such high rates of return from 1978 to 1983 that they were able to select their investors for over half of the capital. Thus, some of the most experienced selectors of venture capital fund management teams are investors in the megafunds. Kleiner, Perkins, Caulfield & Byers raised its megafund in 4 days and claims to have turned away $140 million. It is charging its investors a 50% greater capital gains over-ride than any other venture capital management company in the country.

The demand for megafunds is probably short-lived because there are several negative factors that perhaps outweigh the positive. Three factors are worth a closer look:

1. *Money Burns Holes In Pockets.* Large venture capital funds have never performed as well as small to medium-sized venture capital funds. In 1970, Heizer Corp. raised $81 million, which in 1984 dollars would be one of the larger megafunds. Its annual rate of return has been far from the top of the list. A single large investment in Amdahl Corp, a producer of IBM-compatible computers, helped to erase dozens of losers. Heizer invested its capital relatively quickly. Its personnel were ill-equipped to deal with the 1973–1975 recession and tight money period and as the portfolio companies folded, the personnel took jobs elsewhere.

In megafunds, more capital is invested per deal, in some cases whether the portfolio company needs it or not. For example, a first stage Boston-area software company with sales of approximately $100,000 per month, launched in 1982 by two brothers in their late twenties sought venture capital in late 1982. The company had a single product—a data base management package for the IBM personal computer—an absence of launch experienced management, and a business plan that sought $500,000–$750,000. Much to the entrepreneur's surprise, a Boston megafund invested $2 million. Many smaller venture capital funds would have invested more slowly, perhaps $500,000 to begin, then a layer of bank financing followed by another $500,000 plus a co-investor for $500,000 in a second round.

An educational software company was launched with $5.5 million in late 1983 by 6 venture capital funds, several of which manage in excess of $50 million. It folded its tent in mid-1984, the victim of venture capital overkill. A smaller amount of capital would have forced greater care in entering the market.

In order to avoid the impression that the author has an arbitrarily negative attitude toward megafunds, we assume the hypothesis that megafunds invest more capital per portfolio company. Then it will be shown that there is no positive relationship between size of investment and rate of return. The hypothesis that megafunds invest more money per deal is examined by comparing the investments of well-known venture capital funds when they were relatively small with their investments of today, under the auspices of subsequent, larger funds. Exhibit 5 compares the size of investments of venture capital funds in 1975 with investments made by the same management groups in 1983.

The method of selecting the seven investments in 1975 and the seven investments in 1983 was not scientific or unbiased. The companies were selected, in the case of the earlier investments, because they are start-up investments and they have become very successful businesses, and, in the case of the later investments, because many venture capitalists think they will be successful businesses. The aggregate dollars committed to the seven earlier investments were $4,575,000, or $653,570 per investment. Nineteen investors combined to invest the $4.6 million for an average investment of $240,789 per venture capitalist. The valuations were very attractive to the venture capitalists. For example, a $200,000 investor in Rolm Corp. in 1975 purchased 12.5% of the company. In 1983, IBM purchased a 19% interest in Rolm Corp. for $150 million.

There was more venture capital in circulation in 1982 and 1983. The seven companies that raised venture capital in 1983 in Exhibit 5, amassed an aggregate of $103,700,000 of start-up and first-stage capital, or $14,814,290 per company. The funds were provided by 67 venture capital funds for an average investment of $1,547,761 per venture capitalist. The valuations were not nearly as attractive as they were in 1975. A $750,000 investment in Businessland, Inc. in 1982 purchased 584,620 common stock equivalent shares, or 3% of Businessland's common stock—a start-up valuation of $25 million. Is a start-up telecommunications company worth one-twentieth of a start-up computer and software retailer? Under normal circumstances this disparity would not exist. However, in 1982

EXHIBIT 5.  Investment Sizes of Venture Capital Funds
in 1975 and 1983

### 1975

| Company | Amount Invested | Investors |
| --- | --- | --- |
| Rolm Corp. | $1,200,000 | Institutional Venture Associates, Wells Fargo |
| Tandem Computer Corp. | 1,000,000 | Kleiner Perkins, Mayfield, Asset Management, E.M. Warburg, Data Science Ventures |
| Qume Corp. | 700,000 | Kleiner Perkins, Sutter Hill, Time, Whitney |
| Genentech Corp. | 375,000 | Kleiner Perkins |
| Logisticon | 600,000 | Brentwood, Mayfield |
| Atari, Inc. | 1,500,000 | Mayfield, Capital Management, Time, Fidelity Ventures |
| Collagen Corp. | 100,000 | Institutional Venture Associates |

### 1983

| Company | Amount Invested | Investors |
| --- | --- | --- |
| Businessland, Inc. | $23,500,000 | Aetna Casualty, Arscott Norton, Bessemer, Early Stages, Emerging Growth Partners, John Hancock Ventures, Interwest Partners, Institutional Venture Associates, Kleiner Perkins, Kyocera International, LNII Associates, Matrix Partners, Mayfield, Merrill Pickard, Oak Investment, Oxford Partners, L.F. Rothschild (the eventual underwriter), Sonoita Enterprises, University of Rochester and Venrock |

EXHIBIT 5. (continued)

| | 1983 | |
| --- | --- | --- |
| Company | Amount Invested | Investors |
| Compaq Computer | $28,500,000 | Crown Associates, Kistler Investments, Kleiner Perkins, Mayfield, Oak Investment, L.F. Rothschild (the eventual underwriter), Sevin Rosen, Technology Venture Investors, J.H. Whitney |
| Callan Data Systems | 9,200,000 | Brentwood, Capital Management, Fidelity Ventures, First Interstate, John Hancock, IBM Pension Fund, Morgenthaler, North American Ventures, Richard J. Riordan |
| Filenet Corp. | 4,000,000 | Brentwood, Dougery Jones, Lawrence WPG Partners, Matrix and Olivetti |
| Imagic, Inc. | 12,000,000 | ABS Ventures, H & Q, Kleiner Perkins, Merrill Pickard, Sysorex, TA Associates |
| Spinnaker Software | 6,000,000 | ABS Ventures, Aeneas Venture, New Enterprise Associates, New Venture Partners, L.F. Rothschild, TA Associates, G.E. Pension Fund |
| Pyramid Technology Corp. | 20,500,000 | Burroughs Corp., Capital Management, CH Partners, Chatham Venture, Crown Assoc., Harvest Ventures, IBM Pension Fund, Montgomery Bridge Fund, L.F. Rothschild, University of Rochester, Vanguard Associates |

and 1983, the successful venture capital fund managers raised extremely large pools of capital, some over $100 million, and they invested more money per fund in the start-ups in 1983 than the entire valuation of Rolm Corp. in 1975.

If one steps up his investment size from odd lots when he has only $10,000 to his name to $10,000 individual bites when he has become wealthier, the case could be made that he is a more knowledgeable and experienced investor. In the case of venture capital management companies, although the founders grow in knowledge and experience, it is not the case that they are directly responsible for the venture capital investments of the megafunds. The average age of the megafund staffs, their number of board seats, and their experience in rescuing companies during serious recessions is considerably less. In an age where entrepreneurs expect more from their venture capitalists than capital, they are more likely to achieve that goal with a 45-year-old venture capitalist with more than 10 years of industry experience and are more likely to be monitored by a 27-year-old associate member of a megafund management company, too young to have experienced the 1974 recession.

The tendency of megafunds to let money burn holes in their own pockets is the perfectly normal desire to grow, achieve, and prosper. It would take a management company twice as long to invest $150 million in increments of $1 million as it would increments of $2 million. The younger partners and associates with less ownership in the management company desire to fully invest the $150 million more quickly so that another fund can be launched in which they have greater ownership. They put pressure on the senior partners for larger and fewer investments.

The leveraged buyout industry, a sister to the venture capital industry has sprouted a number of multi-megafunds in 1983–1984, based on some very attractive returns in the 1970's. One of them, Kohlberg, Kravis, Roberts & Co. raised $1 billion in a blind pool from municipal pension funds, and attracted over $6 billion in one week to become one of the three legitimate bidders with Arco and Socal for Gulf Oil Corp. The appetite of investors for get-rich-quick schemes has created the huge pools of money managed by the most successful small fund managers of the 1970's. Is it possible to generate 50% per annum compound rates of return on $350 million as it is on $25 million? That kind of performance would turn

$350 million to $2.7 billion in 5 years. Can one fund generate more capital gains in 5 years than the entire industry with $7 billion does every few years?

*Forbes* writer Allan Sloan said the following about megafunds: " . . . leveraged buyouts are showing signs of wretched excess. The gold-into-dross stage of LBOs is obviously at hand. What used to be a craft practiced by a handful of specialists has turned into a multi-billion-dollar industry with syndicators scouring the earth doing deals, some of which don't seem to make any sense."*

In the capital markets where capital is one's principal inventory, success is measured by rate of return and masked by size. This confusion of size with success has been made by every generation of young investors to ever achieve the right to present deals to investment committees. The megafund is another example of this eternal confusion. We can merely hope that their performance will not be as bad as that of the megafunds of 1970–1971, which turned investors away from venture capital funds for 5 years.

Because of the wretched excesses of venture capital and LBO megafunds, we will soon see work-out and recovery funds formed to salvage troubled companies sprung from the checkbooks of gluttoness venture capitalists.

2.  *The Takedown Rate Is Too Slow.* A second objection frequently voiced by institutional investors is that the megafunds take down their commitments over longer time periods than do the small funds. Thus, if an institutional investor wishes to back certain management teams, the investor is not offered frequent opportunities to do so if the management teams form megafunds rather than smaller funds. Whereas smaller venture capital funds take down their commitments over 2–3 years, megafunds stretch out their takedowns to 5 years.

The staggered or delayed takedown schedule employed by most venture capital managers has three important reasons. These are:

a.  Institutional investors are better able to invest capital in short-term investment instruments than are venture capital fund managers.

---

*Forbes*, "Wrong Banks Overboard?", Allan, Sloane, April 9, 1984, pp. 39–40.

b. Staggered takedowns discipline the venture capitalists to schedule their investments over a 3-year period. This helps to diversify the portfolio over time.

c. There are cycles of innovation and technology change which create relatively better times to invest in entrepreneurial companies. A management team feels the urge to invest if it has all its capital in hand, but that urge may coincide with a relatively weak year. If the management team obtains its capital incrementally, it would be more likely to catch a relatively good year.

In taking down their capital over 5 years the megafunds are possibly failing to meet the needs of the institutional investors to invest a portion of their assets in well-managed venture capital funds each year or every other year. Yet venture capital funds with $150 million in hand and 8–10 people cannot put their capital to work effectively in less than 5 years; unless they invest some of it in regional venture capital funds. If this is true, and only time will tell, the megafunds will lose their attraction to sophisticated U.S. institutional investors and their existence will become a historical footnote.

3. *Megafunds Are Less Able to Syndicate Their Deals.* When a management company of a venture capital fund needs to put upwards of $100 million into suitable entrepreneurial companies within a 3 year period of time, whereas its previous fund invested $25 million to $30 million within the same time period, it is faced with several strategic choices. These include the following:

a. Add to its staff a proportionate number of experienced venture capitalists.

b. Invest in regional venture capital funds and take other actions to increase its deal flow.

c. Put greater amounts of capital into individual deals.

There are other alternatives, such as diversification into public markets, takeovers, and leveraged buy-outs that typically require more capital, but the management company may lack the necessary experience to enter those areas. Thus, the three viable alternatives are to increase the number of experienced staff members, place some of the capital with trusted ferrets in other regions of the country, or invest larger sums per deal.

Megafunds have tested the first two alternatives with less than satisfactory results. There are an inadequate number of trained venture capitalists to add to the staffs of the larger funds, and recently graduated business school students are typically long on analytical skills but unfamiliar with the entrepreneurial process. It takes several painful losses to learn the venture capital business and that means line responsibility somewhere. Following the next major downturn, resumes of former venture capital associates in their late 20's will probably be as plentiful as are resumes of commercial and investment bankers seeking positions in the venture capital industry in 1983–1984. Staffing up quickly is not a viable alternative for the megafunds.

Diversifying into small regional funds that serve as sweepers for the primary fund is a trend that began in 1981. Kleiner Perkins, Brentwood, Mayfield, Rothschilds, and several other large funds supported regional feeder funds in Austin, Texas and Boulder, Colorado. The primary funds control the investment decisions of the regional feeder funds and have the option to coinvest, or to invest at a later stage. The jury is still out on the success of this strategy. It seems that if the regional feeder funds succeed, the principals thereof will seek to leave the nest and begin funds in which they have more authority and ownership. The primary funds may in that case be left holding bags of questionable value. However, there are mechanisms to reward outstanding personnel and to attempt to keep them in the flock, if that is desirable. Thus, a series of regional feeder investments by a megafund may be an idea whose time has come. Some extremely wealthy venture capitalists are using precious capital in this manner and judgment is best reserved.

Yet diversification in this manner will absorb less than 10% to 20% of a megafund's total capital. That leaves $200–$280 million to invest in a relatively short period of time. The third alternative strategy seems to be the road most travelled: investing larger amounts of capital per deal. This trend is observable (see Exhibit 5 above). Not only does it have a deleterious effect on rates of return, but it will lead to more losses.

One of the most effective means of testing one's due diligence process in a venture capital investment is to see if the deal can be sold to another venture capitalist at the same price. This practice, known as syndicating, is one of the fundamentals of successful venture capital investing. Venture capitalist A will see a deal, investigate it thoroughly, agree to invest $750,000 of the $1.5 million requirement and offer the other half to venture capitalist B. The latter may review the same information made available to A, but decline to invest for a fundamental reason. Venture capitalist A then calls venture capitalist C, who after a week of reviewing the due diligence book, turns down the deal because its price is too high. Then venture capitalist D is offered the deal and does extra due diligence which reveals that the patents pending referred to by venture capitalist A are probably worthless because of competitive patents issued to a Japanese company. Then venture capitalist E learns upon further digging that the company's Vice President of Engineering has a false resume.

All of these inputs add materially to the original venture capitalist's due diligence book and sum of knowledge about the company. The inputs also sharpen his pencil on valuing the investment.

Now assuming that venture capitalist A did what he felt was an adequate due diligence process and invested the full $1.5 million at the valuation that he and the entrepreneurs agreed was fair. A few months later the problem of the Japanese competitor may surface with the result of a threefold reduction of the company's gross profit margin and the domino effect of creating a need for more capital. The problem of the Vice President of Engineering leaps out at about the same time when it is discovered that he cannot produce a working model of the company's principal product for a very important potential customer. Locating his replacement eats up 90 important days, which include the last opportunity of a missed trade show and order cancellation. The domino effect of this problem turns out to be the need for more capital as well.

Following another round of venture capital provided by venture capitalist A, the company fails to ramp up against its competitors and loses its opportunity to get out in front of its market. The venture capitalist and the management team jointly agree to seek a buyer for the company. After 120 days of playing host to various potential buyers, the best offer is at a price less than that paid by venture capitalist A. Thus, the company is sold at a discount.

Now, it is not the case that all deals go sour that are invested in by one venture capital fund which has not taken the time to syndicate a portion of the deal with others. Many deals fail after syndication among several experienced venture capital funds. Yet, syndication is one of the best methods for testing one's due diligence process and pricing. If a deal is not good enough to attract an *experienced* co-investor, then it deserves further scrutiny by the lead venture capitalist.

Because of their size and the pressures by their investors to have a full portfolio in 3–4 years, megafunds syndicate less than smaller venture capital funds. In so doing, they do not gain the benefit of having their due diligence reviewed, having their valuation tested, or having a monitoring partner actively involved with them post-investment.

As you may have noticed, many of the syndicate partners in the 1982–1983 investments listed in Exhibit 5 are not experienced venture capitalists. They are passive investors, investment banks, and corporations seeking a window on innovation. When deals are syndicated with investors of this stripe, extra due diligence is not performed, extra monitoring does not occur, and additional value-added services are not forthcoming.

In summary, the optimal size of a venture capital fund is in a range between $20 and $40 million, depending upon the quality of deal flow, the objectives of the management company, and the experience of the venture capitalists involved. The minimum acceptance size of $20 million permits an annual operating budget of $400,000, which could cover three to four salaries plus the investigation costs. Further, the most successful venture capital funds have operated fairly locally; investing in companies on a staggered takedown basis, investing in companies very near their offices, and monitoring them carefully. Investing large chunks of capital on a far-flung, national basis has thus far not proven to be as profitable.

## RAISING A $20 MILLION FUND

In order to raise $20 million to launch a venture capital fund, the general partners of the management company must prepare a business plan, qualify a number of potential investors, and present the business plan in written and oral form in a manner that answers the five following questions satisfactorily:

1. How much can I make?
2. How much can I lose?
3. How do I get my money out?
4. Who says this deal is any good?
5. Who else is in the deal?

These questions are not trivial. They are the five single most important issues that an investor in a "concept" start-up seeks answers to. A concept start-up is an investment pool that intends to place a portion of its investors' capital in a specialized area that is otherwise not available to them. Concept start-ups differ from manufacturing company or service company start-ups because they are money or asset management organizations that conceptually claim to be able to manage the investor's capital more successfully than the investor. Thus, in selling a concept deal, the promoter must provide answers to tough questions in these five key areas:

1. Performance.
2. Protection from loss.
3. Liquidification.
4. Historical track record.
5. Endorsement.

You may have observed the word "promoter" several lines above. How can a person seeking to become a fiduciary of $20 million of investors' capital possibly be referred to as a promoter? Blasphemy. Not at all, for the venture capitalists are promoting their concept for generating superior rates of return on investment to serious and intelligent investors who do not intend to invest a portion of their capital in concepts unless they are *sold on the deal.* Selling a concept deal requires as much promotion as tickets to the World's Largest Alligator at the State Fair.

## PERFORMANCE

This section of the business plan conveys to the investor unique features of the venture capital fund. These have been as many and varied as there are venture capital funds. The features become even more precise as the number of venture capital funds increase. There were approximately 400 venture capital funds in December 1983, according to Stanley L. Pratt, editor of the *Venture Capital Journal*. The quantity of venture capital funds is a function of the number of qualified venture capitalists. If the former outpaces the latter, a self-correcting mechanism called failures and liquidations brings the two numbers back into parallel. Are there more venture capital funds than necessary? Absolutely not. As long as problems exist in society that lend themselves to solution via the entrepreneurial process, there exists a need for venture capital funds.

For a person to become a venture capitalist, he or she must raise a $20 million fund (optimally, although a smaller amount is workable within narrow investment objectives) and that requires, in the first instance, creating a business plan that leaves no doubt in the minds of investors that it will provide them with outstanding performances. The business plan is a function of where the management team is located, the deal flow that it will attract, the ability of the management team to recognize potentially successful deals and the investment objectives of the management team.

The location of the venture capital fund is of particular interest to investors because most venture capitalists have come to believe that propinquity to their portfolio companies is the first step in adding value and close monitoring. Thus, new venture capital funds tend to be located in regions where none existed 5 years ago. For example, Exhibit 6 points out the emergence of regional venture capital funds.

With the exception of the mature entrepreneurial regions such as Northern California and New England, which attract venture capital from all regions because of the quality of the entrepreneurial teams, the regional venture capital funds can press the case, and legitimately so, that their performance will be enhanced because they are the first funds in their areas and will receive the benefits typically accorded monopolists. This means

EXHIBIT 6.    The Growth of Venture Capital Funds Serving Specified
              Geographic Territories

| Region | Number of Venture Capital Funds | | Amount of Venture Capital Available ($ mm) | |
|---|---|---|---|---|
| | 1978 | 1983 | 1978 | 1983 |
| Southeast | 1 | 5 | 10 | 80 |
| Southwest | 1 | 10 | 25 | 150 |
| Midwest | 10 | 16 | 200 | 600 |
| Rocky Mountains | 1 | 9 | 5 | 105 |

that if a quality start-up company in Florence, S.C. visits five New
York City venture capital funds, they are likely to refer the deal to
the venture capital fund nearest Florence. If the regional fund requires co-investors, it can then act as lead investor and syndicate
the investment with the New York funds. The entrepreneur of the
Florence start-up has less negotiating ability when it comes to
valuation because the regional venture capital fund is his primary
source of capital. Thus, the investment will be made at a price
more favorable to the venture capital fund.

A non-regional or national venture capital fund is not able to obtain monopoly prices for its investments. However, to obtain a flow
of deals from the newer regions of entrepreneurial activity some of
the large, national funds invest in smaller, regional funds. Some regional funds with national venture capital funds among their investors are included in Exhibit 7.

EXHIBIT 7.    Regional Funds that Have National Venture Capital
              Funds as Investors

| Name and Location of Venture Capital Fund | Name of National Venture Capital Fund Investor |
|---|---|
| 1. Pathfinder Venture Capital Co. Minneapolis, Minnesota | Crossroads Capital Security Pacific Capital |
| 2. Advanced Technology Ventures Atlanta, Georgia | Welsh, Carson, Anderson & Stowe |
| 3. The Hill Partnership Boulder, Colorado | Mayfield Fund |
| 4. Business Development Partners Austin, Texas | Kleiner, Perkins, Caulfield & Byers, Brentwood, Rothschild |

The management team should go to some length to research the strengths of the region, its ties to providers of deal flow, its covert activities to generate deal flow, and other local features. The existence of large universities, research activities of industrial corporations, national laboratories, broad range of component manufacturing skills, inexpensive labor, major hospitals to beta-test new medical products, management consultants, support services such as a nearby major airport, advertising agencies, vocational high schools, and a life style and climate that is attractive and affordable to young families are among the key ingredients to sow the seeds of a productive entrepreneurial garden. Regions that appear to have these features in the mid-1980's are:

Albuquerque, New Mexico
Atlanta, Georgia
Austin, Texas
Boulder, Colorado
Phoenix, Arizona
Portland, Oregon
San Antonio, Texas
Tampa, Florida

Each of these regions have recently witnessed the formation of one or more venture capital funds. The much-publicized Research Triangle near Raleigh, N.C. has not encouraged a venture capital fund to set down roots; but, rather, has sought out large, high technology companies as tenants. Time will tell which region have been the more successful.

## Management's Track-Record

The venture capital industry is perhaps one of the last professions (to use Milton Friedman's definition of a profession: "a self-governing group of people offering the same service") for which the most significant qualification is apprenticeship. It is virtually impossible to learn the venture capital business from a textbook, at a commercial bank, investment bank, management consulting firm, or as an entrepreneur or manager of a rapidly emerging growth company. Persons with these kinds of backgrounds who have not apprenticed at a venture capital fund, SBIC or corporate venture capital subsidiary who seek to become venture capitalists, generally enter the business in one of three ways:

1. Gain employment with a venture capital fund, SBIC, or corporate venture capital subsidiary.
2. Form a small venture capital fund with 10 to 25 friends to invest in and assist the growth and development of local companies, either on a full-time or part-time basis.
3. Become part of a general partner of a venture capital management company whose other members possess the requisite venture capital backgrounds.

Notwithstanding this seemingly reasonable list of prerequisites, investors have launched venture capital funds that did not have seasoned venture capitalists in the management company. They replaced experience with performance. Sevin-Rosen Management Co., for instance, is managed by L.J. Sevin, a founder of Mostek, Inc., which was acquired by United Technologies Corp. 5 years after start-up for approximately $800 million; and Benjamin Rosen, publisher of an electronics industry newsletter for the securities industry and institutional investors. The Sevin–Rosen team, based in Dallas, identified a highly successful integrated software publisher called Lotus Development Corp. in Cambridge, Massachusetts. Its Lotus 1-2-3 package has been extraordinarily successful throughout 1983, pulling customers away from competitive packages, Visicalc and Supercalc, and generating a market value in December, 1983 of approximately $180 million on annualized revenues of $35 million. Although its valuation is not Genentechian by any means, Sevin–Rosen's success with Lotus enabled the fund to raise a second venture capital fund, twice the size of the first one, thus legitimizing their title of venture capitalist, notwithstanding an absence of apprenticeship. Other non-apprenticed persons have been able to enter the profession and achieve similar, near-term results.

The manner in which a venture capitalist describes his past performance to investors is in terms of the fairly traditional compound annual rate of return. The factors are: amount invested, time elapsed, and realized return. Unrealized returns should be separately cited. As an example, assume that a person started a business in school, which was later sold for a profit, and then became a corporate attorney. A few years later, with the law firm's capital, he formed a small venture capital fund capitalized with $250,000, made four investments with varying results, and finally decided that he preferred venture capital to law. His track record could be presented as shown in Exhibit 8.

What at first blush might appear that one investment produced a gain of 50 times and erased two losers and two small winners, is slightly more than 2 times over 10 years ($550,000/$251,000). The rate of return should be expressed logarithmically, looking at total return rather than the return on $251,000 over 10 years. The logarithmic rendering is more accurate, because it presumes that each company received the same amount of capital rather than the capital available to the investor and it accurately reflects that there was no investment activity for the 8-year period between 1973 and 1981. Thus on a logarithmic scale, the ex-lawyer's track record in five venture capital investments is a compound rate of return of 10% per annum, as is borne out by Exhibit 18 in chapter 4 on page 93.

Each of the five investments requires an accurate explanation of the person's degree of involvement. In the first investment, pre-

**EXHIBIT 8. Presentation of Hypothetical Track Records**

| Name of Company | Date Invested | Amount Invested | Unrealized Gain | Realized Gain | Total Return |
|---|---|---|---|---|---|
| University Equipment | 7/73 | $ 1,000 | $ — | $ 50,000 | 50.0x |
| Hospital Diagnostics | 8/81 | 25,000 | 75,000 | — | 3.0x |
| ABC Paint & Glue | 12/81 | 40,000 | — | — | — |
| Eager-Beaver Software | 4/82 | 100,000 | — | 500,000 | 5.0x |
| Electro-Testing Devices | 7/82 | 85,000 | — | — | — |
| Total | | $251,000 | $75,000 | $550,000 | |

sumably the person was the founding entrepreneur who assumed certain management responsibilities as the business grew, and then he sold the business when he graduated. The other investments occurred while the person invested the law firm's excess capital in several local ventures. These companies should be described in terms of their industry, stage of development, results of operations, and the person's kind and degree of involvement while an investor. The more active his role, the more venture capital apprenticeship he has done. If the person is still a member of the board of directors of these companies, he should state his intentions to resign over a reasonable period of time. Managing a venture capital fund does not permit diversionary activities, although there have been exceptions.

The ex-lawyer it would seem has the kind of track record that would compliment a venture capitalist with a longer record and perhaps portfolio management responsibility at an SBIC or corporate venture capital subsidiary. This person would be perhaps younger than the ex-lawyer but had been schooled for approximately 5 years in the due diligence process, forming syndicates, and monitoring a large number of portfolio companies simultaneously.

A third complimentary partner could be a manager from a high technology company skilled in assessing the technologies that the fund plans to seek out, such as medical diagnostics or electronics industries. This person's principal skill areas would be technical evaluation of deals and adding value to portfolio companies. The track records of these three individuals compliment one another and cover the important areas of deal flow generation, technical audit, due diligence, monitoring, syndicating, adding value, and liquidifying. Unless these areas are covered by qualified members of the management teams, seeking to raise capital for a new venture capital fund may be an exercise in futility.

## OTHER PERFORMANCE ENHANCERS

Managers of venture capital funds have entered into special relationships with various sources of special technical or industrial knowledge in order to enhance their performance. The second

Mayfield Fund, launched by Tommy J. Davis in 1975, had a special relationship with the Stanford University Department of Engineering which performed technical audits of Mayfield's proposed investments in consideration for an equity interest in the management company.

The Centennial Fund which was launched in 1982 to specialize in cable-tv and telecommunications start-ups has a special relationship with Daniels & Co., the country's leading broker of cable-tv stations. The investment banking-related venture capital funds cite their "enhanced deal flow" as a performance booster. Wind Point Partners, a 1984-vintage fund, mostly funded by S. C. Johnson & Sons, cites its ability to utilize the research and development resources of S. C. Johnson & Sons to perform technical evaluations.

Where the management team has worked together at another fund, the obvious benefit to an investor is that the general partners have had hands-on experience as a team with a variety of companies through various phases of the business cycle. Many new venture capital funds are assembling boards of advisors composed of scientists, industrialists, and high technology-backgrounded entrepreneurs to assist in selecting and monitoring investments. Boards of advisors as performance enhancers become dubious, of course, as every new venture capital fund tacks one onto their business plan. There is likely to be a trend away from boards of advisors to other kinds of performance enhancers in the future. These might include connections with small underwriters, an advisory board of work-out and turn-around experts, and perhaps a bankruptcy or reorganization expert. Investing in new companies is substantially easier than growing and liquidifying them.

## PROTECTION FROM LOSS

An investor wants to know at the outset what provisions the venture capital fund will make to protect him or her from loss. The desire is much like wanting to know if the boat has inflatable jackets and floatable cushions before going aboard. The answer to this question is one of *process*: the process by which one audits the principal risks of a deal prior to investing; the process by which one structures the investment to protect against loss and to generate early warning signals to permit the venture capitalist to exercise the controls necessary to protect his investment; and the process by which the venture capitalist monitors the portfolio companies. There are variations in process from one management company to another, but the experienced venture capitalists have thought through the form and rhythm of their processes and are capable of explaining them to potential investors. The audit, structure, and monitoring processes are critical to loss avoidance. They are the three most critical processes in protecting the assets of the fund in order to create value for the investors. If the management company fails to set up a system to maintain the health of its portfolio, it will surely fail in a serious downturn. Hundreds of SBICs have failed since the program began in 1946 because of the failure of their managements to develop processes to avoid losses. Risk averse venture capitalists are more successful in the long run than those who believe that one or two winners will offset the losers. The process is explained in detail in several subsequent chapters.

## LIQUIDIFICATION

The typical means of liquidifying a venture capital investment are (1) sale to a publicly-held company for stock or other currency, (2) registration of the company's stock and sale of a portion of it to the public, and (3) sale to the founders for cash and notes. It is important that the management has experienced in significant detail each of these means of liquidification, that it has contacts with underwriters and merger and acquisition brokers, and that it has a trader's orientation toward its portfolio. Management should have the judgment to know when a portfolio company's management team is sufficiently strong to be a good candidate for a public offering, when it should merge into a larger company, and when the venture capital fund should bail out at the soonest moment for the best price available. This knowledge should be conveyed to potential investors in the form of examples of successful liquidifications.

Selling several successful investments in the height of a bull market for initial public offerings does not demonstrate a management team's ability to liquidify its portfolio. In hot new issue markets, the new issues underwriters are actively seeking product for their customers. They frequently make companies public before the companies are ready for the scrutiny of the public market, as happened in 1983; but demand for new issues occasionally exceeds supply. An investor in a venture capital fund is more likely to be interested in the experience of the management team in liquidifying companies in less bullish new issues markets as well as in economic recessions and illiquid periods in the business cycle such as the years 1974 and 1984. There are approximately 20 methods of raising capital for small, rapidly-emerging companies* and the managers should be conversant with these vehicles to generate cash because an institutional investor will require knowledge and experience in the area of liquidifying the portfolio.

## HISTORICAL TRACK RECORD

When one raises capital to launch a venture capital fund he or she is selling *performance*. The principal means of selling performance is to document how successfully one has performed in the past. Though managers have been involved in launching a new company, managing an entrepreneurial growth company, or providing financing for rapidly emerging companies, their track record is relatively incomplete. A partner is required who has had portfolio management experience in an SBIC or corporate venture capital subsidiary. Without a blended track record, the institutional investor is likely to find it difficult to impute capabilities to the manager that suggest he or she might be capable of generating a performance record that exceeds that of the institutional investor.

For a first venture capital fund, since one's credibility in the area of performance is suspect, it is best to set one's sights relatively low: $20–$25 million in total funding. The terms of the limited partnership agreement could permit the managers to launch a second venture capital fund upon meeting certain predetermined goals in the first fund. A typical hurdle seen in many first funds is that the

*Silver, A. David, *Upfront Financing*, Wiley, New York, 1982.

general partner is restricted from managing an additional venture capital fund until it has achieved a return of 150% of initial capital to the investors in the first fund. Assuming that an institutional investor has the capital and policy approval to invest in venture capital funds, he will select the managers whose performance projections seem to him to be the most credible. The more he can convince sources of capital of the credibility of his projections, the more capital he can raise. There are means of "borrowing" credibility from other more established venture capital funds, as was described earlier, such as regional clones and corporate affiliates. Although they may attract incrementally more capital, it is questionable if their performance will be greater than that of non-hybrid venture capital funds.

## ENDORSEMENT

Investors almost always want to know "who else is in the deal?" There is a novine quality to institutional investors. Over time they have learned that certain of their number tend to develop knowledge and experience in a form of investing and that these institutions can be relied on to investigate and analyze investment opportunities as "lead investors". Their staffs are larger, their legal departments more attuned to venture capital fund limited partnership agreements, and their ability to modify the terms and conditions of the partnership agreements, management fees, management overrides, and other forms of compensation is greater than that of institutional investors for whom investing in venture capital funds is more passive and more casual. Were one to raise capital from institutions without obtaining the endorsement of a lead investor, the marketing effort would be relatively long and difficult. However, if a lead investor could be identified early in the capital-raising effort, the marketing effort could be reduced to the normal time span of about 20 to 30 weeks. Some of the most well-known lead investors among U.S. financial institutions and the approximate dollar size of their commitments to venture capital funds as of December 31, 1983 are listed in Exhibit 9.

Although it is by no means imperative to attract the endorsement of a lead investor, or one of the above lead investors, before

EXHIBIT 9.    Lead Investors in U.S. Venture Capital Funds

| | |
|---|---|
| 1. CIGNA Corp.<br>950 Cottage Grove Road<br>Bloomfield, CT<br>$100 million | 6. Investment Advisors, Inc.<br>Dain Tower<br>Minneapolis, MN<br>$50 million |
| 2. Citicorp Employees<br>Retirement Fund<br>299 Park Avenue<br>New York, NY<br>$100 million | 7. Manufacturers Hanover Trust<br>600 Fifth Avenue<br>New York, NY<br>$250 million |
| 3. Crossroads Partners<br>1 Lewis Street<br>Hartford, CT<br>$100 million | 8. Prudential Insurance Co.<br>Prudential Plaza<br>Newark, NJ<br>$200 million |
| 4. General Electric Employees<br>Retirement Fund<br>112 Prospect Street<br>Stamford, CT<br>$90 million | 9. University of Chicago<br>One First National Plaza<br>Chicago, IL<br>$90 million |
| 5. University of California<br>2200 University Hall<br>Berkeley, CA<br>$60 million | 10. New York State Employees<br>Retirement System<br>New York, NY<br>$75 million |

setting off on a cross-country march to raise $20–$25 million of capital, the journey is made easier by having the support of a knowledgeable, experienced, well-staffed institutional investor. The lead investor must be willing to handle inquiries from other potential institutional investors and to invest a meaningful amount of capital, especially in proportion to its own size and the size of the venture capital fund.

Some venture capital fund managers have offered "special limited partner" status to their lead investors in order to obtain their endorsement. This usually takes the form of providing them with the additional incentive of a portion of the general partner's override. When Mayfield II was raising capital in 1975, it had two special limited partners: Stanford University, whose engineering department provided technical advice and assistance to Mayfield II in exchange for ownership, and Ford Foundation which served as lead investor and increased its investment size in proportion to other investors, and for so doing, received a special limited partner status. Wind Point Partners, Racine, Wisconsin, has accorded special limited partner status to S. C. Johnson's Sons, Inc. in 1984 in consideration for its initial investment of $22 million and technical advice and assistance. Noro-Moseley Venture Capital Partners, Atlanta, Georgia, accorded special limited partner status to The Noro Group, a Swedish technology firm and Interwest Partners, a San Francisco venture capital fund, which was helpful in Noro-Moseley's attracting $45 million, a relatively large amount for a first fund. Some venture capital funds have accorded special limited partner status to well-known venture capital funds in other regions and to investment banks, for a variety of considerations such as monitoring assistance and enhanced deal flow. These latter examples of special limited partners appear to be merely a device to raise capital; and as to their usefulness to the venture capital fund, they fall into the category of gold-plating the crowbar.

Investment banks, for the most part, have not been particularly useful in assisting venture capital fund managers in raising their capital. It is difficult to describe an intangible such as the future performance of a team of venture capitalists if they have an interest in the "product." The value of an investment bank is twofold: (1) once the venture capitalists have attracted a core of institutional investors, the investment bank can call on its clients and relatively rapidly add to the size of the fund; and (2) the investment bank can endorse the venture capitalists in a manner that says to the institutional investors: "We have checked out these people and they are intelligent, honest and qualified venture capitalists." For these two services, a reputable investment bank will expect a fee of approximately 2% of the gross proceeds invested in the fund plus a 1% limited partnership interest.

### The Road Show

As soon as the business plan is written and the management team identified, the venture capitalists begin the arduous task of qualifying and visiting institutional investors. The names, addresses, and telephone numbers of all of the large pension funds, endowment funds, and insurance companies are available in directories found in public libraries or the libraries of commercial and investment banks. In 1982, these three sources invested $770 million or

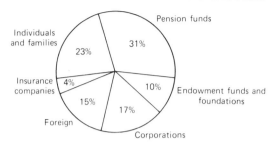

1982 : Total $1.4 billion

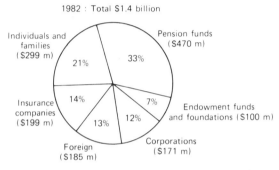

EXHIBIT 10. Capital Commitments to Independent Venture Capital Funds (Source: Capital Publishing Corp.)

54% of all capital invested in venture capital funds. The aggregate sources are shown in Exhibit 10.

When the corporate pension fund manager is qualified—i.e., his positive interest has been determined—the venture capitalist can ask him if the area of primary interest in venture capital is in the corporate planning area—a window into innovation and technology—or in the pension fund area—return on investment and co-investing opportunities.

Because the institutional investors are located in a myriad of large cities and small towns throughout the country, and because they must be visited personally by the venture capitalists, the road show is a time consuming, arduous task. It has very few redeeming features, save for meeting the investors for several hours and discussing the field of venture capital and one's role in it. It is important to be tenacious and systematic in qualifying and visiting investors. Although it can take 6 months to a year to complete the fund-raising effort, like banging your head against a wall, it feels awfully good when it's over.

# 2

# GENERATING A
# DEAL FLOW

Nothing is certain in this contingent world, but you can rest assured that there is absolutely no truth to the adage: "Everyone's money is green." Quite the opposite is true. Some money is greener than other money. Particularly in the venture capital business, one venture capitalist's money can be materially different than another's. A venture capitalist can invest in a company and then be either (1) active, (2) passive, or (3) hurtful. Until recently, when the entrepreneurial process changed from cottage to factory, ad hoc to disciplined, entrepreneurs did not thoroughly investigate the differences among venture capitalists. Perhaps the change came in 1981, when Microsoft Corp., the highly successful computer software company in Bellevue, Washington, was visited by 24 different venture capital funds each offering venture capital. Microsoft at the time had annualized sales of $7.5 million and pretax profits of about $3 million. Bill Gates, the company's founder, told the venture capitalists that the company did not need venture capital, but he would accept $1 million in exchange for 5% of Microsoft's common stock from the venture capital fund which agreed to work the hardest to help Microsoft grow into a professionally-managed growth company. The race was on. The victor was Technology Venture Investors of Menlo Park, California, which agreed to work closely with middle management to assist them in developing professional managerial skills.

Technology Venture Investors was not the first venture capital fund to add value to a portfolio company. But the linkage of

Microsoft and TVI, as it is known, signifies the beginning of a transitional period in the venture capital industry. The transition is from venture capitalists offering capital plus value-added services to entrepreneurs to venture capitalists becoming "destination sources of capital."

## DESTINATION SOURCES OF CAPITAL

The definition of a destination source of capital is a little like a destination resort. For example, a first time vacationer in Hawaii may select a hotel or resort from a directory provided by a travel agent. On the other hand, a knowledgeable traveler will select a destination resort in Hawaii. The choice is first the resort and second Hawaii. If the resort were to be lifted by "sky hook" to the Dominican Republic, for example, the experienced traveler would go to the Dominican Republic rather than to Hawaii in order to vacation at that resort.

Venture capital funds must now learn to become destination sources of capital. They must learn how to compete for the best deals. It will not be an easy lesson to learn, because there are old habits to change and a lack of experience in competing.

In 1967, when there were very few sources of venture capital, an investment banker told a very young associate: "Money walks. Entrepreneurs run." He meant, quite literally, money should not chase deals. Deals should chase money.

Nearly a generation later, with over 400 active sources of venture capital, money has to put on track shoes.

## WHERE THE BEST DEALS COME FROM

Venture capitalists will tell you to a man that the best deals come from other entrepreneurs who received their start from the venture capitalists to whom they refer good deals. That takes the form of a "thank you note." The venture capitalist is more likely to trust the judgment of a successful entrepreneur about a novice entrepreneur, particularly where the former is well-known to the venture capitalist. Thus, in areas of intense venture capital activity, this system of referrals becomes a self-fulfilling prophecy. The more entrepreneurs that one launches, the greater the number of successful ones, and the greater the number of referrals.

Little good that does for the new venture capital fund sinking roots in a new region. Frequently there are relatively few entrepreneurs who have achieved success. This means there are few mentors or persons with launch experience to help new entrepreneurs get over the hundreds of difficult and random hurdles that befuddle and cause problems for the new company. Whereas San Jose venture capitalists and entrepreneurs can benefit from the explosion of new enterprises in Silicon Valley, and Boulder, Colorado venture capitalists and entrepreneurs can tap into the resources created by Hewlett-Packard and Systems Technology, which in fact have made Colorado's electronics industry the largest employer in the state in less than a decade, numerous other regions do not have the mentors to assist their fledgling entrepreneurs. An entrepreneurial community lacking in mentors is destined to create losers more frequently than winners. There is however a mechanism for creating mentors and feeders to assist in producing superior deals and a self-generating deal flow.

## WHERE THE SECOND BEST DEALS COME FROM

While one is busily creating in his regions the coordinates of an entrepreneurial society, it is important to let the rest of the venture capital community know what you are doing. This is very important for two reasons: (1) your venture capital fund may seek co-investors for its deals in the future and to that extent, you will want to have built strong bridges to other venture capital funds; and (2) it is unlikely that your community and your staff is capable of generating all of the good deals in a certain time period—in 1974, the three best start-ups were located in Sunnyvale, California, Memphis, Tennessee and Stamford, Connecticut and two of the three, Tandem Computer Corp., Federal Express Corp., and TIE/Communications, Inc. attracted venture capital. The second best deals come from other venture capitalists who seek syndicate partners normally to validate their investment judgment and raise a sufficient amount of capital to launch the company they have selected for investment. It is also the case that a deal shown to venture capitalist B by venture capitalist A will be monitored primarily by venture capitalist A. This permits venture capitalist B to invest a portion of its capital without spending the additional cost of labor. A number of the Funds of Funds that make some direct investments in venture capital deals, in addition to investing in funds, rely on the funds they invest in to supply them with a flow of deals.

However, the established, successful venture capital funds are not of a mind to telephone the newest venture capital fund in Central City, USA and offer this new fund with untested venture capitalists a $500,000 piece of a $2 million start-up financing in a company they spent 60 days and 150 man-hours investigating and positioning to receive venture capital. The new venture capital fund must first put itself on the map by describing to the venture capital community—at its conventions and through the trade press—that it is creating value in and around Central City. It must also demonstrate that when it invests in a deal its management team works hard to add value, consult with management, locate customers, locate licensing contracts, generate orders, give sound business advice, and unfailingly attend board meetings. It takes time to generate a reputation in the venture capital community as someone the established venture capitalist would look to share deals with. There are systematic methods of putting oneself on the map; for becoming a destination venture capitalist.

### Generating a Deal Flow

One must become entrepreneurial in the manner in which he goes about generating a flow of high-quality deals. To do so is to develop a business plan called "Catch Entrepreneurs." There is a classic formula for launching any new business that I have addressed elsewhere* known as the Pyramid Method. Its objective, within the Catch Entrepreneur's business plan, is to attract 1000 business plans per annum in order to find 10 outstanding deals. It is easier to discuss this process diagramatically (see Exhibit 11).

A potpourri of governors, mayors, economic development agencies, and concerned municipal leaders have engaged the au-

*The Entrepreneurial Life, Wiley, New York, 1983.

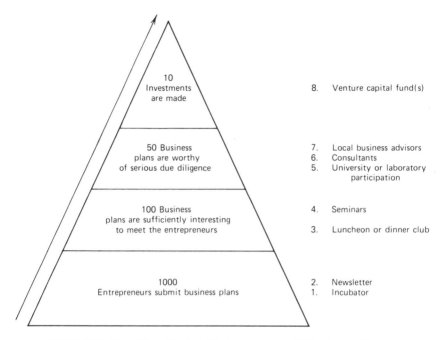

| | |
|---|---|
| 10 Investments are made | 8.   Venture capital fund(s) |
| 50 Business plans are worthy of serious due diligence | 7.   Local business advisors<br>6.   Consultants<br>5.   University or laboratory participation |
| 100 Business plans are sufficiently interesting to meet the entrepreneurs | 4.   Seminars<br><br>3.   Luncheon or dinner club |
| 1000 Entrepreneurs submit business plans | 2.   Newsletter<br>1.   Incubator |

EXHIBIT 11.   The "Catch Entrepreneurs" Business Plan

thor over the last 10 years with one question: "How can we clone Silicon Valley?" The answer lies in the diagram shown above, plus one other exogeneous variable: develop and implement a "Catch Entrepreneurs" business plan. Another exogeneous variable, by the way, is the physical amenities of the area. Having the ocean, the mountains, sunshine, low crime rates, and good schools is required to attract and hold entrepreneurial companies. Small towns such as Champaign, Illinois, Eugene, Oregon, Madison, Wisconsin, Albany, New York and Ann Arbor, Michigan have effectively put out an "Entrepreneurs are Welcome" sign, and added a new coat of paint every year; yet none are conventional sun belt cities and none have venture capital funds in operation. They import their capital or generate local funding programs to hold their entrepreneurs.

As one studies the ad hoc methods used by these small towns and the more systematic plans of Pittsburgh, Pennsylvania, Salt Lake City, Utah, Atlanta, Georgia, Troy, New York, and Fort Wayne, Indiana to catalyze the entrepreneurial revolution on a local level, it is one additional step to transfer that form of regional economic planning to the "Catch Entrepreneurs" business plan.

The pyramid in Exhibit 11 has four principal categories which are indicative of the four quality levels of business plans or the entrepreneurs who generate them. As the eye moves up the pyramid in the path of the arrow, the business plans and the entrepreneurs who generate them are positively affected by the eight variables along the right-hand wall of the pyramid. These variables, created or sponsored at least in part by the venture capital fund managers, add value to the system that pulls the better entrepreneurs up the pyramid with the best ones finally obtaining funding. These eight variables are the catchers that attract the entrepreneurs, improve and enhance their business plans if that is called for, and move them up the pyramid until they are worthy of funding. Along the way, 99% of the business plans and entrepreneurs are either thrown out because of their inadequacies or funded by other means, including a venture fund outside the region, wealthy individuals, government guaranteed loans, the new issues market, suppliers, customers, licensees, lenders, or other competitive sources. If the support services to the pyramid are effective and improve over time, then in the second year the venture capital fund should invest in 20 deals generated and enhanced by the system, and in the third year 30 deals should be funded. This means, of course, that other venture capital funds will move into the market to shoulder some of the investment responsibility and the original fund may need to be augmented with additional capital.


## THE INCUBATOR

The venture capital fund should take a certain amount of responsibility to form an incubator in the local community. The purpose of the incubator is to enable potential or would-be entrepreneurs to test their concepts or business plans without taking the full risk—leaving their jobs, raising money from family and friends, foregoing other securities and comforts—and perhaps falling on their faces. The incubator is not a new concept, but it has become so successful that it is being systematized.

The original entrepreneurial incubator was typically a room in a small venture capital firm or investment bank where an entrepreneur could use a variety of services free of charge and sit in on business plan presentations of other entrepreneurs for the purpose of learning from the better ones and critiquing the poorer ones. Jim Treybig, the founder of Tandem Computer Corp., was plucked out of Hewlett-Packard in 1975 by Tom Perkins, of Kleiner Perkins, and incubated at that venture capital fund while he develped a business plan. The tangible services include telephone, mail, couriers, photostat machines, secretarial, data processing, and a large library. The intangible benefits include reading hundreds of business plans, sitting in on dozens of oral presentations, participating in the due diligence process on the better deals, structuring and negotiating the terms of the superior ones and then helping to launch or add value to the ones that get funded.

The objective of an incubator in a community that heretofore has lacked a venture capital fund and awareness of the entrepreneurial process, at least in a systematic and sustained manner, is to "start an entrepreneurial itch." It is the all-important physical facility that welcomes would-be entrepreneurs and affords them a relatively inexpensive opportunity to test their entrepreneurial ideas. It is important that the facility be stocked with all of the resources that a potential entrepreneur needs to test his or her idea and be staffed by people who can provide support services. Most communities are utilizing old school buildings for incubators. They have large rooms, good security and parking, and big halls for informal meetings among the entrepreneurs and managers.

In an ideal world, the financial support for an incubator would come from three sources: (1) the venture capital fund; (2) the local research institution or university; and (3) a small band of local businessmen and investors who have the time, skills, and inclination to assist emerging businesses. These three groups are the entrepreneur's mentors.

The financial return to these three groups for funding the incubator's annual budget can be one or two of several forms of consideration. A simple form of consideration is that the local investors are businessmen who will invest the necessary seed capital to enable the entrepreneur to pay for rent and other services offered by the incubator. A second form of consideration is that the incubator will receive a royalty equal to a percentage of the net profits before taxes of every entrepreneurial opportunity that occupies an office at the incubator. A third form of consideration is that the incubator will receive a combination of cash payments for rent and other services plus a royalty. Or, perhaps there are other workable variables. In any event, the would-be entrepreneur should be required to pay relatively little for the services of the incubator. However, the incubator should be launched in tandem with a seed capital fund made up of local investors and businessmen who can assist the entrepreneurs. There is nothing like equity to glue disparate interests together.

Because the incubator will incur losses for at last 5 years, it might be appropriate to set it up in a form that permits the losses to be used optimally. Venture capital funds, for example, cannot use losses nor can universities, but individuals can. Thus, although an incubator might be funded equally by a university, a venture capital fund, and a small group of businessmen/investors, the former groups might be larger owners of the potential profits of the incubator while the individuals receive a greater amount of losses.

The legal structure of the incubator should be such that there is fluidity in and out of the ownership. For example, the venture capital fund may go out of business or move to another town; or its key personnel might die or lose interest in venture capital investing and thus seek to sell the interest in the incubator to a third party. A science-based corporation may move into the community and seek to play a helpful role in generating an entrepreneurial spirit among its employees. It may feel that it is in the corporation's best interests to encourage employees to test their entrepreneurial ideas at the incubator, and in order to participate in possible successful ventures, it would like to buy into the ownership of the incubator. The university or research institution may have a budget crisis and seek to sell all or part of its interest. Finally, the individual investors will come and go and there should be a fluid means for their estates to be able to sell their interests to an approved third party. Systems such as this have been used in condominiums and attorneys can be located who are aware of the most flexible legal structures to meet the needs of the parties.

The annual budget of the incubator is probably not less than $150,000 nor more than $300,000, depending upon the numbers of potential entrepreneurs the facility must service in a given year. If an incubator will have extensive utilization, there will be a need for more telephone lines, greater maintenance, extra personal computers, more furnishings, and perhaps additional staff members. If a university or research institution has some unused space that it wishes to make available to the incubator, then that portion of the budget devoted to rent would be saved. Perhaps some tables and chairs could be donated by local corporations or banks, which would reduce the capital equipment and furnishings requirement. Some incubators receive an important impetus from the local university, which donates the time of its business school students—totally free and eager labor—thus saving a material amount of the staffing budget. Finally, the library can be partially stocked with 1-year old directories that would otherwise be discarded by local manufacturers and financial institutions. The library is one of the most expensive components of an incubator; therefore, because of necessity, it must be as full and complete as possible. One potential entrepreneur might want to check prices on semiconductors, thus requiring a fairly extensive directory of semiconductor manufacturers, while another may wish to check locations and square footage of all of the hotels in North America, thus requiring another volume of specific information. It is not necessary to begin with every directory or every industry, but to properly service a community of fledgling entrepreneurs, a beginning library would certainly need to include The Thomas Register of Manufacturers, Dun & Bradstreet's Million Dollar, Middle Market, and SIC Code Directories, Standard & Poor's Directories of Publicly-Held Companies, The Department of Commerce's Industrial Directory, statistics published by the U.S. Government and essentially based on census data, the yellow pages of the 100 largest cities, the Encyclopedia of Associations, catalogues of the principal suppliers of components to small companies, plus subscriptions to several dozen trade journals and business newspapers and magazines. The incubator should also develop a simplified indexing service to "electronic directories" that are able to provide answers to inquiries by downloading information through the incubator's modem and onto its computer for print-out. Other useful indexes are those that one finds in a well-stocked business school library, such as the New York Times index, Business Week index, and indexes of articles pertaining to subject classifications such as oil, electronics, energy, health care delivery, and other relevant areas. In building the incubator's library, the relevant issue is this: each potential entrepreneur must initially involve himself, with the guidance of the staff, in measuring the size of the problem he or she says that he can develop a solution for. That means locating information about the number of selling sites for the solution and the potential price that a selling site is likely to pay. This will involve researching the group of people who ostensibly have the problem and ascertaining the likelihood of their willingness to pay for a solution. The library must be created to make it relatively easy for the potential entrepreneur to audit the size of the problem fairly rapidly. If not, discouragement may set in which could infect attitudes of other entrepreneurs. Investigating the size of the problem or as some say, "market research," is the least fun part of the entrepreneurial process. It is also the part that most entrepreneurs perform in a weak and incomplete manner. Thus, it is incumbent upon the incubator staff to assist the entrepreneur in completing his market research in an extremely thorough manner, before going onto the next step.

The most critical component of the budget is the capital equipment cost. Depending upon one's location and the industries that the potential entrepreneurs are most likely to address, the capital equipment budget must accommodate a variety of tools from electronic test instruments, lathes, and welding equipment to printed circuit board layout, and apparel cutting tools. Once again, these tools should not necessarily be purchased before the first potential entrepreneur rings the doorbell, but a shop should be set up and nicely furnished with plenty of room for expansion. In some cases, a successful graduate of the incubator may wish to purchase the analog to digital convertor or oscilloscope that he used in the incubator and either use it or bronze it. There is no particular reason to purchase new equipment for the incubator, when used equipment in good repair will suffice. Equipment purchases over a certain dollar amount should be referred to an executive committee, with the intent not to deprive the entrepreneur of testing his entrepreneurial ideas, but rather to determine if there might be a way of not tying up capital in a large piece of equipment that may never be used after the first time.

A hypothetical first 3-year budget for an incubator appears in Exhibit 12.

The incubator's hypothetical budget for its first 3 years of operation in Exhibit 12 is dependent upon a number of critical factors,

EXHIBIT 12. Hypothetical First Three Year Budget for an Incubator

| | Year One | Year Two | Year Three |
|---|---|---|---|
| *Operating Expenses*: | | | |
| Salary: Receptionist, Secretary | $ 16,000 | $ 18,000 | $ 20,000 |
| Assistant Secretary | — | 9,000 | 20,000 |
| FICA, Benefits | 3,000 | 6,000 | 8,000 |
| Rent—3000 sq.ft. | 36,000 | 36,000 | 36,000 |
| Telephone | 12,000 | 18,000 | 24,000 |
| Utilities, Insurance | 6,000 | 7,000 | 8,000 |
| Postage, Couriers | 4,000 | 5,000 | 6,000 |
| Consummables | 4,000 | 5,000 | 6,000 |
| Library, Subscriptions | 5,000 | 5,000 | 5,000 |
| Maintenance, Repairs | 5,000 | 6,000 | 7,000 |
| Subtotal | 91,000 | 115,000 | 140,000 |
| *Capital Costs*: | | | |
| Word processors | 8,000 | 6,000 | 4,000 |
| Leasehold improvements | 20,000 | 2,000 | 2,000 |
| Shop set-up; Tools | 15,000 | 5,000 | 5,000 |
| Electronic equipment | 25,000 | 25,000 | 25,000 |
| Reserve | 25,000 | 25,000 | 25,000 |
| Subtotal | 93,000 | 63,000 | 61,000 |
| Total | $184,000 | $178,000 | $201,000 |

including demand for the incubator's services and the role of key members of the community in supplying goods and services on a free or very low cost basis. For example, the hypothetical business plan depicted herein lists relatively large expenditures for capital equipment and relatively little for skilled labor. It assumes that a university or research institution in the community will make available faculty or students to assist potential entrepreneurs in formulating their new business idea. The benefits to the potential entrepreneurs and to the students of this kind of cross-fertilization are both lasting and substantial. When managers of local factories and businesses are brought into the process along with academicians and potential entrepreneurs, the gains are spread further.

The interrelationships between the incubator and the university are primarily the interpersonal ones that develop between students and entrepreneurs. The students are assigned certain times during the week in which they staff the incubator. It is assumed that the faculty will have approved a certain number of hours each week of incubator time as being credit worthy.

While staffing the incubator, the students will be responsible for logging in the deals, interviewing the potential entrepreneurs, explaining their contractual arrangements with the incubator and summarizing the procedures of the incubator in its relationship with the potential entrepreneurs. Once the process is understood and agreed to, the potential entrepreneur becomes the client and the incubator becomes the agent. The goal of the agent is to produce a professional service for the client that will lead to his either happily burying his idea or happily launching a new company.

It is assumed that the students who staff the incubator will have had a 1-year, graduate level business school education and understand economics, accounting, and marketing at least well enough to matriculate into their second year of business school. It is further assumed that they are enrolled in a course on the entrepreneurial process or on managing the small company. To the extent that they will be hand-holding potential entrepreneurs through the "problem formulation" or market research stage of exploring their idea for a new company, the students should be familiar with portions of the venture capital process, primarily the due diligence stage. This subject is dealt with in Chapter 3.

If the flow of deals is relatively slow, several students may be assigned to one client. This should have the effect of researching the market more broadly and determining with greater thoroughness if the problem for which the client has a solution exists and if the client would respond favorably in a marketplace to the solution. The students should involve the client in the market research activity in order to gain insights from him in designing the questionnaire and so that he may hear precisely what the people with the problem are saying about his potential solution. The response may enable him to redirect his efforts or modify the solution to fit the problem. After all, Columbus thought he was sailing to India in 1492 and Thomas J. Watson, Sr. thought IBM might sell 12 computers in total. Planning errors have been known to produce the occasional pleasant result.

If it is determined that the client is addressing a responsive potential marketplace eager for his solution, he must develop and produce the solution. At this point, the student involvement may become less, depending upon whether the solution is a product or a service. If the former, then the incubator must provide the tools necessary for the development and prototyping of a product. The local manufacturers who have a relationship with the incubator could become helpful at this stage.

An optimum number of clients simultaneously being serviced by a newly-formed incubator in its first year is probably between five and eight. Incubators in Philadelphia, Pittsburgh, and Salt Lake City have grown to over 30 tenants in 2 years. This assumes that one-third are in the process of entering the incubator with their projects in a planning stage; one-third in an active investigation stage, which could last from 60 to 90 days; and one-third are in the solution or product development stage. A full house of eight clients serviced by 18–25 students, several faculty members, and a handful of representatives from local manufacturing companies, scheduled in some intelligent manner from 10:00 A.M. to 9:00 P.M. 5 days a week and on weekends would exhaust a secretarial staff of two, particularly if the secretaries were new to their jobs and to word processing. There is a trade-off to consider. A highly successful incubator could create an electrically charged entrepreneurial environment, which is at first blush extremely positive for the local venture capital fund. On the other hand, it could lead to confusion, disarray, and a negative attitude toward the incubator, which could lead to criticism of the venture capital fund. Consultants in the field of incubator launching and management are available to minimize the mistakes. When asked what their biggest past mistakes in previous incubators have been, these consultants have said the following: (1) taking government money and having to take in all entrepreneurs from the state; (2) trying to be all things to all people; and (3) not acting in a businesslike manner at all times.

To avoid the problems identified by incubator-launch consultants, the incubator's executive committee should encourage the development of guidelines for the acceptability of entrepreneurial projects and for the timing of the investigation phase, as well as the product development phase. For example, as to guidelines for acceptability, a workable statement might read as follows:

The incubator agrees to assist any potential entrepreneur from the region whose idea for a new business addresses one or more of the following goals:

1. Could effectively treat a disease presently affecting large numbers of people.

2. Could assist or enrich the lives of a disadvantaged sector of the population.

3. Could improve the productivity of an industrial sector, thereby reducing costs.

4. Could add efficiency to a distribution or marketing system, thereby reducing product costs.

5. Is otherwise deemed a *potential* social benefit by a simple majority vote of two clients, two students or agents, and one member of the executive committee.

Although an exclusional system might seem to contradict the purpose of an incubator, there are individuals whose destiny it is to take advantage of any inexpensive support system. At a banquet set for potential entrepreneurs, mentors, and venture capitalists, these individuals come early, stay late, and eat from everyone's plate. Their entrepreneurial ideas range from floating icebergs from the North Pole to Saudi Arabia to stopping hurricanes. Inventors are frequently colorful and charming, though rarely successful entrepreneurs.

The executive committee of the incubator implements the policies of the board, facilitates its decisions, serves as an intermediary between the activities of the incubator and the board, and pays the bills. A five-person board made up of three of the incubator's investors, one member of the faculty, and one independent outside business person, would be a feasible structure. The board of directors, by the very nature of desiring to obtain the involvement of the community, must be somewhat larger. Representatives of local manufacturers, the university, the venture capital fund, possibly an engineering firm, vocational high school, and commercial bank would.be suitable board members. The people, rather than the institutions they represent, will hold the key to the success or failure of an incubator. The Research Triangle, in Raleigh, North Carolina, has not been particularly successful at launching entrepreneurial companies. One reason is because the predilection was that large high technology companies spawned entrepreneurs. The opposite is the case. They must be ferreted out of corporations, laboratories and universities with the offer of mentors, business plan writers, and capital.

A directory of the current incubators in the U.S. appears in Appendix I.

## NEWSLETTER

In the classic new industry launch, a newsletter presages the coming of the problem-solvers. And so it is when one wants to trumpet the coming of incubators, seminars, and venture capital funds to a new region. The newsletter is the principal means of getting the attention of the target market. Its purposes are to index the entrepreneurial activities in the region, announce various events that the readers may wish to attend, and feature the burgeoning entrepreneurial companies in the region. For potential entrepreneurs. who lack the courage to visit the incubator with their idea, the newsletter helps to inch them out into the open. Its message is, clear and simple: "There are lots of problems in need of solution and an increasing number of hearty souls, no brighter than the rest of us, are testing their ideas with other people in the community." The temptation to put into practice the often-used phrase— "What this country really needs is . . ."—eventually becomes too great, and the potential entrepreneur avails himself of one or two of the monthly events listed in the newsletter. It also helps, of course, to situate the incubator on a busy street and have lights kept on until midnight every night. The entrepreneurial itch will eventually catch up with even the most stoic company man who yearns to be his own boss someday.

There is a science, or perhaps an advanced art form, to the publication of a newsletter, which is explained in several interesting books on the subject. In classical entrepreneurship, the newsletter is used to generate customer financing via its subscriber base. In the case of a newsletter, the purpose of which is to generate entrepreneurs in a region, it would be difficult to charge more than $1.00 per month or $12.00 per year. To meet the deficit, the newsletter would need a grant, which has been heretofore available through the National Science Foundation, or advertisers. Let's examine first the layout and contents of a typical monthly newsletter and then review its hypothetical budget.

## Layout

The cover of the four-page, tabloid-sized newsletter published by the Utah Economic Development Division, shown in Exhibit 13, has an important, significant appearance.

Its running title, over-sized appearance, and feeling of spaciousness practically compel the reader to look at the headlines and read a story or two. The purpose of the newsletter is to attract readership with stories about entrepreneurial activity in the region, and an open, spacey layout is friendlier than a small, compact "grey" cover. Tabloid size is more unusual than the more conventional 8½" × 11" and an odd size will make the newsletter stick out in the mail and compel readership as well.

The use of photographs is suggested, because they will point out more vividly the faces of the entrepreneurs, the directors of the incubator, and other persons actively involved in catalyzing entrepreneurial activity in the region. Drawings and photographs are useful to show more clearly how a complex product operates, the organization chart of a company, the flow of a product or service through a distribution system, and to uncomplicate other subjects. As much as possible, the newsletter should stretch to be more than black or white, with lots of type. Exhibits that employ bar charts, line drawings, and the occasional introduction of another color can brighten the pages and help to create an enthusiastic readership. The objective of the newsletter is to create a positive, friendly environment that will coax entrepreneurs out of their laboratories, corporate offices, and classrooms and into the incubator, seminars, or venture capital club meetings.

As to the subject matter of the newsletter, the overriding goal is to index entrepreneurial activity in the area. Thus, the relevant subject matter is as follows:

The entrepreneurial process.

Governmental activities vis-à-vis entrepreneurs.

Institutional activities vis-à-vis entrepreneurs.

Examples of local entrepreneurs.

National venture capital and entrepreneurial activity.

Calender of events.

Book reviews.

Letters to the editor.

Classified advertising.

## The Entrepreneurial Process

This topic, perhaps in the form of a regular interview with a local entrepreneur, could discuss the sequence of events that led him or her into entrepreneurship and the events that followed: identifying a large problem in need of solution, researching the problem, developing the solution, testing the solution, building the management team, conveying the solution to the problem, raising venture capital, overcoming obstacles, and so forth.

## Governmental Activities Vis-à-Vis Entrepreneurs

It is frequently the case that state and local government must be prodded to remove obstacles that impede the entrepreneurial process. For example, state blue-sky laws are frequently too constraining, historical revenue bond financing is too limiting, industrial zoning designed for the Industrial Revolution should be reexamined in terms of the digital revolution, or the state pension fund should consider setting aside a portion of its funds for venture capital investing. Interviews with state and local officials in other states, whose achievements could then be correlated with the entrepreneurial achievements of that state, can effect change.

## Institutional Activities Vis-à-Vis Entrepreneurs

Local universities, vocational schools, and corporations from time to time make more than a passing gesture towards entrepreneurs. Indeed, universities are increasingly becoming the catalysts for entrepreneurial incubators. In Philadelphia, 24 universities approved the incubator launched in 1983.* Corporations in the state

*Forbes, December 21, 1983, p.135.

# the Utah Experience

A Publication of the Utah Economic Development Division

Vol. 1, No. 4 Spring, 1984

## Kimberly-Clark Selects Utah For Plant Site

Utah's economic well-being received a major infusion of good news in mid-March when Kimberly-Clark Corporation, the paper products giant, announced it will build a 430,000 square-foot facility to produce disposable diapers in northern Utah. The firm is a Fortune 500 company and recorded sales last year of $3.3 billion.

The development will create 300 jobs and will be located at the Weber County Industrial Park north of Ogden where the Neenah, Wisconsin-based firm has acquired options on 137 acres. Darwin E. Smith, board chairman and chief executive officer of Kimberly-Clark and Governor Scott M. Matheson made the announcement.

Mr. Smith said the facility will have an annual payroll of $6 million with nearly all employees to be hired locally.

The plant will manufacture Kleenex Huggies, the nation's leading brand of premium diapers, and will be Kimberly-Clark's second new plant to serve western and southwestern markets for that product. The other is in Paris, Texas, and it was completed in 1983.

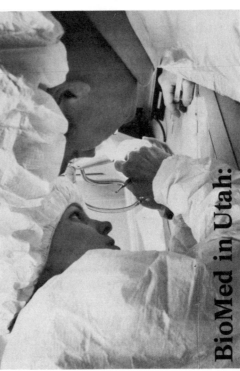

Photo courtesy of Kalil N edical Inc.

## BioMed in Utah:

## From World-Class Research To World-Wide Marketing

The scenario is played often in board rooms across the country: corporate executives assessing the resources of five or six "target cities" which are the most beneficial for a company planning to either move or expand its bio-medical/bio-technical operations.

So it was with Catheter Technology, a biomedical research company which has patented a new type catheter. Its officers hired a private consulting firm to assist in selecting a manufacturing site which would incorporate the company's expected production and employment levels three years into the future.

First, the consultants constructed a model of Catheter Technology and then projected the company's figures into the costs of doing business in six western cities—Salt Lake City, Utah; Portland, Oregon; Tempe, Arizona; Boise, Idaho; Vancouver, Washington; and Sunnyvale, California.

Salt Lake City proved to be the best location for economic reasons and rated number one on a separate measure of non-economic factors.

The favorable economic factors of a Utah site were:

Equity of the tax structure (property tax, income tax, sales tax); labor costs; unemployment insurance costs; worker compensation costs; and land costs.

Utah's favorable non-economic considerations influencing the decision were:

Availability and suitability of labor skills; productivity of the work force; higher educational and vocational training facilities; sound transportation (air and ground); attitude of local government and the state legislature toward business; community appearance; similar industrial technology; and transfer receptiveness (willingness of employees to move to Utah).

But Catheter Technology is not the only firm to cite these reasons for locating in Utah. Officials of Deseret Medical, Inc., a subsidiary of Warner-Lambert say labor and operating costs are moderate in Utah. And Harold Rossberg of Sorenson Research, a subsidiary of Abbott Laboratories, adds that a good work ethic and industry-oriented vocational training centers are additional attributes to the area.

Another major catalyst for the burgeoning bio-medical industry in the state is the University of Utah's world-renown research capability which has spawned several high-tech firms, including companies developing artificial blood vessels, an artificial ear, artificial nerves and the now-storied permanent artificial heart.

Dr. Robert Jarvik, developer of the Jarvik-7 artificial heart at the University of Utah, notes that "Utah has a can-do attitude" and does not stifle research but encourages the commercialization of products which are beneficial to mankind. He is president of Kolff Medical which is developing an artificial ear, in addition to refining its artificial heart.

An October 1983, study for the Utah Economic Development Division by the University of Utah Bureau of Business and Economic Research reveals there are nearly 5,000 persons employed by 34 firms in the medical supply and biomedical industry in Utah.

Pointing to the study, Evelyn Lee, director of the economic development division for the state, says the medical supply industry includes large mass manufacturing firms and small specialized companies engaged in batch production. The two largest, the aforementioned Deseret Medical and Sorenson Research, are involved in the mass manufacture of disposable medical supplies. Fifteen of the 29 manufacturing firms produce electronic medical devices.

See page 2, col. 1

Construction on the Utah facility is scheduled to begin in May, take 12 months to complete and will include an automated warehouse.

Mr. Smith said, "The plant will be very attractive and we believe it will be a valuable asset to the community as an employer, tax payer and corporate citizen." He described the manufacture of disposable diapers as a clean process that would have little, if any, affect on the environment. "All of the materials for the diaper would be shipped to the plant and converted into the finished product," he said.

Kimberly-Clark has plants in 19 states and in 19 countries outside the U.S. The Ogden operation will be its first in Utah. In addition to diapers, Kimberly-Clark's other consumer products include Kleenex facial tissue, Kleenex and Hi-Dri household towels, Kleenex and Delsey bathroom tissues, Kotex and New Freedom feminine pads and Depend incontinence products.

Kimberly-Clark has 34,000 employees in its worldwide operations, including 18,000 in the United States. The firm has 22,500 shareholders.

In making the announcement on selecting Utah for the new facility, Mr. Smith lauded Governor Matheson, the Utah Economic Development Division, the Weber County Industrial Development Corporation, and others "who were so cooperative during the site selection process." He said, "All had an important bearing on our decision" to locate in Utah.

Governor Matheson said, "I welcome such an internationally prestigious company as Kimberly-Clark as the newest member of Utah's business community. This announcement reflects the success of Utah's economic development efforts to enhance Utah's image as an ideal site for business and industry.

"It also is consistent with the state's policy to create jobs and provide a broader tax base," the governor continued.

**EXHIBIT 13. Cover of the Utah Economic Development Division's Newsletter**

could be interviewed to determine their willingness and desire to farm out work to smaller companies in the community, notwithstanding their under-capitalization or other standard deficiencies.

## Examples of Local Entrepreneurs

This topic is possibly the highlight of the newsletter. A successful entrepreneurial company should be the feature story each month and it should be seen as an achievement to reach that level. The newsletter editor, it goes without saying, should be cautious to select companies that are more substance than smoke. Frequently in a community there is a rapidly emerging company that attracts investors and publicity with ease, but is more hard pressed to deliver revenues or create value in the marketplace.

## National Venture Capital and Entrepreneurial Activity

Every community is interested in how it compares with other communities or with "national averages." For example, entrepreneurs are concerned if their state is receiving its "fair share" of venture capital; if it is to become the next clone of Silicon Valley; if its community leaders are as aggressive in paving the path for entrepreneurs as they are in Austin, Texas, or Columbus, Ohio. This column could be written to bring relevant national news to the area's entrepreneurs. The newsletter entrepreneur must be careful to do more to extract information from *Forbes, Inc.,* and *Venture.* He or she should call economic development agencies routinely to discuss developments in their communities, particularly with regard to innovative financing methods, such as R&D limited partnerships with equity features rather than royalties; formation of seed capital funds that will support entrepreneurs in their incubation stage; or new state legislation that assists entrepreneurial companies.

## Calendar of Events

This topic requires very little expansion. Every event of the next 30 days that might be of interest to entrepreneurs should be announced and briefly described. Events outside the state, such as regional conferences, should be listed. The newsletter should be open and responsive to all requests for listings.

## Book Reviews

There is much written for entrepreneurs and managers of rapidly emerging companies, and a cogently written book review in each issue of the newsletter could be of invaluable assistance to entrepreneurs who read very little, owing to the pressure and demands on their time. A review of a book on marketing, recruiting, or raising venture capital could provide a busy entrepreneurial team with a breath of insight that it might have otherwise done without.

## Letters to the Editor

In order for a newsletter to index all of the entrepreneurial news in its community, it must avail itself to the letter writers. Although entrepreneurs and people involved in the "chase" have precious little time for writing letters, there are people who have an insatiable curiosity to know why events occur, frequently in a manner not totally favorable to themselves. These people are frequently complainers; but the problems they raise should be responded to in a careful and intelligent manner. Occasionally, most of the readers can benefit from the questions and answers.

## Classified Advertising

Much of the entrepreneurial process is aided by networking in the community to obtain resources, such as marketing, public relations, management assistance, and so forth. The classified advertising could serve as a means for entrepreneurs and managers to form alliances, or for an entrepreneur to locate a hitherto unknown logo designer, product packager, or production engineer. The price of the advertising should be relatively inexpensive in order to service the needs of the community.

These sections appear to be obvious ones, those of the most topical and immediate interest to a community interested in stimulating the entrepreneurial process. From time to time and from community to community, there may be news of great importance that will need headlining. The formation of a new venture capital fund or the introduction of a new state grant program would be an appropriate cover story.

## THE VENTURE CAPITAL CLUB

Once each month it is pleasurable for the entrepreneurs, venture capitalists, and affiliated parties to push aside their day-to-day cares and come together for cocktails, dinner, and conversation. A properly run venture capital club elevates its audience primarily by inviting outstanding speakers chosen from the ranks of successful entrepreneurs or venture capitalists. The audience can usually relate to either, and the question and answer session that follows any topical speech can last for over an hour.

The format for the venture capital club must fit the audience that it serves. For example, the New York Venture Capital Forum is a monthly luncheon club, attended primarily by venture capitalists and leveraged buy-out fund managers. The speakers are generally enlightened, successful individuals whose relationship to venture capital may be, at best, tangential. The purpose that many members feel that the club serves is to find co-investors for their deals.

New York and San Francisco are unique in that hundreds of venture capitalists live in the area, of whom 50–75 are available to meet for lunch once each month. In smaller towns where the venture capital initiative is being created, the audience mix is more heavily would-be entrepreneurs. The format of this type of club in a community such as this is typically composed of 40% would-be entrepreneurs, 20% entrepreneurs, 20% investors, and 20% other (attorneys, advertising agents, consultants, and government personnel). The most successful program includes a forum, during which entrepreneurs seeking capital or management assistance and managers seeking entrepreneurial companies to join may address the group for 5 minutes. Each speaker must be prepared to answer questions from the audience. The local venture capitalist or incubator staff member can "plant" some questions that will direct the speaker into the proper channels, such as: "Have you researched the market?" "Have you begun thinking about a marketing strategy?" "How large do you think the market is for that product?" And, in that manner, the speaker can think about the *entrepreneurial process*, rather than building the proverbial better mousetrap that ends up languishing on the shelf.

After the 5 minute forum speakers, the guest speaker is introduced. Preferably, he or she has achieved some visible success as an entrepreneur or a venture capitalist. He or she can explain the *process* they went through to launch their company, fund it, staff it, and market the product or service. If the speaker is a venture capitalist, his or her topic is typically "What Criteria Appeals to Our Venture Capital Fund," sparkled with war stories of investments that soured and investments that succeeded.

It is useful, from time to time, to inject principal speakers who can bring another dimension to the community of entrepreneurs and mentors: securities lawyers, tax shelter packagers, leverage buy-out entrepreneurs, and communications consultants. A menu of speakers who essentially work different sides of the same street becomes a little tiring. Nothing has the shocking effect on engineers thinking about black boxes as a communications or marketing consultant showing how to sell, cajole, persuade, and otherwise convince people to do something for you that they had no intention of doing. Frequently, an evangelical, off-the-wall speaker whose subject is "Getting in the Door" or "Closing the Sale" can be the most memorable speaker of the year.

Rather than have a full 12 month program of dinners and speakers, it might be practical to consider a 10- or 11-month program in order to accommodate vacations in July and August. Further, too many programs make them less special, while skipping 2 months heightens the desire for a renewal of the club's dinners.

To initiate a venture capital club, one must generate a mailing list of persons likely to be interested, engage a speaker, and rent a hall. For the latter, hotel or large motel conference rooms are ideal. The price of dinner is generally under $12 per person. The club is able to charge as much as $15 per dinner and apply the slim profit to postage, stationary, the free meal of the speaker, and the cost of his or her board or transportation.

To locate speakers is less difficult than might be at first perceived. There are frequent articles in trade journals and the magazines that service entrepreneurs about successful venture capitalists and entrepreneurs. By telephoning and writing to them, and by being fairly tenacious in one's pursuit of them, a reasonable proportion of them will agree to speak. The would-be entrepreneurs for the 5-minute forum will speak with far less coaxing, primarily because they are anxious to form networks with mentors, consultants, and investors. Word will leak out through the community of the opportunities presented by the venture capital club and a variety of promoters may attend in order to present their "unique investment opportunity" to the investors in the audience. Unless their number gets out of hand, the inclusion of "promoters" during the 5-minute forum can serve as ballast for the weightier, less promotional presentations of the engineers and scientists.

To generate the mailing list requires networking with attorneys, accountants, and advertising agencies that service the small businesses in the community. Although entrepreneurs and small business people are not necessarily one and the same, the distinction is frequently not made by the general population. If the incubator is in operation, its membership should be contacted. The faculty of the nearby business and engineering schools, as well as their graduate students, should be invited, as well as corporate planning officers and plant managers of the local large industrial companies. To obtain a larger initial following, one could rent from the more entrepreneurial magazines the lists of their readers in the community. *Venture* and *Inc.* generally rent their lists, as do high technology publications, such as *Discover, Science Digest, High Technology,* and *Byte.* Finally, the yellow pages are a tried and true method of obtaining names of businesses that appear to be operating in entrepreneurial fields. At the present time, those fields might be listed under the headings of computer services, health care, and electronics.

The venture capital club dinners (or luncheons) should be relaxed and spirited. The host should engender an air of spirited innovation and the sense of a forum of optimistic people pulling in the same direction. Persons with negative attitudes from the audience or a clique of financial consultants who pounce on unsuspecting would-be entrepreneurs offering loans from Middle Eastern banks should be quietly removed from the mailing list.

In the event that it becomes necessary to pay more to obtain quality speakers, the club can charge annual dues. A dues charge of $25–$50 per year is a means of discouraging non-participating people from attending. For example, some clubs have found that without dues an interested entrepreneur might bring his or her date for the evening, who is uninterested in the entrepreneurial process. When dues are introduced, less interested people remain at home.

## SEMINARS

One of the most interesting phenomena in the entrepreneurial process is the seminar. It is, in its simplest form, an all-day, or several-day, series of speeches in which answers are supposedly available to an audience whose members, for the most part, have the same questions. In successful seminars, there is quite a bit of interplay between all of the attendees—speakers and audience—during the seminar, during the coffee breaks, and before and after the seminar. The audience comes to a seminar when they are at a point in their awareness of a new area at which they would like to share information with other people like themselves who have the same kinds of unanswered questions. The seminar is successful when the audience's hands are raised for several hours after the presentation is over.

In the first year of operation of an incubator and venture capital club, a fairly large group of would-be entrepreneurs will have received exposure to the entrepreneurial process. Perhaps 300 will have attended the venture capital club dinners and perhaps 50 will have attended the incubator. Of these, 20% or more may have the entrepreneurial bit placed squarely in their teeth and be eager to absorb more sophisticated information about other rungs in the ladder of entrepreneurship. The initial seminar, then, should respond to the needs of this 20% group, plus any others who might benefit.

Some of the more viable areas of interest in a full day of speeches and panel discussion are the following:

1.  Various sources of financing.
2.  Legal aspects of the new company.
3.  Accounting aspects of the new company.
4.  Designing and implementing marketing plans.

5.  Building a management team.
6.  Setting up a production line.

Naturally, these topics require skilled speakers in order for the seminar to succeed. The community may possess some, but not all, of the speakers in its universities and corporations. The seminar sponsor will have to import qualified speakers in order to satisfy the attendees. This may require paying the transportation and board of speakers, and possibly a small per diem, to assure a quality program. An alternative or possible solution to holding down the price of the seminar is to enlist the financial assistance of a local sponsor or perhaps several sponsors. Possible candidates for sponsorship include accounting firms, universities, and commercial banks.

It would be difficult to charge in excess of $150 to $200 per attendee for the community's initial seminar. Would-be entrepreneurs are among the least financially solvent people, certainly in proportion to the size of their dreams, in the community. They have an appreciation of the extraordinary value to them of the seminar, and it is in the best spirit of starting an entrepreneurial itch in the community to set the price of the seminar at a very affordable level. The entrepreneurs should come away knowing that they received a considerable amount of value for their $150. At the end of the seminar, the attendees should be asked to fill out a questionnaire that rates the program overall, each individual subject, and each speaker. In this manner, the seminar may be improved each time.

The frequency of the seminar is subject to the needs of the community. Two seminars per annum of the type outlined above will probably be adequate for a community of 75,000–150,000 total population. Larger communities may beckon more or perhaps other kinds of seminars. For example, cities the size of Atlanta and Dallas, which are attempting to spawn enlightened entrepreneurial valleys, have invited venture capitalists to attend seminars at which the speakers are entrepreneurs. The latter have numbers, and after a day in which 20 entrepreneurs present their business plans to several hundred venture capitalists, the better numbers meet with the interested venture capitalists to explore a possible investment in greater detail. Smaller communities have less need to become involved in these auction type seminars, as long as enough venture capital funds begin to inhabit the community or send emissaries to speak at the venture capital club dinners or at the seminars.

It is also important at seminars that a professional, articulate promotion is made for the incubator, the newsletter, and the venture capital club. Booths should be available for attendees to become subscribers to the newsletter, members of the club, and to have questions answered about the incubator. Attendees may also wish to purchase cassettes of the seminar in order to refresh their memories in 30 days or so; or to listen to one or two of the seminars that they were unable to attend. As to the budget of the seminar if 70 persons attend and pay $150 each, the $10,500 in gross revenues should cover rental of the meeting rooms, brochure preparation, postage and handling, a light buffet and $300 in expense reimbursement for each of the six speakers. If fewer than 50 attendees are expected to attend then a sponsor may be needed. It requires reiteration that the attendees should feel that the seminar sponsors seek to add value at a nominal price, rather than to make a profit by gulling the unknowing and untravelled entrepreneur.

## UNIVERSITY OR LABORATORY PARTICIPATION

Incubators in most communities have received the endorsement and active sponsorship of the nearby engineering school or laboratory. The reasons for this are several, including the obvious one that Silicon Valley, the legend has it, was initiated by Dean Terman of the Stanford Engineering School recommending his brightest graduates to local investors in and around Palo Alto. Some of the unsuccessful attempts to clone Silicon Valley bear the heavy hand of state governments and large corporations, rather than universities and laboratories. The former have shorter time horizons, need to show increased employment between elections, and approach problems with sweeping, top-down solutions. Universities and laboratories have longer time horizons and far more patience.

Some incubators have been located on university campuses or adjoining them, in order to enhance the university's real estate. The incubator, thus, may have sprung from the off-hand comment:

"Why don't we do something with that empty barracks behind the engineering school's parking lot." A short research effort leads to the awareness that other schools have been starting programs to assist graduate students in testing their black-box ideas as possible new businesses. The logical conclusion is to provide this facility for graduate students as a means to anchor their brains and energy locally, and at a facility that enhances the university's real estate.

The university may see a profit potential in sponsoring an incubator. University endowment funds have been important investors in venture capital funds since the early 1970's. The entrepreneurial process has been taught since 1978 at an increasing number of business schools. In the not-too-distant future, the existence of an incubator on or near campus will be an important means by which graduate schools attract students. Alumni frequently respond positively to their alma mater's studied incursions outside academia. They feel, perhaps incorrectly, that a successful incubator might breed some new enterprises that will spawn microprocessor factories around the perimeter of the university, creating two long-term salutory effects: (1) a reduction in pleas for donations and (2) a reputation for the university as the womb of high technology entrepreneurs that enhances the value of the university's name in one's curriculum vitae.

Laboratories have become interested in incubators, as well as the entrepreneurial process, for some of the same reasons. However, their overriding reason is a growing shortage of capital. The Federal Government has recently reduced the amount of financial support it is willing to give to national laboratories. In searching for supplemental donors, the laboratories have discovered the private sector: technology-based corporations and venture capital funds. They have invited the two groups to review technologies that are suitable for licensing, a process that is now known as "technology transfer." The licensor provides the capital for the laboratories to continue their technological development and the corporation or venture capital fund obtains a proprietary product around which to build a new division or company.

Laboratories have a second need: cheap labor. They have historically attracted cheap labor in the form of post-doctoral graduates by offering exciting research projects and a community of scholars. With Federal funding in decline, the research projects become fewer. Local technology licensors and venture capital funds provide an offset, and the presence of an incubator adjacent to the laboratory is an advertisement to the post-doctoral graduate that, should he or she develop a possible solution to a large problem, there is a support system to take it from the drafting table to an emerging new company.

Business schools have been sticking their noses under the incubator tent, as well. There appears to be a growing awareness on the part of business school faculties that the nation's economy is becoming entrepreneurial and, once defined, the process of entrepreneurship (to the extent that it is science rather than art) should be taught. Furthermore, in order to attract students, business schools necessarily began offering courses in entrepreneurship or, at least, courses in managing the small business. The existence of a nearby or on-campus incubator provides an outlet for the business school students, whose interests lie in smaller enterprises, to assist the would-be entrepreneurs in testing their new products or services; while at the same time, learning something about the entrepreneurial process. The plus to the community is that the business school graduates will be less likely to leave town to seek their future in New York or San Francisco, but will join a local entrepreneurial company—that which is in shortest supply is management. The active involvement of business school students in the incubator, the seminars, working on the newsletter, and interning at the local venture capital funds helps attract and hold managers in the community. This involvement should be encouraged in all ways, and with whatever stimuli are available.

## CONSULTANTS

As the marketing afficionado Carl Ally once said, "A consultant is someone who borrows your watch to tell you the time, then charges you for it." A necessary evil are consultants. In a local community bent on creating, attracting, and holding entrepreneurs, the consultant fills an important gap: interim management. Consultants are able to see ingredients in a new enterprise that are missing and to recommend their inclusion. Frequently, consultants have some familiarity with management principles and are able to implement them in a manner that lifts up the entrepreneurial process a notch or two. The incubator may operate at too slow a pace for the would-be entrepreneur; so, he or she leaves in order to work directly with a consultant who speeds the product along to final design, test, and assembly, and begins to find customers. The acceleration of the entrepreneurial process may be a positive or a negative influence on the entrepreneur and the incubator sponsors can but wish their graduates well, even when they leave the next prematurely.

Entrepreneurs are produced, in a sudden transformation of a formerly non-fanatical human being, when someone becomes (1) suddenly dissatisfied with an employer, (2) has the insight into a large problem and a solution for it, and (3) has the energy to develop the solution and bring it to the market. Consultants go through a period of dissatisfaction, as well. They have lots of energy, but they are short on the insight that is the "driver" of the entrepreneur. The consultant has a desire to be on his own because he has identified a problem in need of a solution. However, he has not conceived of the solution. Inside every consultant beats the heart of a frustrated entrepreneur. Usually, the consultant understands the scope of the problem, as well as a variety of management disciplines, and can provide very useful advice and assistance to entrepreneurs who are past their start-up stage.

Unfortunately, would-be entrepreneurs are not ready for the kind of service consultants have to offer and they frequently waste their money engaging the services of a consultant. Inventors are frequently abused by consultants who paint visions of wealth and fame in front of their eyes and ask for large ownership positions or percentages of the royalty stream in order to be helpful. Would-be entrepreneurs are subject to being persuaded that their enterprise is the next Polaroid.

The incubator sponsors should advise their clients that consultants can be very helpful in the area of management until the area builds up a large supply of managers, but that their fee arrangements should be reviewed with experienced people to determine their reasonableness. The incubator library might maintain lists of qualified consultants, as well as articles on how to use the services of a consultant optimally.

## LOCAL BUSINESS ADVISORS

One of the many positive events that occurs when a small nucleus of people begins to create a garden of entrepreneurial delights in a community that has ignored the subject for a century or more, is that experienced people begin to surface and to offer their experience on favorable terms. Entrepreneurs need mentors. And mentors need entrepreneurs to validate their existence. The process of a young entrepreneur being guided by a local board of advisors, made up of experienced business people, represents the culmination of many of the efforts of the incubator, the seminars, the newsletter, and inputs of the university and area consultants.The business advisors, in some cases, can combine their resources into a seed capital fund that provides capital to the entrepreneurs just as he or she leaves the incubator. With an ownership position as their consideration, the local business advisors throw themselves into the project to assist the entrepreneur with the launch. When this process works well, the momentum propels the entrepreneurial company much faster than other propellants. Venture capital funds generally like to see a strong local board of advisors, because it helps monitor and add value to the emerging company.

## VENTURE CAPITAL FUNDS

The culmination of the Catch Entrepreneurs Business Plan is that the entrepreneurial companies, when launched correctly, will be funded by the local venture capital fund. It is inevitable that communities that build the structure and the system for attracting, developing, and holding entrepreneurs described herein will also attract capital from financial institutions to form a venture capital fund. Further, the community that can attract a venture capital fund will also, in all likelihood, develop a deal flow that will keep the venture capital fund's capital and interests focused locally. When that closed loop system occurs, Silicon Valley has been cloned.

# 3

# THE DUE DILIGENCE
# PROCESS

The quantity of business plans submitted to a venture capital fund, especially one that raises an optimum amount of funds and builds important communications networks in its primary region of focus, beggars the imagination. Business plans come with the mail, by courier, through brokers, from lawyers and accountants, via telephone, at seminars, in classrooms, and occasionally on airplanes, at sports events, and at parent conferences. For example, Rupert Murdoch, the founding entrepreneur of News Corp., an Australian-based communications conglomerate, met Stanley Schuman, a partner at Allen & Co., creative and astute investment bankers, at a parents conference at Dalton School in New York in the mid-1970's. News Corp.'s financial support for its acquisitions of the *New York Post, Chicago Sun Times, New York, The Village Voice* and other communications companies was unquestioned thereafter. The point is that the heavy volume of incoming business plans, irrespective of their source—children's or adult's playgrounds—must be dealt with rapidly and systematically. The mechanism for dealing with a large quantity of incoming business plans is to create a sifter with purposely shaped tiny holes that permit only certain kinds of deals to be carefully reviewed. It is the careful review of business plans that is known as the *due diligence process*. A deal that survives a meticulous due diligence process, generally receives an investment proposal from a venture capitalist.

At the front end of the due diligence obstacle course is a mechanism for turning down deals that do not meet the venture capital fund's predetermined criteria. To weed out unacceptable deals at the front end, most venture capital funds adopt a deal log and deal log summary mechanism, which permit the general partners to scan the cogent elements of a large number of business plans in a relatively short period of time.

When a business plan is received, an associate or intern reads it quickly looking for significant facts. One of the reasons that cacophonous voices cry out for more literate business plans is that venture capitalists are so lacking in time to read them. The better-written business plans are more carefully read by more senior people. Turndowns occur more frequently for poorly written business plans. The significant facts that the associate attempts to locate in the business plan are the following:

1. At what stage is the company?
2. What problem is the company attempting to solve?
3. Is its solution proprietary or conveyed to the problem in a unique way?
4. Is the entrepreneurial team experienced and competent to manage a rapidly emerging company?
5. Has the company, its product or solution or its management team, been endorsed by a responsible and highly regarded customer or investor?
6. How much capital is required?

A typical deal log that encompasses all of this information plus additional, useful data is shown in Exhibit 14.

A venture capitalist should be able to read a deal log such as the above, filled in with accurate, concise information, and determine if the fund manager should devote manpower and financial resources to investigating the market size, determining the proprietary nature of the product, or exploring the claims in management's resumes. Let's discuss some of the key points to scan for.

### Address

The company should be located within a one hour's drive or flight time from the venture capitalist, particularly if it plans to be an active investor. If the company is both a start-up and located far away, its attractiveness diminishes, unless the entrepreneur will relocate to the venture capital fund's region.

## EXHIBIT 14.   Sample Deal Log

Date received: _____

Name of company: _____

Address: _____

Telephone no: _____

Stage of development: _____

Capital invested to date: _____

Capital requirement: _____

Description of business: _____

_____

Entrepreneur name: _____

Age, background: _____

_____

Manager(s) Name(s): _____

Age(s), background(s): _____

_____

Recommendation: Turndown _____/ _____/ _____/ _____

                     Market size audit _____ / _____ / _____

                     Technical audit _____/ _____ / _____ / _____

                     Entrepreneur audit _____ / _____ / _____

                     Request meeting _____ / _____ / _____ / _____

Disposition: _____

Review by: _____

## Capital Invested to Date

It is important to know the amount of capital contributed by the founders and the sources of the capital. Occasionally an entrepreneur will have sold an excessive percentage of his company's ownership for a relatively small amount of capital which reflects poorly on the entrepreneur's conviction in the company he is attempting to launch. It could also infer a potential problem area in the future when the venture capitalist attempts to reorder the ownership of the company in a more realistic manner.

## Description of Business

In a clear and concise deal log, this section is the only one with a section of thoughts strung together as a short paragraph of several sentences. The associate who prepares the deal log must strive to synthesize information as completely as possible, but with an economy of words. The readers will make decisions based on this section that could make the fund its greatest rate of return or its largest missed opportunity. The style of this section can be modelled after the "Introduction" section of prospectuses for new issues written by securities lawyers. Some examples follow:

> Company intends to design, develop, manufacture, and market hyperthermia equipment and related software for the treatment of cancer. Beta-test site at a Boston hospital over last 6 months with 75 patients shows positive results in 80% of cases on early-stage, subcutaneous carcinomas.

> Scientist has designed a test for home use to enable women in the high-risk age group to give themselves an annual check-up for cervical carcinoma. An inexpensive diagnostic device must be developed to withdraw a specimen, mix it with a reagent, pass it through a recording device, and print out the results.

Both of these deals are in the health care delivery field, the former is a treatment and the latter a diagnostic. It is clear to the venture capitalist that the hyperthermia deal is a start-up and the cervical cancer diagnostic deal is in the product development stage. Development stage companies frequently occupy a very small proportion of a venture capital fund's portfolio because of the length of time required for them to generate a return. Although development stage companies may have higher rates of return, the additional risk—the product development risk—is not generally borne by venture capital funds. Thus, the deal log should explain the company's stage of development and the problem that it is attempting to solve. If the solution has been developed and can be demonstrated, a venture capital fund can react more favorably.

## Entrepreneur: Name, Age, Background

The profile of the potentially successful entrepreneur has become more clearly understood by venture capitalists. It is important that the preparer of the deal log summarize certain of these profile characteristics in order for the fund manager to quickly determine if the entrepreneur will pass through the sifter. Some of the more important characteristics, as we will see further on in this chapter, include the entrepreneur's age, marital status, prior position and length of stay, and technical abilities. In the event that the entrepreneur is not acceptable, but the other characteristics of the business plan seem interesting, the entrepreneur can be removed to a middle management or technical position within the company or bought out in the first stage financing. However, in many cases the entrepreneurial qualities are as important as the solution he or she has developed, because of the entrepreneur's knowledge of the problem and the solution and because of his or her leadership qualities. The preparer of the deal log should look for negatives in the entrepreneur's background to summarize in the deal log. Negatives might include previous bankruptcy, no business experience, and numerous job changes in a short period of time.

## Manager: Name, Age, Background

The objective in providing a short synthesis of the manager's background is first to determine if there is a manager and second to see if he or she fits the profile of the potentially successful manager of an entrepreneurial company. This profile will be discussed in greater detail further along in this chapter. The preparer of the deal log should be looking for the manager's record of corporate achievement, that he or she is approximately 13–16 years older than the entrepreneur and that he or she has had management experience in rapidly growing companies in an industry or industry segment related to the one described in the business plan. If the manager does not meet these requirements, the venture capitalist will know from the deal log that there may be a need to replace him or her in the near future. Entrepreneurs are not necessarily the optimal selectors of their managers. Frequently venture capitalists or executive search consultants are better at matching entrepreneurs with managers. The deal log can indicate to the venture capitalist if the probability of locating a new manager after the financing is high or low. Further, if the problem and the solution appear marginal, the deal can be quickly turned down based on the failure of the entrepreneur and the manager to meet minimum acceptable profile characteristics. On the other hand, if the problem and solution seem exceptional the venture capitalist will intuit a need to consider people changes in the months following the financing.

## Disposition

At the bottom of the deal log are action words indicating the recommended disposition followed by an underline and slash marks. The slash marks separate the underline and allow room for the three fund managers to place their initials. For example, after reading the deal log summary, one venture capitalist whose initials are "RGD" might feel that the market size should be audited, in which event he would initial "RGD" on the line after the words "Market Size Audit." He would then pass the deal log onto another fund manager who would prefer to turn it down, and so indicate by initialing after the words "Turn Down." The third partner may feel that the problem, or potential market, was well explicated in the business plan and he recommends moving right along to the technical or solution audit. He would so indicate by placing his initials after the words "Technical Audit."

Assuming there is a weekly meeting of the fund managers and staff to review the deal log and other matters, the divergent opinions on this particular deal can be aired. The fund managers may adopt an operating policy that two of the three of them must agree on procedure in order to go forward. Another policy might be that if a deal gets two votes for a turn-down, out of three possible opinions, it will be turned down. The issue of operating policy is not the relevant subject; because policies reflect individual preference.

What is important is how to review a massive deal flow in a thorough and expeditious manner. A fast "no" is as helpful to an entrepreneur as a long "yes." If the entrepreneur is turned down quickly, he or she can go on to the next source of capital without a serious delay. A long "no," on the other hand, is very expensive to the entrepreneur in terms of time and working capital.

## The Turndown

Many venture capital firms have developed turndown letters which are churned out by their word processor in flat and cursory words. The turndown letters are clipped onto the entrepreneur's business plan and the two are mailed back. The entrepreneur has not learned anything from the venture capital fund except that the deal did not find interest there.

There are seven non-substantive turndowns that venture capital funds use. These turn-downs provide very little information to entrepreneurs, and frequently incorrect information. Upon receiving one of these, the entrepreneur should recontact the venture capital fund and attempt to determine if his deal (1) was indeed reviewed and (2) if reviewed, could there have been a mistake in interpreting it. The seven non-substantive turn-downs are listed in Exhibit 15.

---

**EXHIBIT 15.    The Seven Non-Substantive Turn-Downs**

---

1. We cannot review your deal at this time due to unusual time constraints.

2. We are not investing in start-ups (or first-stage companies, etc.) at this time.

3. We are not investing in your industry at this time.

4. We are not investing in companies located in your region of the country at this time.

5. Although one or two of us liked the concept, we were unable to obtain unanimous consent at the committee level.

6. We are not investing in companies that require less than $500,000 for ($1,000,000, etc.) at this time.

7. We are not investing in companies that lack an experienced manager (or local board of directors, or some other factor) at this time.

---

When the venture capital fund's word processor churns out turndowns that sound something like the above, the entrepreneur can be fairly assured that the business plan was not thoroughly read. With a little tenacity, the entrepreneur can locate one of the fund managers on the telephone and obtain a more thorough reason for the venture capital fund's not electing to pursue the deal. It could be that the venture capital fund is busy doing work-outs, or is short-handed for health reasons, or that some other problem exists. A tenacious entrepreneur is referred by venture capitalists; and a particularly persistent series of telephone calls may lead to an investment.

There is no good reason for a carefully written business plan which is turned down by a venture capital fund to receive one of the above style form letters. Occasionally, ill-informed would-be entrepreneurs will send one or two page letters to venture capital funds asking them for their interest in a "concept" or "idea." Certain entrepreneurs feel that their solution is "too confidential" to be circulated to venture capitalists via a business plan. These are time wasters, which should receive cursory treatment to match the cursory treatment they have given the venture capitalist. But, a well-prepared business plan deserves a helpful turndown from the venture capitalist.

A helpful turndown provides information to the entrepreneur as to why his or her deal did not make the cut. If the venture capital fund does not wish to put the reasons in writing, it can telephone the entrepreneur and then follow-up with a return of the document.

For example, assume that the problem the entrepreneur has identified is relatively small and that other companies have begun developing solutions there as well, although slightly different. The venture capital fund should have no difficulty saying in a letter that "We think the market you have identified is smaller than we would like to make investments in and that several other companies are geared up to sell into that market which makes your potential share even smaller." Another reason for a turndown might be a young, inexperienced entrepreneur who has not taken the time to find a manager partner, or build a local board of mentors. The venture capitalist should let him or her know that "We would prefer to see your management team strengthened by a strong local board of advisors and perhaps an experienced marketing manager to assist you in launching your new company."

A venture capital fund that takes the time to provide some advice to the entrepreneur along with its turndown is building a stronger deal flow for the future. The entrepreneur will in many cases take the venture capital fund's comments to heart and rebuild the business plan adding into it the deficiencies pointed out by the venture capital fund.

Notwithstanding the venture capital fund's desire to build networks to entrepreneurs with helpful turndowns, the venture capital fund must handle its turndowns rapidly and efficiently in order to make room for the important business of the fund: making investments, adding value to them, and then selling them.

A venture capital fund can convert turndowns into positive advertising for the fund, by enclosing a pamphlet for the entrepreneur to study on the subject of "Characteristics of Successful New Businesses." If a pamphlet such as this accompanies a helpful turndown letter, the entrepreneur is almost certain to have positive feelings about the venture capital fund.

## Deal Log Summary

At the end of each week, the deal flow should have been entered onto the deal logs, typed and circulated to the fund managers for review and comment within a 10 day to 2 week period. On the last day of each week, the deal logs should be summarized onto the deal log summary, a sheet of paper that lists the names of the companies that appear on the deal logs, their addresses (city and state only), the date the business plan was received, and the description of business section essentially retyped. To the right of that, if the status is known, it can be entered in code form such as "MA-1," meaning that one partner recommends a market audit. Or TD-2, meaning that two partners recommend a turndown. The deal log summary can be clipped to the deal logs and the package sent to travelling fund managers and given to non-travelling fund managers for weekend review. Then, at the fund's weekly meeting—usually Monday morning—the deal log and the deal log summary can be reviewed.

An absence in the in-flow of certain kinds of deals can be detected from a well-assembled deal log summary. For example, if vertical market computer software applications companies are attractive investments, but the venture capital fund is receiving horizontal market deals, such as accounting packages, tax packages, and integrated software packages, the fund managers can take the initiative and attempt to encourage the flow of deals that they wish to see.

Venture capital funds occasionally send copies of their deal log summaries to their institutional investors. The purpose of this is to permit them to see the tempo of the deal flow and to read summaries of new company descriptions in innovative areas. In this manner, the institutional investors can get a feel for the possible impact on their equity portfolios of possible new competition, notwithstanding that it may be a few years away.

## THE THREE LAWS OF VENTURE CAPITAL

Venture capital investing is a discipline. Just as in other sciences there are certain rules, or guideposts, which must be committed to memory, tattooed on one's brain if you will, and never forgotten—because to do so is to lose all of one's money and be forced out of the venture capital business. Someone once said, quite prophetically, that venture capital investing is like a pinball game: you have to keep the ball in play. When you run out of balls to play, you are out of the game.

The three laws or guideposts of venture capital, then, are the following:

1. Accept no more than two risks per investment.
2. $V = P \times S \times E$, where $V$ = Valuation, $P$ = the size of the problem, $S$ = the elegance of the solution, and $E$ = the quality of the entrepreneurial team.
3. Invest in big $P$ companies, because the public market will accord to them unreasonably high $V$'s, irrespective of $S$ and $E$.

Prior to discussing the due diligence process, the three laws of venture capital will be elaborated upon, because they form a frame into which the picture of due diligence will be placed.

## THE LAW OF RISK AVERSION

There are typically five risks in a start-up or early stage company. It is up to the venture capitalist to accept no more than two of these risks; and the two that the venture capitalist can control most effectively are numbers three and four: marketing and management. The five risks are given in Exhibit 16.

The acceptable risks are marketing and management, because they are the most controllable. The development and production risks should be borne by the entrepreneur prior to his seeking venture capital. The growth risk is typically borne by public investors after the venture capitalist has liquidified his investment. To remain an investor in a company after one has nursed it through its start-up, first stage, second stage, and initial public offering is to assume the non-controllable risk of the company's stock price declining and giving back much of the hard-earned profit. There is an old saying from the Wall Street district, whose winding streets were laid out in the 17th century by farmers following their pigs to market: "Bulls win. Bears win. Pigs go to the slaughter house." Venture capital investments should be sold when a reasonable return has been achieved and the venture capitalist holds marketable securities.

To better understand the five risks in a start-up or early stage company, we refer to Exhibit 17.

It is the function of the venture capitalist to provide capital and management assistance to the start-up company after the product development and manufacturing risks have been eliminated. The

---

**EXHIBIT 16.    The Five Risks of A Start-Up Company**

---

1.  The Development Risk: Can we develop the product?
2.  The Manufacturing Risk: If we can develop it, can we produce it?
3.  The Marketing Risk: If we can make it, can we sell it?
4.  The Management Risk: If we can sell it, can we sell it at a profit?
5.  The Growth Risk: If we can manage the company, can we grow it?

---

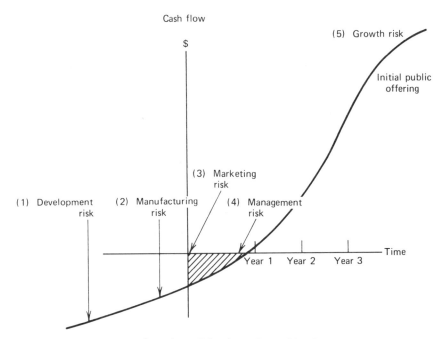

**EXHIBIT 17.** The Five Risks in a Start-Up Company

development risk is normally assumed by the entrepreneur upon his having identified a large problem in need of a solution. The solution is the product or service that the entrepreneur has developed. If venture capitalists could conceive of solutions to large problems they would be entrepreneurs (or their equivalents; i.e., artists, writers, scientists) rather than venture capitalists. There have been venture capitalists who funded on a regular basis the development stage, but they are no longer playing pinball.

The development risk is typically assumed by one or more of the following providers of capital:

1. Wealthy individuals who hire tax attorneys to structure their investments in a manner that generates a reduction or elimination of their income taxes.
2. State and federal governments via grant programs the intent of which is job creation.
3. Customers, such as large corporations, who invest in consideration for an ownership position plus the rights to market the product once it is developed.

4. Suppliers who see a large market for certain of their products if the product is successfully developed.

5. Family and friends who, because of emotional ties, are willing to invest in the entrepreneur's dream.

Rarely is it appropriate for a venture capitalist to invest in a company prior to the development of a new product or service. However, every rule has its exceptions. A development risk may be assumed with not more than 5% of a venture capital fund's assets in the very earliest years of its life, and then only with a corporate customer or suppliers as an investing partner. The reason for corporate co-investors is that the product, if developed, will have to be manufactured. The co-investing corporate partners are most likely to know how to produce the product, once developed. For example, Chester Carlson, the inventor of Xerography, was funded by the Haloid Corp. which engaged Battelle Memorial Laboratories to develop the Xerography process with Xerox Corp. (nee Haloid) then produced.

The manufacturing or production risk is also inappropriate for venture capital. What if the solution to a large problem cannot be produced at a price low enough to make it more attractive than (a) continuing to live with the problem or (b) competitive solutions? What can the venture capitalist do to lower the production costs? Not a thing.

What if the solution can be manufactured at a low enough cost to attract customers, but for a component that resists all attempts to produce it? What can the venture capitalist do to produce it? Not a thing.

Venture capital should not seek companies that are unable to demonstrate a completely operative product or service. Clearly, the product or service can be in prototype form, and it frequently is. But, can it be demonstrated, tested, and placed on a potential customer's site for testing? The venture capitalist can inquire of the potential customer: "Did it solve your problem? Would you purchase it? How much would you pay for it?"

There are exceptions to averting the manufacturing risk, which are similar to those for averting the development risk. If the venture capital fund is in its formative years and if a co-investor exists that is able to manufacture the product, then a small amount of the venture capital fund may be used to invest in companies at this stage of their development. The product, of course, must be absolutely proprietary, protected by a bullet-proof patent filed in the key countries, in order to make adding a third risk acceptable.

In service companies, the delivery system must be very difficult to duplicate in a short period of time and heavily underrated by existing competition using other delivery systems. For example, Federal Express Corp. introduced a new means of delivering small packages overnight. Among its more unique features was that it "absolutely, positively" guaranteed next day delivery. The competition relied on commercial airlines to deliver their freight. Before Federal Express could attract venture capital it hired two management consulting firms to measure the demand for the service, the size of demand and price elasticity, the key cities to begin, and every other factor they could think of. In this manner, the production risk was investigated and venture capital was raised.

As for the growth risk, one could argue that venture capitalists are as equipped, perhaps more so, than anyone to measure and deal with this particular risk, since they know the company from its infancy and are familiar with its products, markets, and management team. The other side of the coin is that the investors who hire the venture capitalists do not engage their services to invest in publicly-held companies: rather, it is their task to distribute to their investors the shares of publicly-held companies, which the investors can determine to hold or sell as they choose. It would seem that the more reasonable approach is to sell the companies once they are public or distribute them to the fund's investors to hold or sell. The overriding issue it seems is how long can a company continue to grow at a rate acceptable to a venture capitalist? The target rate of return of most venture capital funds is approximately 5 times in 3 years or 10 times in 5 years, which works out to a compound return on investment of approximately 70–90% per annum (see Exhibit 18).

It is one thing to achieve a 70–90% compound annual return over 3 years or over 5 years. But to maintain it beyond that requires the continual introduction of products and services that solve a continual group of problems for a large number of people. Very few companies can develop a succession of managers who are capable of maintaining near miraculous growth records. IBM comes the closest to achieving that kind of performance, and it is often

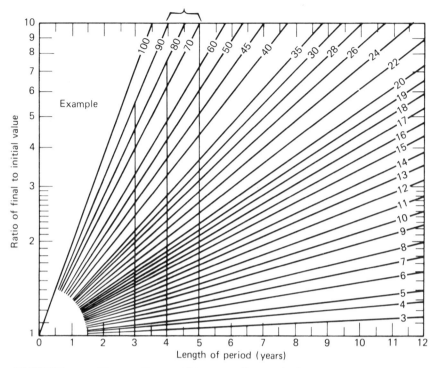

**EXHIBIT 18.**   Target Rates of Return of a Typical Venture Capital Fund

hailed as the only megabillion dollar extrepreneurial company in the United States. The exception proves the rule. The entrepreneurial period in a person's life is a stage of development lasting about 5 years, after which, if one succeeds, he enters a time period of being a manager. In this period, he is more cautious, because there are assets to protect. The same is true of companies. When they mature from an entrepreneurial to a managed stage, their growth slows down, because they are more cautious. There are assets to protect. This is the primary reason that companies in this stage address a certain kind of risk better understood by public investors than by venture capital investors.

In summary, venture capitalists should accept only two of the five risks addressed by start-up and early stage companies: the marketing and the management risk. Three other risks—development, production, and growth—are best understood by other kinds of investors. By minimizing the number and kind of risks that they are willing to accept, venture capitalists are risk averters rather than risk takers. Although this may make the breed less attractive to the financial press who would prefer to think of them as "gun slingers," it is axiomatic. The most successful venture capitalists understand when to get into and when to get out of deals; that is, which risks to accept and which ones to avoid.

## THE LAW OF $V = P \times S \times E$

The second law of venture capital investing, $V = P \times S \times E$, defines the components of high valuation. The law says that if one selects companies with high quantitative values for the components, $P$, $S$ and $E$, he will achieve high valuations, or wealth.

### The Second Law of Venture Capital

$$P \times S \times E = V$$
where $P$ = problem, $S$ = solution, $E$= entrepreneurial team
and $V$ = solution

The most important of the three components is P, because if there is no problem, then a good solution conveyed by an outstanding entrepreneurial team, will not generate revenues.

Examples of non-$P$ industries in the 1970's have included feminine deodorant sprays, safer automobiles, automated voting systems, windpower, electric cars, and a variety of food products that appear on supermarket shelves one month only to vanish the next. It is impossible, of course, to avoid investing in non-$P$ and low-$P$ industries and companies, because one person's valuation of $P$ is different from another's. However, there are certain methods for identifying big-$P$ investment opportunities. And if one continually attempts to diligently place venture capital into big-$P$ opportunities, the amount of capital wasted because the $P$ is low rather than high will become less. When venture capitalists run penguin-like into the same industry over and over again, as they did into disk drives, work stations, portable computers, entertainment software, and integrated software in 1982–1983, and as they did 15 years before that in computer time-sharing and day care center franchisors, they are not addressing the solution of large problems. Rather, they are trying to succeed by copying others and trying to catch a trend.

The problems of our society are addressed by problem-indexers. The best of these are the *New York Times* and *Washington Post*. These two daily newspapers have taken it upon themselves to index the problems of society. Of the two, the *New York Times* is the more thorough, eliminating the space normally reserved for cartoons. The day's events in our world are not humorous to the *New York Times*. It describes social, industrial, and physical problems on most of its pages. A venture capitalist, or any other investor, can be made aware of big-*P*s in search of solutions by a careful reading of the *New York Times*.

The technique of measuring a society's concerns has been used successfully by John Naisbitt, author of *Megatrends*, whose firm counts lines of print devoted in various topics in hundreds of local newspapers. In so doing, Naisbitt spots the things that concern large numbers of people, or megatrends. Pollution, civil rights, womens liberation, energy, AIDS, and other megatrends are indexed by Naisbitt, the *New York Times*, and other serious problem-locators.

In *Megatrends*, Naisbitt sees the transformation from an industrial to an "information economy" as a megatrend. He writes: "The transition times between economies are the times when entrepreneurship blooms. We are now in such a period."* There seems to be a Naisbitt every few years who summarize the forces that drive our society forward and the obstacles that stand in its way. It is these obstacles that create entrepreneurial opportunities.

The venture capitalist should assign numerical values to the factors *P*, *S*, and *E* and accept only those business plans whose product of the equation $P \times S \times E$ exceeds a pre-determined minimum acceptable level. For example, an efficient rating system is 0 to 3, where 3 is the highest possible value for *P*, *S*, or *E* and *O* is the lowest possible value. The highest valuation or *V* factor that an incoming deal could have then, is 27, or:

$$P \times S \times E = V$$
$$3 \times 3 \times 3 = 27$$

*Naisbitt, John, Megatrends; Ten New Directions Transforming Our Lives, Warner, 1982.

The existence of a high $P$ factor in an incoming deal of more than 2.5 on a scale of 0–3, is extremely critical for success in venture capital investing. It seems obvious, and not in need of reiteration, that solutions for which there are no problems result in a waste of time and money. Without a large problem in search of a solution, a new business is doomed to failure. Big-$P$s change over time, and one must not lock in to the obvious big-$P$s of disease, hunger, and cost of health care. For example, in the mid-1960's, fast food chains addressed the large problem of women entering the work force and the consequent need for a fast, reliable family dinner. In the mid-1980's, there is probably only the smallest justification to launch a new restaurant chain no matter how unusual its menu or other features.

The staff of the venture capital fund manager should decide among themselves and their advisors which problems they consider greater than 2.5, or their minimum acceptable level; or stated more conventionally, which problems they would like to solve with their capital. The values assigned to the various problems can be altered every year as they are mitigated. When a company or group of companies begins earning a profit, by definition it has begun solving a problem for its market, which reduces the size of the problem and makes it a less interesting investment area for venture capitalists.

Some of the big-$P$s, circa 1984, are listed in Exhibit 19.

These problems easily warrant values of $P$ in excess of 2.5 on several scales: number of lines of print devoted to the subjects in

EXHIBIT 19.   Large Problems Seeking
Entrepreneurial Solutions, Circa 1984

Hunger
Disease (cancer, heart attack, diabetes)
Increasing size of elderly population
Rising cost of health care
Chemical abuse
Computer literacy for adults
Computer literacy for children
Selecting efficient software quickly
Rising cost of government
Costs associated with criminal justice

the *New York Times,* dollars raised to research the problems annually, and the number of people willing to pay for a solution times the price they would pay for a solution.

It is undeniable that cancer is one of the biggest problems in the United States in 1984, with upwards of 400,000 deaths attributed to it each year. According to the American Cancer Society, 855,000 Americans became cancer victims in 1983, and 2.6 million Americans were being treated in 1983 for cancers they had gotten earlier. Multiply 3.4 million cancer patients times the market price for the solution and it is readily apparent that cancer nets a value of 3. Heart disease, diabetes, and other killing diseases are not far behind.

To attempt to solve the problem of AIDS, for example, a large medical problem in mid-1984, a venture capitalist might invest $1 million at a $10 million valuation, while an equally competent entrepreneurial team that addresses a problem in office automation would have its start-up company valued at less than $2 million by the same venture capitalist. In mid-1984, the aggregate market valuation of the five leading, publicly-held, US genetic engineering companies was equal to the market valuation of the nation's third largest bank, Chase Manhattan. These five companies—Biogen, Cetus, Genentech, Genex, and Molecular Genetics—had no material revenues and negligible earnings; but their dreams and plans were viewed as being worth in the public marketplace an aggregate of nearly $2 billion.

Experienced venture capitalists know that they can take big-$P$ companies public before they have achieved earnings because of the public's desire to invest in companies that chase after real-life Darth Vaders: cancer, hunger, diabetes, and other killing diseases.

The values of $S$ are more difficult to calibrate, because $S$ is composed of two factors, $B$ and $T$.

$$B \times T = S$$

where $T$ = the existence of low-priced technology and $B$ = the business plan or the solution-delivery mechanism. Let's assume the range of values for two factors of $S$ are from 0 to 3. Thus, the technology factor, or $T$, might warrant a 3 if it involves microprocessors, state-of-the-art software algorithms, or recombinant DNA techniques. The value of $T$ might drop to 1 if the technology involves relatively expensive photovoltaic cells, or to .5 if the government could block or delay entry.

Experienced venture capitalists look for an "elegant $S$." This means that if the solution is a product it should be proprietary, and if it is a service it should have a non-duplicable distribution system. Anything short of these requirements makes the $S$ factor fall under minimum acceptable levels. The $P$ and $E$ factors would have to be relatively high to cause an experienced venture capitalist to invest in a non-elegant $S$ company. Venture capitalists call these kinds of companies "JA" deals, as in "JAWS" or "JAISP," which means "just another work station" or "just another integrated software package" company.

The $T$ or technology component of the $S$ factor is important in achieving an elegant $S$. New technologies can be protected via basic patents, process patents, or lead time, and these three kinds of protection are of great importance to the investor. There is an axiom in the company launching business:

"Anything worth doing is worth duplicating."

This means that if an investment opportunity is attractive to one group of investors or to one entrepreneurial team, it will surely be attractive to several others. A better-faster-cheaper system or device, no matter how thoroughly protected by patents or an elegant, non-duplicable delivery system will very shortly be copied, duplicated, simulated, and, in short, attract significant competition. Natural monopolies simply do not last more than 3 years, unless protected by the government. Thus, the emphasis placed on the $T$ sub-factor by venture capitalists.

In the case of non-proprietary companies, such as one frequently finds in the service industries, venture capitalists tend to prefer delivery systems that are either non-duplicable or very expensive for the second or third company in the industry to copy or emulate. Perhaps the best example is Federal Express, which identified an opportunity to deliver time-sensitive, small packages overnight on a guaranteed basis. The established freight forwarders were using commercial airlines to carry their packages. If the commercial airlines were delayed due to weather or strikes, the packages simply would not be taken. If the destination was off the main route of the commercial carriers, they didn't get there next day: maybe not for 3 days. To fill this gap Federal Express' founding entrepreneur, Fred Smith, conceived of a delivery system that involved flying all packages into Memphis, Tennessee, a city with an airport rarely closed due to bad weather and located near the center of the country. The packages were sorted between 1 and 4 A.M. and then flown to their destination for next day delivery. The start-up costs of this unique delivery system were expensive and Federal Express nearly died several times before it lived. The competition—Airborne Freight, Emery, and Purolator—merely scoffed at the upstart. But by the time Federal Express was passing them by, as well as the U.S. Postal Service, the cost of duplicating Federal Express' unique delivery system would have been several hundred million dollars. Thus, the entrepreneurial company beat the established competition with a difficult to duplicate delivery system.

Weight Watchers International, Inc., the first of the weight-loss service companies had an extremely easy to duplicate delivery system. However, no competitor bothered to attack Weight Watchers using the same or similar delivery system, until Weight Watchers was the established leader in the field of weight-loss systems; and then it was too late. At the time it was acquired by H. J. Heinz, Weight Watchers had a recognition factor of 92%; that is, over nine persons out of ten questioned knew the name Weight Watchers and what the company did. Heinz, on the other hand, had a recognition factor of 17%. The advertising budget of Heinz exceeded Weight Watchers by tens of millions of dollars. Among other things, this fact shows that entrepreneurial achievements can come quickly and capture the awareness of many; but when they mature, such as Heinz, they are more or less forgotten—another reason for venture capitalists to avoid the "growth" risk discussed a few pages previously.

Jean Neditch, the founding entrepreneur of Weight Watchers, conceived a rather simplistic business plan that read something like the following: "I will invite overweight ladies to come to a hotel conference room once or twice a week, and pay $2.00 for the privilege of standing up in front of other overweight ladies and saying how fat they are. At the end of the session I will sell them books, tapes, and diet plans in the back of the room as they leave." This business plan was so simplistic that many venture capital investors turned Mrs. Neditch down when she sought venture capital in the late 1960's. Thus, when she sold Weight Watchers to H. J. Heinz for $120 million in 1979, she kept most of the proceeds.

On reflection, Weight Watchers' business plan is relatively complex. And the delivery system for the service, when it is launched simultaneously in several dozen metropolitan markets, is difficult to duplicate. A similar system would be deemed a copy-cat, a "number 2," and probably not "the genuine article." The Weight Watchers delivery system required effective newspaper advertising, renting convenient, attractive conference rooms, positioning a knowledgeable person in the conference rooms to greet the customers and lead them in a weight-loss program, having products available at the conference room, taking the cash and accounting for it properly, and most important, making sure that the system worked. Indeed, a careful reading of Weight Watchers business plan would indicate that the conveyance system, if done well, would obviate competition for a number of years. Once Weight Watchers gained sufficient size, it began marketing food products under its own brand name. The conversion to a proprietary company came immediately thereafter.

If, therefore, the service company's delivery system is believed to be non-duplicable, to the point of eventually becoming unique and *suigeneris*, then it qualifies for the same quantitative valuation as a proprietary technology, or $T$ factor company.

The $B$ sub-factor, or business plan component of the $S$ factor, is quite another matter. It is important for entrepreneurs to take the time and make the effort to develop a thorough and competently presented business plan. The venture capitalist ultimately makes his investment decision on the *credibility of the operating statement projections*—sometimes referred to as the "hockey stick"—in the business plan. If there is no business plan, then the venture capitalist must request that one be prepared in order to determine (1) how much capital is required, (2) the projected profitability of the enterprise, and (3) the valuation to be placed on the business at the time of the venture capital investment.

The solution, or $S$ factor, that the entrepreneurial team claims that it can convey to the problem must be investigated thoroughly in terms of the uniqueness of the solution and the nonduplicability of the conveyance system. An investigation of these components, coupled with a thoroughly prepared business plan, are the audits of the $B$ and $T$ sub-factors of $S$, the most time-consuming activities in the due diligence process.

The quality of the entrepreneurial team, or $E$ factor—placing a value on it between 0 and 3—is the final component in the second law of venture capital: $V = P \times S \times E$. The venture capitalist has more control over this factor after he has invested, if the terms and conditions of the venture capital investment permit changing members when the company defaults on the terms. Notwithstanding its ability to change the $E$ factor post-financing, the investment should not be made unless the entrepreneur and his or her manager partner meet minimum acceptable character-istics to justify an investment. However, the venture capitalist is able to effect the greatest amount of change in a deal via the $E$ fac-tor. It is not possible for a venture capitalist to change the $P$ factor, and modifying the $S$ factor is done usually via a committee ap-pointed by the board of directors, via a consulting organization, or via contracting a production job to another firm to design a new $T$. The component of a new company that can be changed by the venture capitalist is the entrepreneurial team: the entrepreneur or his manager partner. The mechanism that permits the venture capitalist to change members of the management team is the Pur-chase Agreement. If the entrepreneurial team is in default under the terms of the Purchase Agreement, the venture capitalist can bring to bear a number of changes to protect the capital entrusted to his partnership to invest wisely. A venture capitalist who fails to change members of the entrepreneurial team quickly and as nec-essary is abdicating his fiduciary responsibility. For, indeed, to in-vest mostly in early-stage, unique companies without benefit of controls over the entrepreneurial team, is irresponsible. It is the equivalent of locking yourself into a room without doors.

Notwithstanding the necessity of having the ability to make changes in the entrepreneurial team, it is possible to select entre-preneurs and managers based on certain criteria that suggest the likelihood of their achieving success. Potentially successful entre-preneurs and managers can be weeded out before the investment is made. If the values of $P$ and $S$ are extremely high, but the entre-preneur and his manager partner do not get high marks for their potential to launch a new company successfully, they can be asked if they would mind stepping aside or out. Chairmanship of a board of scientific advisors is one possible and frequently used innocuous position; technical consultant is another. If the company's board of directors is large enough, the entrepreneur and/or the manager can be hidden thereon.

If moving them to the side is not acceptable, it may be necessary to buy their interest. This can be effected by offering them a certain dollar amount—perhaps 5% of the amount to be invested, as if the founders were finders or brokers. A carried interest in the equity of 1 or 2% may be required to sweeten the offer. If the removal of the founders to a more passive position cannot be effected by persuasion or compensation, then the deal should be rejected. Random events, it should never be forgotten, will continually collide with a new company and knock it off its business plan. It takes an excellent entrepreneurial team to get the company back onto its path. On the other hand, an inferior entrepreneurial team will be unable to maintain the company on its business plan. It will lead it off the path without the provocation of random events. Whereas a superior entrepreneurial team can overcome low values for $P$ and $S$ and achieve a fine success, an inferior entrepreneurial team will virtually guarantee failure.

## THE CHARACTERISTICS OF SUCCESSFUL ENTREPRENEURS

The venture capitalist can give himself some comfort in selecting entrepreneurs and managers by comparing their relevant personality characteristics with those of successful entrepreneurs and their manager partners. These characteristics were explicated at length in *The Entrepreneurial Life: How to Go For It and Get It.*\* They are summarized herein as follows:

1. *Age, Appearance, and Other Outward Signs.* Entrepreneurs that have a high probability of succeeding are generally between 27 and 33 years of age, married or divorced (but never a bachelor), and simply dressed (no extra wearing of pins, buttons, or items of clothing). Their hair is short and easy to care for, and they fre-

---

\*Silver, A. David, *The Entrepreneurial Life: How To Go For It and Get It*, Wiley, New York, 1983.

quently have beards and moustaches, possibly because shaving takes too long. They speak quickly, again because time is so precious to them. They generally live in the city, vote liberal, and drive a European car. The latter because of the long mean time to failure rate.

2. *Origins Are Middle-Class Homes*. In extremely culturally deprived families, there is little attention given to upward mobility. Success in others is derided; it is assumed that the successful person had breaks, cheated, or got lucky. The day is spent eking out survival. Without supportive parents or an older mentor, the child of a dirt-poor family will not strive to achieve more than his or her parents.

Occasionally a person will break out of a survival background and attempt to become an entrepreneur. Frequently he is over 50 when this happens and resentful that he has so few years left to launch his own company. In middle-class homes the children are encouraged to succeed in accordance with the middle-class community's definition of success (i.e., make good grades, go to college, become a doctor, lawyer or other professional), marry well and produce gorgeous grandchildren. The script is studied, rehearsed, memorized and followed, until at some point it is discarded if, indeed, the heart of an entrepreneur lies beneath the surface.

3. *The Absent Father*. When you are the only kid on the Little League team whose father isn't in the stands, you learn to live without a safety net. If you slide into second base and bang your knee, you wash away the blood by yourself and limp home alone. The emotional hurt lasts long after the knee has healed. Successful entrepreneurs are generally raised in homes where the father is absent. The hurt of not having a father in the stands to cheer your achievements, great and small, is converted later on to entrepreneurial drive and perseverance. The entrepreneur's early value system generally comes from a strong, supportive mother. The entrepreneur's father is generally absent due to death, divorce, or being kept away from home by business. Many male entrepreneurs have attributed the strength of their mothers as strong motivating forces. Female entrepreneurs, on the other hand, seem to be more motivated by their fathers and learned how to compete at a very young age.

4. *Entrepreneurs Are Usually Guilty.* Many entrepreneurs are guilty for having not lived up to their parents' or mother's expectations. A large number have obtained professional degrees, or were on that track, when they cast the American Dream aside to start a business. Edwin H. Land dropped out of Harvard to devote all his time to developing a system to polarize light. Dr. Leonard H. Schoen, founder of Arcoa Corporation, the U-Haul company, is a medical doctor. John Y. Brown, founder of Kentucky Fried Chicken, was a lawyer. Dr. An Wang was a Harvard Math professor when he left to launch Wang Laboratories. The reputation of entrepreneurs as drop-outs is accurate; about as many drop out before obtaining a professional degree as after.

The guilt that derives from disappointing the parents is a powerful force. The guilt in a divorced entrepreneur to show that he or she can succeed without the "impatient" spouse frequently unleashes a volcanic burst of energy. Further, entrepreneurs are frequently the target of ridicule and derision by journalists and economists who tend to classify all entrepreneurs as promoters and opportunists. Entrepreneurs think of themselves as socially useful, on the same level as microbiologists attempting to find a cure for cancer. The greater the misunderstanding, the more powerful the drivers.

Bachelors tend to have less to be guilty about. They are not concerned that they are away from their families. If their spouse has left them, they are not guilty that they were unable to hold the family and the business together simultaneously. Bachelors have not shown a commitment to a spouse and family; thus, there is no measure of the firmness of the bond they have struck with the people in their new company and with their investors. In short, committed bachelors do not make successful entrepreneurs.

5. *Entrepreneurs Were Deprived as Children.* A highly successful computer-industry entrepreneur told me about his childhood. "I was the youngest of three sons. My father had died and my mother supported us. We moved from town to town so she could find better jobs. Whenever she would send me to the store to buy a bottle of milk, the grocer would always say in front of other customers, 'Remember to tell your mother that she owes me money.' I've been chasing that grocer ever since."

Entrepreneurs carry a considerable amount of emotional baggage. The heaviest weight is the pain of a childhood in which they were deprived of what others had: a healthy body (Fred Smith, whose father died when he was 4, had a form of cystic fibrosis), athletic ability and peer recognition (dozens of entrepreneurs are short—David Sarnoff, founder of RCA, furnished his office in undersized furniture to make him appear larger): or enough money ("Hey, look at the little Greek kid—he has to help his mother at the store"). Ask an entrepreneur about the deprivation in his or her childhood and be prepared for a long story.

6. *The Ability to Focus Intensively on a Single Subject for a Sustained Period of Time*. Christopher Columbus attempted to gain an audience with Queen Isabella for 6 years. Edwin H. Land worked on polarizing headlights to reduce their glare for 7 years. When Detroit turned him down, he worked another 7 years to develop the Polaroid camera. Chester Carlson pursued a corporate sponsor for xerography for 12 years.

In the early months or years while developing the product, formulating the market, hiring people, locating customers, finding capital, and dealing with dozens of other problems, most of them new and unfamiliar, entrepreneurs close themselves off from previous groups, old friends, golf or racquetball partners, church groups. Entrepreneurs are too busy. Their minds are too full of new challenges to permit family, old friends, or community activities to enter. They are so totally focused on the liftoff of the new company that they appear fanatical. It is in this focused period that the entrepreneur's marriage is likely to dissolve.

7. *Entrepreneurs Have Uncommon Courage*. The courage possessed by entrepreneurs is a basic quality not unique to them. It is also possessed by successful athletes.

Courage is the quality of not being able to permit failure. You hear it in the interviews of certain spectacular athletes after their conquests: Jack Nicklaus in his prime, Edwin Moses, Martina Navritalova, and the Olympic figure skater, Scott Hamilton, who overcame a crippling childhood disease. You can see it in the way Alberto Salazar tortures his body in order to win marathon races.

Successful entrepreneurs cannot conceive of failure. Obstacles may have to be jumped, danced around, crawled through, or require a new path. But obstacles will not stop them. In the words of David J. Padwa, founder of Agrigenetics Corporation, the entrepreneur's attitude toward obstacles is: "Shoot at me. It doesn't matter. I'm going to do it anyway."

Although the obstacles may deter entrepreneurs and may knock them off the path and cause a variation in the business plan, they will not kill the company. New businesses die for a variety of reasons; but if entrepreneurs possess most of the characteristics listed here, they succeed. If entrepreneurs possess only half of these characteristics, but are long on courage, the company will thrive as well.

A quick test for the existence of an entrepreneur's courage is to ask him, during the first interview, how he intends to achieve his hockey stick. If the response is, "With venture capital," the courage factor may be weak. A more encouraging answer would be something on the order of this: "I hope to attract venture capital, but in the event I do not, I am negotiating the sale of the European rights to Nixdorf, my lawyers are packaging an R&D limited partnership offering, my secretary's father has put up $100,000 for us to borrow $500,000 under an SBA 502 loan, I have submitted an SBIC grant, and I have begun discussing with certain suppliers converting my payables into equity. So with or without your venture capital, I will carry out the business plan." That response identifies an entrepreneur with courage, heart, and a healthy respect for the possibility of failure.

8. *Entrepreneurs Are Creative.* "He has the ability to see the whole market" is a frequent description of entrepreneurs. It means that entrepreneurs problem-formulate very well. Whereas a small businessperson opens a store that is conveniently located to sell a product that he or she likes, an entrepreneur formulates a problem (some prefer the term "see the market opportunity") to see the various levels of demand and then creates a solution that the people with the problem will purchase.

The "better mousetrap" attracts no mice and no money, even though it is a new and improved way to catch mice. The creative aspect of the entrepreneurial process is in problem-formulating. Entrepreneurs can take a peripheral encompassing view of the problem that they have formulated and determine which segment needs to be informed about the problem, which segment wants to meet with others who share the problem, which segment is ready to spend a little money to explore solutions, and which segment is suffering from the problem and needs the solution immediately.

9. *Entrepreneurs Have Insight.* Some call this the judgment factor. Peter Drucker said it something like this: "Entrepreneurs must do the right thing. They can hire people to do things right." Entrepreneurs have a sixth sense about their customers. They know when to press for the order, what services to add on to the order, and when to ask for the check. They have market sense in their fingertips.

The careful interviewer can listen for incidences of the entrepreneur's abilities. Did he hire a "corporate achiever" for a manager partner or an old friend who worked at the telephone company who had $20,000 to invest and one or two middle-management credentials? Does he speak like he knows what he's doing, or like he knows how to promote? This key factor requires careful listening to discern.

10. *Entrepreneurs Are Happy and Good Communicators.* Even though their lives are spent trying to stay upright in a wind tunnel, entrepreneurs are not sad or depressed. They are too busy for cocktail parties, community service organizations, spicy conversation, hobbies, vacations, and even a good book or movie; yet they are very happy people. They never tell Polish or Black jokes, or denigrate others even in jest.

Entrepreneurs are happy because they keep score against the system, and small victories over bureaucracies such as airlines, airports, and car rental companies are pleasing, if only briefly. Convincing one's banker that a sales call will soon result in a receivable, then getting him to loan against it to make payroll, that's happy.

Entrepreneurs tend to prefer sports that are open-ended and rely on the performance of the individual, rather than the team. They do not, as a rule, prefer fixed-time-limit team sports such as football and hockey. More popular are baseball, the racquet sports, and golf. Entrepreneurs do not usually jog, or if they do, rarely alone. Jogging is not sufficiently intense or competitive. It is a lonely activity and entrepreneurs tend to avoid things that are lonely. It is not easy to be happy and alone; sharing pleasure makes it more pleasureful.

Entrepreneurs understand that in order to convince people to change their minds and do something for the entrepreneur that they had no intention of doing, the entrepreneur must control the questions. In any situation in which an entrepreneur is speaking, he or she is the seller and the other person is the buyer: bankers, investors, customers, and suppliers are always the buyers and the entrepreneur is trying to convince them to give him money, a purchase order, or extended payment terms. It is impossible to pull a "yes" out of a buyer who is trained in problem-finding if the buyer controls the questions. If the seller asks the questions, he opens up, relaxes the buyer, and wins his approval.

Raising money is talking—an axiom frequently stated by entrepreneur watchers. An entrepreneur long on communications skills will persuade them to invest. It should be noted, though, that in this area many entrepreneurs fall short due to boundless enthusiasm that is unstructured and not yet organized.

These characteristics are my personal set, and other venture capitalists may espouse a different set of criteria by which to judge entrepreneurs. The 10 characteristics that are described herein have many years of successful entrepreneur-selecting to their credit, as well as interviews with approximately 400 entrepreneurs who have made over $5 million by launching new companies. These characteristics are by no means carved in stone. Yet, it is good to begin somewhere, and a new venture capitalist can do worse than look for the 10 characteristics summarized above.

Whereas the entrepreneur formulates $P$ in all its myriad aspects and conceives, designs and develops $S$, it is usually the manager that is responsible for delivering $S$ to $P$. After all, it is the function of management to develop and implement a business plan.

There are some exceptions to the rule, but in most new companies, the entrepreneurs require assistance in hiring managers. This task is generally undertaken by the venture capitalist. It is fairly common for a venture capitalist to spend approximately one-third of his time hiring managers to assist entrepreneurs in launching their new companies. To believe that entrepreneurs are capable of taking their companies from zero sales to $1 billion in sales or valuation, without standing down as their chief executive officer, is to believe in Santa Claus. Name 10 entrepreneurs who have achieved this kind of success in post-World War II America, and you have all of them: Charles McCowen (MCI Communications), Robert E. Noyce (Intel), Kenneth E. Olsen (Digital Equipment), David Packard (Hewlett-Packard), H. Ross Perot (EDS), Dr.

Henry E. Singleton (Teledyne), Saul Steinberg (Reliance), Charles Tandy (Tandy), and Dr. Ansu Wang (Wang Laboratories).

Prospects such as Intel Corp. do not stroll into the venture capitalists' offices and ask for capital. Most deals are not as complete as Intel. With Intel, not only were the values of $P$ and $S$ high—low-cost, light-weight, high-speed electronics was the $P$, and putting tens of thousands of transistors on a single chip of silicon was the $S$—but the entrepreneurial team had launch experience at Fairchild Semiconductor Corp. There were risks, to be sure, but the $E$ factor—Messrs. Noyce, Moore, and Grove—had encountered similar risks at Fairchild. Venture capitalists place Intel on a pedestal as the finest work of art in the entrepreneurial gallery; the greatest, fastest return on venture capital.

Professional managers make successful companies when they are harnessed to the vision created by the entrepreneur and given the capital and support to run with. The entrepreneur builds the stagecoach and charts the course. The manager drives the stagecoach. And the venture capitalist buys the team of six white horses. Assorted managers are brought along to feed the horses, shoot at the hold-up men along the way, repair the stagecoach if needed, but keep it moving at all costs. Inside the stagecoach is the product or service being conveyed by the team from its origin to its destination. Entrepreneurs do not make companies successful. It is their insight, drive, creativity and, above all, their heart that launches a new company. If it were otherwise, we would see more entrepreneurs with absolute authority at the top of their companies.

Venture capitalists should anticipate that the manager selected by the entrepreneur is incompetent, and that he will have to be replaced by a competent one found by the venture capitalist. This frequently means convincing the entrepreneur that his "cousin Herbie," who had a middle-management job at the telephone company and who invested his life savings of $50,000 at an earlier stage and then came aboard as chief operating officer, must be replaced.

The replacement of "cousin Herbie" is best done with the aid of executive search consultants. Classified advertisements do not produce the quality resumes that executive search consultants are able to achieve.

The characteristics of successful managers of entrepreneurial companies are those described as follows:

1. *Age, Appearance and Other Outward Signs*. The manager partner is, on average, 13 to 16 years older than the entrepreneur—40 to 50 years of age. He is generally male. He is married about 80% of the time. He is more formally dressed. Whereas the entrepreneur is more likely to wear loafers, the manager partner will take the time to put on lace-up shoes. His hair is more treated, perhaps blown dry, and he may wear a button-down shirt or collar pin. It is unlikely that he would be wearing cufflinks or cologne, which accoutrements come at a more advanced stage of maturity.

The manager partner generally lives in the suburbs where he owns a house and perhaps other assets. Although he is not wealthy, he generally votes Republican because he has assets to protect. The manager partner generally drives an American car, unless he is from the electronics or computer-related industries where foreign cars have become acceptable in large corporations.

2. *Corporate Achiever*. The potentially successful manager has a documented record of corporate achievement. He can point to sales or productivity increases in his division, rapid advancement, and recognition in the form of increases in rank, responsibilities, and remuneration. Frequently this individual began his career in engineering or the technical side of his chosen industry, gravitated to sales, achieved and bettered his sales goals and was promoted into marketing. Reference checking will later reveal that the manager partner was respected by his superiors, who regret his departure; adored by those who worked for him, who will miss his wit and wisdom; but disliked by his peer group, who felt that he stepped on them and over them, over-committed and "rubbed people the wrong way."

3. *Dissatisfaction and Energy*. In one's maturation process, if the entrepreneurial characteristics listed above make up one's personality, the transformation to entrepreneurship is the result of a three-step process known as dissatisfaction, energy, and insight. That is, the potential entrepreneur grows dissatisfied with the refusal of his employer to recognize his idea for a new market, product, or service. He has the insight into a large problem and how it might be solved, and he has the energy to go out and solve

it. A serious writer or painter also sees lots to be dissatisfied with and has the insight to describe the problems or paint them, as well as myriad solutions for them.

The corporate achiever, on the other hand, who will make a superior partner for an entrepreneur, has dissatisfaction and energy but lacks the insight into a large problem in need of solution or its possible solution. If the dissatisfaction is sufficiently strong, the corporate achiever will leave the corporation and become a consultant in the same industry until he finds an opportunity that fits his needs. There may be an incorrect career move between his period of employment and being tapped by a venture capitalist to join an entrepreneurial company, but generally that experience will be with a smaller company, hence transferable to the entrepreneurial company.

4. *Heart*. Whereas much of the entrepreneur's strength of spirit and drive has to do with the size of his heart, the corporate achiever's heart has been removed by his corporate employer. To accelerate within the company, the corporate achiever had to stab co-workers in the back, leverage his employees, take credit where others accomplished the task, support a co-worker then write a CYA memorandum to mitigate the support and, in general, learn how to climb to the top in the corporate jungle.

This process does not build moral fiber or strength of character. It makes the person with heart lose it and become so disgusted with back-stabbing as a means to an end that he wants to get his heart back. There is some stealing that goes on in large corporations that the corporate achiever goes along with for awhile, then becomes too dissatisfied to condone. It involves expense account padding, failing to turn in "frequent flyer" bonuses, turning in first class tickets for coach and pocketing the difference, and other minor crimes. The potentially successful entrepreneurial company manager eventually grows dissatisfied with the jungle and wants his heart back. A tip that he has entered this period of searching is usually his wandering from the nest, disintegrating relations with his spouse, and perhaps marriage counselling. Until he finds, though an entrepreneur, the *insight* that he lacks, he will continue wandering.

The insight gives him meaning and a purpose. He can then use his years of corporate experience to help make the entrepreneur's dream come true. His toughness can temper the entrepreneur's optimism. He can refine the entrepreneur's ideas and reduce them to a cogent plan.

5. *Practicality, Thoroughness, Capacity for Work.* The corporate achiever is generally the author of the business plan, lending practicality to the entrepreneur's vision. He is more thorough than the entrepreneur. Whereas the entrepreneur can think of 10 new segments of the market between 8 A.M. and 12 noon and will surely drop them on the manager partner's desk with a request to implement them, the latter will thoroughly review them and reject all but the best. He will instinctively know how to implement them by 3 P.M. that afternoon and have a group assembled by breakfast to explore their practicality.

The manager partner has enormous capability to allow the entrepreneur the spotlight and center stage, the appearance of power and dictatorship; but he is pulling many of the strings, with those in the company who require more substance than form gravitating to him. He can outwork anyone in the company, save the entrepreneur, but he also respects the need to stop and step back occasionally to see where the company is heading and whether or not it is getting there.

The track record of a venture capitalist will owe as much to carefully matching entrepreneurs and managers as it will to almost any other aspect of is profession. Successful teams, such as Henry Taub and Frank Lautenberg (Automatic Data Processing) or Stephen Jobs and Mike Markulla (Apple Computer), are constructed by design, not by accident. The venture capitalist who accepts the team he is delivered, because the $P$ and $S$ factors seem so large, will rue the day he failed to investigate the personality characteristics of entrepreneurs and their manager partners. The failure rate in the venture capital business can be mitigated by intensively auditing the $E$ factor before the investment is made and matching high value entrepreneurs with corporate achievers from the same or similar industries.


## THE LAW OF THE BIG-$P$

The third law of venture capital is the Law of the Big-$P$. The law is as follows:

*In Big-P Companies, the valuation is
equal to the size of the problem,
rather than its solution.*

This law helps to explain certain prices of publicly-held stocks, unjustified by earnings. It also explains, perhaps, why our stock market is vibrant while stocks languish in other countries that lack the optimism of the U.S. stock-buying public.

Just as Americans seem to love movies that have important "chase" scenes—"Star Wars," "The Empire Strikes Back," and "Chariots of Fire"—so too do they love new publicly-held companies who claim to be chasing disease, hunger, and illness with weapons such as interferon, monoclonal antibodies, and breakthroughs in medical technology. Cetus Corp. fights the big-$P$ of hunger by genetically engineering seeds that will affix to the sandy soil of the Sudan. It has a market value in excess of $300 million, with the prospect for earnings many years off into the future. Genentech, armed with gene-splicing and recombinant DNA skills, chases diabetes, cancer, hoof-and-mouth, and dwarfism. Its market value once reached $800 million and significant earnings are very much into the future. Cetus, Genentech, and other biotechnology companies are chasing big-$P$s with elegant $S$'s and experienced managers. They are able to go to the public market and to R&D limited partnerships for bales of capital, because the typical investor loves a good chase.

Thus, a venture capital investor can usually become liquid more quickly in a big-$P$ company and at a relatively higher market value ($V$) than in a lower-$P$ company. One is able to achieve financial successes with big-$P$ companies before they are successful businesses. All the more reason for investing in companies that attempt to solve serious problems rather than in more mundane companies.

Big-$P$ companies, once they begin to achieve earnings, frequently drop in price. Analysts begin to scrutinize their earnings and financial ratios and a price/earnings ratio is assigned to their industry. As earnings arrive, so does the solution ($S$). And as a problem becomes solved—i.e., earnings indicate a solution is happening—it is no longer a big-$P$. The venture capitalist should have sold his position long before.

## THE FIVE AUDITS

Given the definition of the principle laws of venture capital investing, it is pertinent to discuss the due diligence process and the application of the laws. There are five principle audits that comprise the due diligence process. These are:

1. The Audit of $P$.
2. The Audit of $S$.
3. The Audit of $E$.
4. The Financial Statement Audit.
5. The Legal Audit.

Should an investment in any company be made without a full five audit due diligence process, then the resulting losses can be traced back to the areas overlooked in the investigative process. Certainly there are reasons for business failures that cannot be located via pre-investment due diligence. These reasons include bad luck and bad timing. However, in any portfolio of venture capital investments, certain companies are pushed forward accidently by good luck and good timing while others are held back by bad luck and bad timing. These two accidents of time and place seem to be mutually offsetting. The major losses in a venture capital fund's portfolio arise because someone forgot to ask a critical question during the due diligence process.

It is not necessary that the five audits be done in any particular sequence. However, the order given above is the usual one for several reasons. For instance, the audit of $E$, the entrepreneurial team, generally follows the audits of $P$ and $S$ because reference checking individuals who intend to join the new company, once funded, could possibly interfere with their current employment. The venture capitalist should be encouraged by the audits of $P$ and $S$ before exhaustive reference checking on members of the entrepreneurial team, because it could lead to their termination and loss of income prior to the venture capital financing. The audit of the legal agreement and contracts is usually done at the end, because it costs the entrepreneurs legal fees to pull together all of their contracts, leases, and agreements and it costs the venture capitalist legal fees to have its counsel review the documents. These fees are normally paid out of a portion of the proceeds of the funding, if there is a funding. Certain issues are treated as "conditions precedent" to the funding, and contracts and legal agreements prepared in an orderly manner is normally one of these "conditions precedent." For example, the entrepreneur might say to the venture capitalist during the course of one of their interviews, "We have a 5-year lease on this office space at $1.20 per square foot per month, renewable for another 5 years at $1.80 per square foot per month." The venture capitalist will probably jot down that information and will not think about it in any great detail, because the lease of office space will be picked up by his attorney during the legal audit. Leases on equipment, automobiles, office space, and other legal documents must be in order as a condition precedent to the funding. If the lease on office space is indeed *not* $1.20 but, rather, $3.50 per square foot per month, and is not a 5-year renewable lease but rather a month-to-month lease, the venture capitalist may compare the legal agreements with his notes prior to the funding and ask the entrepreneur why these are inconsistent. If the inconsistency troubles the venture capitalist, he can cancel the funding without remorse. The entrepreneur provided misleading information which, in itself, might not have been harmful to the future success of the company. But the very notion of providing untrue or inaccurate information may be, in the mind of the venture capitalist, a deal breaker.

Entrepreneurs are frequently not the most methodical of businesspersons. It is completely within their nature to *think* that an understanding that they have reached with a customer, supplier, lessor, lender, or landlord is set in concrete when in fact it is either (a) a verbal understanding or (b) quite a bit different than the entrepreneur believes it is. The audit of the legal agreements, then, must be effected giving consideration to the audit of *E*. For example, if the company is a start-up and has neither a manager partner nor a controller nor administrative officer to memorialize in legal document form all of the entrepreneur's agreements, it should surprise no one if more than half of the agreements mentioned by the entrepreneur are unlike that which he described. In fact, entrepreneurs who are altogether too concerned and too meticulous about the legal aspects of their company are frequently insufficiently daring and courageous to guide the new company through competitive and economic storms. Good legal agreements may help avoid losses, but they rarely make for successful companies.

## THE AUDIT OF $P$ AND $S$

The audit of the size of the problem should be done first, in order that the deal may be turned down quickly if the potential market size that the new company faces fails to meet the venture capital fund's criteria. In this manner the entrepreneur can be given a "fast no," which permits him to look elsewhere for venture capital. A "fast no," many entrepreneurs will say, is as good as a "long yes."

What is a suitable criteria for market size? Some venture capitalists say they will not invest in a new company unless they can see the possibility of $500 million in fifth-year sales. Perhaps a more intelligent approach is to estimate the size of the total market that the new company will address and estimate what its market share is likely to be once the field becomes crowded with competition. A plausible maximum market share is on the order of 10–15%. There are cases of new companies obtaining greater market penetration and holding on to it for a sustained period of time. Certainly Scientific-Atlanta with antennae, Federal Express with overnight small package delivery, and Apple Computer with personal computers, captured market shares in excess of 40%. However, if you can name a small group of anything, they probably represent exceptions rather than rules. Market penetration of 10% is a safe bet, and 15% is probably optimistic. Then if one's goal is to invest only in companies with a possibility of achieving fifth-year revenues of $100 million, the audit of $P$ must result in a problem size of more than $1 billion.

In start-up companies where there is no market, the measurement of the size of the problem, although systematic, is very difficult and time-consuming. Let us examine a few of the newer investment opportunity areas to see how one prudently goes about measuring the size of $P$.

The rising cost of health care is the generic problem area that we will select for investigation. Entrepreneurs in the mid-1980's are proclaiming that opportunities exist to remove expensive medical services from hospitals and perform them in mobile and stationary clinics and in the patients' homes. Let's examine a hypothetical entrepreneurial claim for the existence of a chain of medical diagnostic clinics.

The entrepreneurs claim: "Worldwide sales of medical imaging equipment, including conventional X-ray, computerized axial tomography (CAT) scanner, nuclear medicine and ultrasound devices, and equipment for nuclear magnetic resonance (NMR), and position emission tomography (PET) procedures, will tap $6 billion in 1985. However, most of this equipment is so expensive that only the largest and most financially sound hospitals can afford them. Further, with the change in the manner of federally insured payments to hospitals for patient care, known as diagnosis related grouping (DRG), there will be a tendency on the part of hospital administrators to postpone the purchase or leasing of equipment. Therefore, the company intends to establish an electronically-linked network of diagnostic radiology centers in selected demographic areas in the United States that will include the following imaging modalities:

Nuclear Magnetic Resonance (NMR)
Computerized Axial Tomography (CAT)
Digital Subtraction Radiography (DSR)
Ultrasound

We believe that a mature chain of 25 diagnostic clinics could achieve service fee revenues of more that $250 million per annum."

Your first reaction to the above paragraph might be that the $P$ factor is described in a relatively incomplete fashion. That is, the entrepreneur has failed to cite the assumptions that lead him to estimate fifth-year revenues of $250 million. It is certainly possible to telephone the entrepreneur and/or invite him in for an interview; but at some point the venture capitalist must investigate the size of the radiology business to determine if $2.5 billion in out-of-hospital service fee income is realizable.

The first test is to multiply the number of radiologists times their average annual gross income. A telephone call to the American Society of Radiologists, or reference to an index containing market size data, will produce the number of 18,000. Using $100,000 for a doctor's annual gross income is probably reasonable. Thus, the size of the radiology service industry in the United States is about $1.8 billion per annum. How much of that is concentrated in 25 demographic centers? Perhaps a review of census data would reveal the figure of 60%. Multiplying 60% of $1.8 billion produces a little over $1 billion. A 10% market share would be approximately $100 million in projected annual revenues.

The audit of $P$ does not end there. It begins there. The next step is to determine what portion of the 18,000 radiologists perceive the problem and would be willing to purchase the entrepreneur's solution; a variation of Gertrude Stein's famous question, "Is there a market there?"

For the venture capital fund whose manager has medical advisors, which is an essential in the audit of $S$, the investigation of the radiologists' perception of their problem of affording NMR imaging equipment and ultrasound devices is a simple telephone call away. One call leads to a call back from the medical advisor with the names of radiologists and perhaps some articles from current publications that address this subject.

For the venture capital manager who does not have medical advisors, a network of contacts must be built with the same objective of interviewing radiologists and asking them if they have a need for a mobile diagnostic imaging service. Magazine articles are helpful because they frequently provide the names of radiologists interviewed by the journalist. If there are no magazine articles, the venture capitalist should refer to Nexus, the medical information computer-based search system developed by Mead Data Corp. By accessing Nexus, the venture capitalist can obtain substantially every piece of published information on any medical subject in a matter of a few hours. If Nexus is not available (although most large hospitals or university connected medical institutions are subscribers), the venture capitalist can contact Find SVP or Disclosure, or one of the other 24 to 36 hour information-gathering organizations. Their prices are not inexpensive, but their data gathering ability is superior.

However, the most useful information is that which is provided through direct contact and conversation with potential users of the entrepreneur's product or service. Questions such as, "Do you have the so-and-so problem," and "Would you buy the such-and-such solution to remove it?" are an important kind of investigation of the size of $P$ that a venture capitalist must undertake, because he can engage in conversation with potential users, hear reasons why the product or service would be useful to them, ask the price they might be willing to pay for the solution, and, if they would not be interested in buying the solution, finding out why. Is it a reason peculiar to them? Is it related to the size of their medical practice? Do they have access to NMR imaging devices at the hospital where they are affiliated? Are there technological concerns? Price concerns? Do they know the names of other radiologists with whom the venture capitalist could speak?

In just this manner is the size of the problem measured—through inquiries, investigations, interviews. The important target is to qualify the size of a market before it develops, to find evidence that indeed it will develop. Some of the greatest losses in the archives of start-ups have been due to inadequate investigation of potential market size. For example, hundreds of millions of dollars were invested in the production and marketing of feminine deodorant spray in the latter half of the 1970's. Yet, aggregate sales of all of the sprays over the several years that they were in existence did not top $50 million. There have been numerous black boxes, the euphemism for technological solutions, for which no problems existed. Hundreds of millions of dollars were invested in computer time-sharing, modular housing, solar energy, and in other solutions for which no problems were significantly large. It is extremely important for the venture capitalist to respect the audit of $P$ and to respect the fact that most of the losses in his portfolio can be avoided if the market into which he intends to fund the delivery of a product truly exists. And to determine its existence requires long hours, and interviews with people who are most likely to have the problem and will pay for its solution.

For example, returning to the 18,000 radiologists, it is highly unlikely that those connected with large urban or university-affiliated hospitals will be candidates for the use of a diagnostic NMR imaging and ultrasound service. This could reduce the number by one-third, to 12,000 radiologists, perhaps living in surburban, exurban, and even rural communities. The venture capitalists learns that, although smaller in number, these radiologists may have a serious need for diagnostic imaging and that a mobile service that swings by their offices twice a week would be most welcome.

To quantify the market size, the venture capitalist must transfer his investigations to the small town radiologists and ask a large number of them to estimate the number of images they will take in a week and what the market will bear in the way of price. The interesting part of the inquiries at this point is that the rural doctors may have a tendency to overstate the number of images in order to start the business. The reason for this is that the rural doctor needs and wants the diagnostic imaging service because it creates for him an additional source of income. Without NMR imaging and ultrasound, the small-town radiologist has perhaps lost business to radiologists in larger towns. Now he does not have to refer patients to other places, rather, he can do the work himself and earn the additional fee income. Thus, if the venture capitalist hears from 25 small-town radiologists that they would each be able to treat 20 patients a week who would be able to pay approximately $400 each, should the market size be projected at $4.8 billion per annum (12,000 $\times$ $400 $\times$ 20 $\times$ 50 $\times$ weeks)? That appears to be a vast overstatement of market size. After all, established medical practices such as dentistry have a market size of $20 billion per annum—large towns and small towns, as well. Clearly the practice of diagnostic imaging in small towns cannot be one-fifth the size of dentistry. How large is it then?

Another approach to the problem is to measure the size of the market in large towns where the large hospitals have been doing sonograms, CAT scans, and the like for years, and NMR imaging fairly recently. Perhaps a correlation can then be made as follows:

$$\frac{\text{Revenue of large-town radiologists}}{\text{Revenues of small-town radiologists}} \times \frac{\text{Revenues of large-town diagnostic imaging}}{N}$$

$N$ = Revenues from small-town diagnostic imaging.

Although certainly not an exact measurement of potential market size, this method has a ring of closer approximation than any of the other methods.

Certain markets, health care delivery chief among them, have institutional barriers to entry. The venture capitalist cannot get a true picture of the size of $P$ without determining the cost of piercing the institutional barrier. In the case of a non-invasive diagnostic system, the Food and Drug Administration does not become a factor, as it does with a new drug. The barriers in this instance are local boards of health determining that there is a need for the service, and state governments determining that a diagnostic imaging and ultrasound service is able to receive direct payment by insurance companies. Without insurance payments, the market will never develop. The venture capitalist must investigate the difficulty of penetrating the institutional barriers in order to enter a market. If they are too formidable the deal must be rejected.

In addition to institutional barriers to entry, there are seven other important factors that make a market more or less attractive. These factors must be reviewed one by one by the venture capitalist.

1. Existence of qualified buyers.
2. Existence of competent sellers.
3. Homogeneity of buyers.
4. Large number of buyers.
5. Word-of-mouth is principal form of advertising.
6. Optimum price/cost relationship.
7. Invisibility of the new company can be maintained.

These factors, along with absence of institutional barriers to entry, have been referred to elsewhere as the "DEJ" factors, which stands for *Demonstrable Economic Justification*.\* If a new company possesses all eight DEJ factors, its success is virtually assured. Its valuation, or V-factor, should exceed $1 billion in less than 5 years. Moreover, it will probably not require significant amounts of ven-

---

\*Silver, A. David, *Upfront Financing*, Wiley, New York, 1982.

ture capital in order to lift off. Examples will be provided below; but for now, the DEJ factors require some explanation in order for the venture capitalist to know what he is looking for and to know them when he sees them.

### The Existence of Qualified Buyers

Very simply put, if the people who are supposed to have the problem are not sufficiently aware of that, then they assuredly will not pay for a solution. If the entrepreneur intends to sell them a solution, he or she will have to spend millions of dollars educating a demand curve. Several situations of this nature come to mind. Corporate alcoholism is believed to be a larger problem than many corporations are willing to admit. The problems associated with the high cost of the American prison system—in excess of $50,000 per prisoner per year—are from time to time paraded before the public by politicians or journalists, but the budgets of wardens are frequently inadequate to countenance a new product or service, and legislators are loath to write a check for the wardens to try something new because the political risks of failure are too great. Notwithstanding problem awareness in this instance, the buyers simply are not qualified. They are not able to order and pay for a solution.

Speaking of politics, a problem that every voter is painfully aware of at the polls is the difficulty of casting a vote. Although we could vote from our homes very easily by dialing a coded number and tapping our votes into the telephone, the politicians seem to prefer the 19th century manner of voting. This problem is well understood by those able to pay for a solution and those willing to provide a solution. However, the buyers are uninterested in the solution and as such, are not qualified.

The absence of qualified buyers means instant death for a new company. So critical is this component in the audit of $P$ that many venture capitalists are loath to invest in new areas where a demand curve has never before existed, because they recognize their vulnerability in properly measuring the quality and quantity of demand once the new product or service is launched. Service company start-ups serving individuals, such as Weight Watchers International, historically have had the greatest difficulty attracting venture capital because, among other reasons, quantifying the quality and quantity of buyers of the service is extremely difficult.

## The Existence of Qualified Sellers

The issue that is addressed by this component of the $P$ factor is simply: is the entrepreneurial team able to build a sales organization that the buyers will respond to? Would-be entrepreneurs frequently, and inventors nearly continually, believe that if you build a better mousetrap the world will beat a path to your door. Nothing could be further from the truth. Even the best solutions to the largest problems must be marketed.

Venture capitalists frequently err on the side of optimism. The most typical error is to believe the entrepreneur's revenue projections. Particularly charming entrepreneurs input a certain liveliness and animated quality to their projections which make them seem more believable. Inexperienced venture capitalists—particularly those who have not lost enough capital in situations where revenues failed to materialize—can be lured into investing in fast ramp sales projections.

Alas, when sales do not materialize a culprit is sought out. It is usually the absence of a qualified sales and marketing organization. The business plan may have included the resumes of members of a marketing organization, but they were unable to deliver the sales.

How does the venture capitalist determine if the company's sales and marketing team is qualified? In a start-up, how does the venture capitalist hire competent sales and marketing people? The answer lies in history. Sometime in the early 17th Century there came into usage in France the word *competeré*, which means "to be able to fly." Shakespeare used it several times in his plays, without the accent, to produce the image of a competent soldier. The Oxford Etymological Dictionary of the English Language states that *competere* is the root word of both *compete* and *competent*. The implication that one can draw from this historical coincidence is that to be competitive one must be competent and to be competent, one must be competitive.

For example, in the launch of an educational software firm, the product may be developed by educators and the contacts with

school boards and educational advisors may be the domain of educators in the entrepreneurial team, but the marketing team most
certainly should not be educators. Competition is a foreign subject
in academia. The marketing team should be achievers from the
packaged goods industry: men and women who learned the
packaging, marketing, and sales techniques for getting shelf facings in supermarkets for their plausibly nutritional freeze-dried
flakes over some other company's. Notwithstanding the absence of
a solution for what they were breaking their back to sell to consumers, the record will show that they introduced the product,
developed an advertising campaign for it, communicated the marketing message to the sales organization, and increased sales from
$n$ to $n^7$ over a 5-year period. This person performed competitively
and in a competitive environment. Every new company must have
this kind of person in its entrepreneurial team just as soon as it
has a product or service to market. Any delay will result in an opportunity foregone, a slower revenue ramp.

How important is the people factor to a new company? General
Georges Doriot, Chairman of American Research and Development
Company, Inc., and the founder of the post-war U.S. venture capital industry in 1946, said, "There are three all-important facets to a
new company: people, people, and people." Arthur Rock, who brilliantly represents the generation that followed Doriot in the 1970's
with such stunning start-up investments as Teledyne, SDS, and
Apple Computer, among others, has often stated that he frequently invests in start-ups where there are development or production risks if the entrepreneurial team is outstanding.

How does one identify competence—the *competeré* factor?
The entrepreneur should display judgment, the ability to do the
right thing. The people he selects to manage should display competence, the ability to do things right. The football quarterback has
the hirable skill; the team owner builds the team into a profitable
franchise. The World Football League folded, whereas the United
States Football League is thriving. The business plans for the two
leagues are mirror images of each other. Why is one succeeding
where its identical twin failed? The answer lies with how competently the USFL has been marketed: a different season, well-
financed franchises, and the ability to attract top rookies.

Some venture capitalists prefer a three-man start-up team nicknamed People, Pencil, and Paper. People is the entrepreneur, the Mr. Outside, the front end of the gun. He is the driving force, planner, and sometimes dreamer. He is a concept man. His eventual responsibilities will be marketing, because he can motivate people and is an excellent' communicator.

Pencil is the thorough executor of People's plans. He is Mr. Inside, a good administrator of an idea. He cannot sell. He can produce a product. He can describe a product or service, and put a pencil in his hand and he will give you a nuts and bolts description of the production process.

Paper is the nay-sayer, the financial man, the numbers man. He is more like a green eyeshade than a person. His world is green columnar paper with budgets, projections, cash-flow statements, purchase orders, and bank statements. Paper is responsible for bank relationships, financial controls, payroll and cash management, insurance and other administrative duties.

If the new company appears to be an attractive investment with less than these three typologies, the least dispensable of the three is People.

## Homogeneity of Buyers

It is important to the new company's ability to make a profit that it solve one identical problem shared by all of its customers. For example, if the problem is clothing for the body, the solution may be marketed in different shapes, sizes, color, and fabrics, but it should remain a standard solution to a standard problem. The Polo line of clothing, developed by Ralph Lauren, solves a standard problem for a large number of men and women clothes buyers: it creates an image of the person they would like to be.

Frequently an entrepreneur will have conceived an important solution which could be used to solve a number of problems all at the same time. Holography is such a product. Holography can be an art form. It can see diseases in bone marrow. It can locate stresses in steel. Should the entrepreneurial team address all three problems at once and select the one that ramps the fastest? Clearly not. The market with the most homogeneous buyers is the most efficient to address.

Henry Ford said that he would make the Model T in any color

you wanted, as long as it was black. His entrepreneurial brilliance cannot be taken lightly, nor has it been by Toyota, Nissan, Subaru, BMW and Mercedes-Benz, which offer a far narrower range of colors each year than do the less profitable U.S. auto companies. Founders of new companies who bid on a variety of different contracts, each calling for a variation of their basic product, will end up with manufacturing losses and no marketing program with which to grow. The Model T Ford could have been produced in many colors, but it did not have to be. The market for automobiles is essentially homogeneous.

If you want to measure the great entrepreneurial fortunes in this country, think of the most universally demanded, standardized, off-the-shelf products and you will see the largest fortunes: autos, oil, electronics, foods, department stores, but not the professions (law, medicine, education) and not advertising executives, book publishers, accountants, architects, designers, or other customizers of services.

The homogeneity factor is also known as the "multiplier" or "cookie cutter." If it costs $100,000 to develop a standardized product that will sell over and over again at a significant markup, the investors will achieve a higher multiple on their $100,000 investment than if each sale has to be customized or tailor-made to fit the customer's needs. If a new product or service is knocked out the way your grandmother cut cookies from a big piece of dough, the profits will be greater and more rapidly achieved.

In the late 1970's and 1980's, a number of young men and women, lacking any significant previous business experience, have launched successful new companies by pulling into retail chains formerly disparate unprofitable operations that under one management team become profitable and rapidly growing. These have included cookie stores, barber shops, general contractors, travel agents, real estate brokers, and mail and package shipper-receivers.

The basic problem caused by sellers to non-homogeneous buyers is a need for a substantially greater amount of start-up capital, hence reduced rates of return. Between 1967 and 1970 approximately 400 computer time-sharing companies were launched. Time-sharing is the ability of a customer to lease time and storage space on a computer, along with 100 or so other customers and without interfering with the access to the computer of any other customer. Computer time-sharing had a crisp logic to it: why should small companies own or lease entire computers, which at the time cost millions of dollars, when they need to store and retrieve data only a small portion of the time?

In the late 1960's, when time-sharing was the darling of the venture capital industry, approximately 150 venture capitalists, as well as the public market, invested approximately $600 million in start-up time-sharing companies. Fifteen years later only three of these companies continue to exist and their revenue streams are predominantly from sources other than renting out computer time. Many of the failed companies were deficient in several of the DEJ factors, but the principal reason generally cited for their failure is that they ran out of capital. Since they had no earnings to attract second-stage investors, many were unable to raise additional capital and quietly folded their tents.

Time-sharing customers are non-homogeneous. Their problems differ. They must be sold individually. They must be serviced individually. In order to attract a time-sharing customer, the seller had to write programs for him. Programming is labor-intensive. The programs could not be resold to others. They were customized. Operating expenses exceeded revenues.

A new group of venture capitalists in the 1980's is repeating the mistakes made by time-sharing investors some 15 years ago. They are launching portable computer manufacturers with an enthusiasm that borders on frenzy. Approximately 40 portable computer manufacturers have been launched with roughly $200 million dollars, irrespective of the fact that they buyer of a 21-pound computer with a carrying case and a handle is non-homogeneous. To generate significant sales, special applications packages will have to be developed for each market. The insurance industry will want software packages to enable its salesmen to carry portable computers to the customer's homes and generate a variety of financial planning formulas on the kitchen table. Journalists will want packages that enable them to type a story on sight, set the type, justify the margins, and download into the newspaper's central processor from a pay telephone.

Other industries with mobile salespersons or service representatives will desire customized portable computers as well. With this much heterogeneity in the marketplace, is the portable computer industry worth investing in? And there is IBM Corporation, after all. Not only is IBM a potent competitor in the computer industry, but the $2.1 billion that it spent in R&D in 1982 exceeded the $1.8 billion invested by the venture capital industry in the aggregate that same year.

If the potential marketplace is non-homogeneous, it is probably not a market in which to ship venture capital. To determine homogeneity, the venture capitalist must make many inquiries of potential customers and users. He must ask what features they would like to see on the product: maintenance requirement, bells and whistles, upgradability, and so forth. If each potential buyer has a unique requirement, the marketplace is probably not one that should attract venture capital.

Assume that two companies simultaneously visit a venture capitalist. Christopher Columbus Explorations, Inc., requires $500,000 to sail three ships to India in search of precious metals. Americus Vespucci Maps, Inc., needs $500,000 to purchase a printing press in order to produce and sell maps of India after Vespucci returns from the voyage with Columbus. Both entrepreneurs, Columbus and Vespucci, are willing to give up 50% of the ownership of their companies in exchange for the $500,000, and both entrepreneurs project third-year net profits after taxes of $800,000; Columbus Explorations from selling gold and Vespucci Explorations from selling maps. Which of the two entrepreneurs do you invest in?

The clear choice is Columbus. Gold is attractive to all customers, but maps have to be customized—topographical, flat, black and white, in color, names of key cities, with or without time zones, and so forth. Rates of return to the contrary notwithstanding, if you want your name to get around, the map business is a pretty good place to be. Maybe a new country will see your name on the map and use it.

## Large Numbers of Buyers

Ideally, the market for the new product should contain an infinite number of buyers. This is usually attainable if the problem is a fairly ubiquitous one that people are unable to solve or solve completely, such as managing money, managing leisure time, transportation, education, healthcare, aging or disease; or if the product obsoletes or replaces itself—razor blades, time-sensitive services, cosmetics, communications, and entertainment.

For example, the market created by our inability to mitigate tooth decay and gum disease has been an exciting area for new products. The electric toothbrush, introduced by the Swiss company, Broxodent, achieved an 8% market share of the United States toothbrush market in 1968, because it claimed superior tooth-cleaning ability. The "Water Pic" oral hygiene device manufactured by a Teledyne subsidiary is a popular gift, graduation, and wedding shower item because of similar claims. Sugarless chewing gum has grown in popularity, and ultrasonic denture cleaners made a small dent in the market. The tooth decay market is a marvelous area for entrepreneurs. It involves hundreds of millions of customers making billions of purchases each year. Assuming there is no one-shot solution for cavities, the oral hygiene market is infinite.

On the other hand, if the number of potential buyers of a solution is relatively small—less than 1 million—the unit price of the product must be fairly large and there must be either (1) repetitive sales or (2) sales of ancillary products and services. For example, NMR imaging equipment manufacturers sell products costing over $600,000, plus expensive service and maintenance contracts. There are 5500 hospitals in the U.S., of which approximately one-third have the need and the capital to afford expensive diagnostic equipment. Some products require the purchase of replacement or spare parts. CAD/CAM software used in the design of integrated circuits costs as much as $300,000 for a one-time installation on the IC designer's computer. However, there are approximately 1000 selling sites throughout the world for CAD/CAM software that makes IC design more efficient.

CAD software for the home computer is as inexpensive as $15 per copy (to the dealer), although it is very useful for designing construction projects or landscaping the garden. To make it an attractive area for venture capitalists, however, inexpensive software must be able to run on all significant models, not just the 900,000 Apples (a market size of $13.5 million) or 1.2 million Commodores. In fact, the company would need two lines of 15–20 inexpensive products if there were less than 1 million selling sites to warrant a venture capitalist's attention.

Computer software for the factory floor to manage production scheduling, labor, and inventory, known as MRP software, has attracted several start-ups, because the prices of the software are around $1000 per module and there are roughly 200,000 U.S. selling sites. At five modules per selling site, MRP is a $1 billion market.

Markets with large numbers of selling sites that are renewable annually, or more frequently, present the ideal opportunity for venture capitalists. This has led more and more venture capitalists into the health care field where there have been extraordinary success stories, with many more to come, in both diagnostic and therapeutic products. The high cost of health care—in 1983 the health care costs per automobile manufactured in the U.S. exceeded the steel costs per auto—has created opportunities for entrepreneurs and venture capitalists in clinics and home health care.

Demographic changes can create entrepreneurial opportunities. Women entering the work force in large numbers in the late 1950's fostered the birth of fast food chains in the 1960's and other situations. For example, amniocentesis testing—diagnosing embryoes in utero for Downs Syndrome and other genetic defects—is recommended for women who are having their first child at age 36 or greater. In 1983, approximately 1.1 million women had amniocentesis tests at an average cost of $400. In specialized clinics the cost of these tests could be at least 50% less, which might attract more patients. The patient market is renewable over a 5–10 year period, as well.

There are different market size benchmarks for different venture capitalists. Some mention $1 billion per annum as a target market size; others $1 billion in the aggregate. Some say they would like to see portfolio companies grow to $200 million in 5 years; others are pleased with $50 million in 5 years.

A practical, flexible target is to make the following two assumptions: (1) anything worth doing will be copied by others who have substantial and excellent management, and (2) no single company will obtain more than a 10% market share. Thus, if a venture capitalist can measure the potential size of $P$ as $1 billion, he will be pleased if his entry into the market will be 10% of that, or $100 million in annual sales. At $2.5 billion in potential market size a new entrant should be considered successful if it achieves $250 million in fifth-year sales.

Setting standards is an important part of the venture capital process. Assisting companies in reaching those lofty heights is quite another matter. Most business plans are knocked off their tracks by unexpected and random events, such as strikes, floods, recessions, accidental deaths, and other exogeneous occurrences. Thus, achieving projections requires more than hard work and good timing. The carrot and stick is still the best way to move a company up a growth curve.

Niches, or segments, of large markets have never developed broad appeal among venture capitalists because, it is believed, there is a lid or cap on their growth. The possibility of explosive growth, as occurred among the telecommunications companies—TIE/Communications and MCI—that challenged AT&T for part of its $30 billion annual market, is simply not available to a company that has set its cap on capturing a niche. Frequently an engineer employed by a multi-billion dollar electronics or industrial products firm will develop an elegant technological solution to a small problem in an industry addressed with several products by the large firm. The engineer will demonstrate for his supervisor, who might ask someone from the marketing department to look at it. The latter thinks it might have potential as an addition to one of the corporation's product lines and demonstrates it for a few salesmen. They in turn think they can sell a few, so they take it to a couple of customer sites where the product becomes instantly successful. The salesmen thus inform the marketing manager, who informs the engineering supervisor, who asks the engineer to get together with someone in marketing to prepare a business plan for the launch of the product.

The engineer does so and, after learning quite a lot about PERT charts, submits the business plan to his supervisor. It calls for an investment of $1.5 million to complete product development and to begin production and then launch a direct sales campaign.

Revenues are projected to be $500,000 in the first year, $2.5 million in the second, and $7.5 million in the third, with a $750,000 contribution to income. The supervisor okays the plan and sends it up to the divisional vice president for approval. He immediately rejects it as being too small for a multibillion dollar corporation to fuss over, and probably too short a product life cycle.

The engineer, rejected, leaves the company to make the product on his own. He grants a license to the large corporation to produce and market the product in competition with him at some future date, should it so desire, buys some tools and parts for $20,000, and begins an entrepreneur stage of his life. The business plan is edited and shown to venture capitalists. The entrepreneur is turned down by all venture capitalists because he has a single product company addressing a niche market.

Even if the entrepreneur succeeds and the projections are met on schedule, a $500,000 investment would require that the venture capitalists own more than 50% of the company after the first round, as we will see in the discussion of valuation on page 200 and in Exhibit 29 on page 201 below. Should the venture capitalists control the company from the ouset, that would not leave equity should the entrepreneur wish to launch a follow-on product that requires another $500,000.

Niche markets are best left alone by venture capitalists, no matter how tempting, simplistic, and manageable they may seem at first blush.


## Lack of Institutional Barriers to Selling

Companies in the same industry and people sharing the same problem frequently form associations to *prevent* the introduction of solutions to their problems.

The thickest book in the libraries of many venture capitalists is called *The Encyclopedia of Associations*, and in it are the names of all of the associations in the United States, their addresses, telephone numbers, and the names of their executive directors. The Encyclopedia is used to telephone Association Directors to obtain market size data, brochures, dates on conferences, and so forth.

Associations are don't-rock-the-boat oriented. Are the politics of the American Medical Association associated with forward looking, progressive, fresh new approaches to health care, or keeping the established order safe from intrusion? The latter, for the simple reason that the members of the association use it to maintain their high incomes. When an industry begins to mature, its members form an association to keep out innovators who could lower the cost of the product or service. In so doing, they make the cost of entering the industry more expensive.

How important are institutional barriers to entrepreneurs? Ask the entrepreneurs, venture capitalists, and commercial bankers who lost more than $200 million in the 1960's and 1970's in modular housing. State and local zoning codes began coming out of the woodwork to prevent the on-site erection in residential areas of homes built in factories. The housing industry, too, has its incompetencies to protect. The State of Iowa prohibited the transport of modular houses over its highways.

Entrepreneurs with ideas for safety products for autos have not had an easy time selling these ideas to Detroit. An entrepreneur in Santa Barbara, California, built a car in 1979 so safe—yet attractive—that passengers could survive a head-on crash into a brick wall at 55 mph. He could not attract Detroit's or any other investor's capital.

What about informal barriers to entry? There are certain television sets that emit more radiation than an X-ray machine, but were an entrepreneur to invent a cheap consumer device to measure radiation from home television sets, who would you get to run your ads? Not television. And not the newspapers who are affiliated with television through common ownership. There are hundreds of formal and informal associations aimed at keeping out the problem-solvers.

Associations are created by their members to prevent the solution for one member without the solution for all. For example, assume that an entrepreneur brings a venture capitalist a business plan for New Farm Implements Corp. New Farm has developed and provided an apple picker so revolutionary that it picks, peels, and cores apples in the field, and bottles applesauce and applejuice on the ride back to the shipping dock at a total cost of one-tenth of what it presently costs just to pick apples. The price of applesauce and apple juice can be reduced dramatically.

The entrepreneur at New Farms could elect to manufacture and sell direct to apple processors, or license a farm implements manufacturer to produce and sell the new product, or build the equipment and lease it to apple processors, or enter into contracts with apple processors to manage their picking-canning process at a fee equal to one-half their present budget. Offering licensing or similar opportunities to the established apple processors and canners would be dangerous to the proprietary nature of the product.

Thus, the entrepreneur is blocked from the easiest form of entry. Building the equipment and going into business as an equipment manufacturer, or alternatively as a processor, is probably the only feasible method, but it is considerably more expensive.

Problems don't cost anything if those with the problem do not admit they exist. Solutions cost the establishment something. Associations, confederations, bureaucracies, unions and groups are formed by the members to lock the problem in and keep the solution out. The venture capitalist must ascertain the nature of the institutional barriers to entry and determine how much additional cost they add to entering the market. How is this measurement made?

Formal institutional barriers to entry have in many instances in the past barricaded certain markets from entrepreneurial companies. The most glaring example of a wall too high to leap has been the Food and Drug Administration (the "FDA"). This agency places stringent requirements on the testing of new pharmaceuticals and medical diagnostic devices before permitting their general use in the U.S. The FDA has been severely criticized for the various costs it places on society, for delaying life-saving and pain-mitigating drugs, as well as on pharmaceutical companies which must wait several years and collect large quantities of clinical data in order to obtain FDA approval to market a new drug or medical device. Were the judgment of the FDA infallible, it would warrant, perhaps, the costs it exacts on society. But as Milton Friedman* has pointed out, the FDA's practices have probably cost more lives than they have saved. As a result, many venture capitalists have turned their backs on start-ups whose products require FDA approval. The Pavlovian reaction to deals that must pass through the FDA's sifter has been a result of the extended time required for FDA testing and the added cost of the tests. Venture capitalists, after all, should avoid product development risks whenever possible.

However, the avoidance of FDA-related deals by venture capitalists may be coming to an end. Smith Laboratories, Inc., a start-up pharmaceutical company in 1981, when it was backed by the ven-

---

*Friedman, Milton, *Capitalism and Freedom*, University of Chicago Press, 1967.

ture capital firm of Cable Howse Partners, developed a new drug that effectively treats slipped discs and obtained FDA approval in 12 months. Revenues for the 5 months ended March 31, 1983 were $6,597,000, on which the company earned $3,590,000 before taxes. An unusual fact about Smith Laboratories is that Baxter Travenol Corp., a leading pharmaceutical company, had been licensed for several years after Dr. Lyman Smith, its developer, was issued a patent in 1967, subject to Baxter's obtaining FDA approval. Baxter failed to do so. Dr. Smith took back the drug, formed Smith Laboratories, raised $1,200,000 from Cable Howse Partners and obtained the necessary FDA approval. At Smith's initial public offering valuation, Cable Howse Partners earned approximately $30 million on its investment.

The fear and awe of the FDA may be receding to mere respect. Venture capitalists and entrepreneurs, always in a hurry to do and accomplish, seem better prepared in many cases to deal with the FDA than do large pharmaceutical companies, which are in many ways as slow moving as the government agencies with which they deal.

Another means of dealing with the FDA is to syndicate a pharmaceutical start-up with an established healthcare delivery company. Its experience in FDA applications and testing, coupled with the entrepreneurial energy, could lead to greater speed and cost reduction in obtaining FDA approval.

The possibilities for structuring this kind of joint venture are many and varied. The simplest is that the venture capital firm and the pharmaceutical company each purchase shares of stock in the therapy developer, but the venture capital firm pays a lower price per share because it is not receiving additional benefits, such as marketing rights. For example, the venture capital firm could purchase 25% of the therapy developer's common stock for $1 million, while the pharmaceutical firm invests $2.5 million in the therapy developer's common stock, but receives a 20% interest along with U.S. marketing rights. The marketing relationship will necessarily have to be memorialized with the proper "arms length" agreement, which sets minimum royalties, a proscribed termination date, a proscribed territory, and mechanisms for separating. This is to prevent the therapy developer from giving up its marketing rights to a large pharmaceutical company, which then puts the product on the shelf or fails to put a maximum effort into marketing the new product.

The pharmaceutical partner must be carefully selected on the basis of its ability to achieve results in applications to the FDA. It should be able to demonstrate success with many previous filings and applications.

There are other formal institutional barriers to entry, similar in their total power to the FDA. The venture capitalist should determine if negotiating with them is feasible within the time frame of the venture capital's need to generate a return. In the case of the launch of Federal Express Corp., it became necessary in 1975 for Federal Express to begin using larger aircraft. It had entered the overnight small package delivery business in 1973 with small Falcon Jets; but after OPEC's forced increase in the cost of jet fuel, "Fuel costs represented 15 percent of the company's total variable costs and were expected to escalate rapidly. An individual Falcon used 366 gallons of fuel per hour at a burning cost of $140.09 per hour in 1975. The company estimated that burn cost for 1976 would be $156.51 per hour. This was another compelling reason for Federal Express to gain approval from the civil Aeronautics Board to fly larger, more fuel efficient aircraft to complement the Falcon fleet."*

The Civil Aeronautics Board, or CAB, is an essentially unknown entity to venture capitalists. Not many of the government's agencies are familiar to the venture capital community, except the Small Business Administration. What is known about government agencies, such as the CAB, is generally not positive. They act slowly, are not responsive to requests for speedy decisions, and in the area of innovation and change their approach is negative. Milton Friedman has written in several of his books that the employees of government agencies realize that their jobs are to regulate the companies in the industries they address; and that without the profitable existence of these companies, the agency employees would risk their jobs becoming obsolete. Thus the regulators, Dr. Friedman argues, favor actively the companies that they regulate. Hence, "It was no coincidence, then, that every

*Sigafoos, Robert A., *Absolutely, Positively Overnight*, St. Luke's Press, Memphis, 1983, pp. 95–96.

scheduled airline objected to Federal's request to fly DC-9s, except powerful United Airlines . . . The influential Air Transport Association (also know as ATA), a Washington-based lobbying group for the scheduled airlines, spearheaded the opposition, an opposition in which Delta and American Airlines were among the most vocal."*

While being put through several years of delays at the CAB, Federal Express was running out of capital, yet gained the lead in overnight, small package delivery. Because of increased competition in 1976 and 1977, the company was unable to put through badly needed price increases, and the rising fuel costs narrowed its margins and forced it back into the capital markets. Many of the venture capitalists who had participated in the first two rounds of financing for Federal Express could not accept the risks of continued operating losses and failure to obtain CAB approval. Thus, in order to raise capital the lead venture capitalist, Rothschild, Inc., lowered the price of Federal's common stock from $29.34 per share in the 1973 second round, to $2.50 in the 1976 third round. The dilution to the venture capitalists who could not take the institutional barrier risk was substantial; the public offering price of Federal's common stock in 1978 was $24 per share. Few examples point out as clearly as does Federal Express the cost to the venture capitalist and the entrepreneur of institutional barriers to entering a market.

## Word of Mouth Advertising

The less money that a new company must spend on advertising, the greater the enthusiasm of venture capitalists. Advertising expenditures, it may be said, are in direct proportion to venture capital interest. If a new product or service must be heavily advertised to attract customers, the venture capitalist must ask himself, what is its demonstrable economic justification?

On the other hand, if a product or service leaps out the door of the production department time after time without the benefit of advertising, it is believed to have a great deal of economic validity.

In start-up companies, advertising dollars have not been spent

*Ibid.

nor have sales been generated. The venture capitalist must project the future need of advertising to generate sales. How is this done?

The function of advertising is to create *solution awareness*. It is not so much educating a problem or demand curve; rather it is identifying the source of supply. To paraphrase the philosopher, John Dewey, the first advertisement occurred when someone asked someone else a question, and the latter raised his hand and pointed. The question evidenced demand for something, such as, "Where can I catch fish?" The answer identified the source of supply. The pointed finger said, "You can catch fish over there." The first advertisement, then, was the finger point.

Frequently, many new products or services require a point to identify their location or the solution they provide. The Yellow Pages, or their equivalent, are the principal location identifier. Restaurants are typical users of Yellow Pages advertisements. Their advertisements frequently define their cuisine, meals they serve, and location. Not all restaurants purchase more than a line of Yellow Pages, so well-established are they. Newcomers frequently purchase a quarter of a page. The advertising budget of a new restaurant is not high as a percentage of sales. The Yellow Pages plus an occasional radio, television or newspaper advertisement is about all one might expect to generate a customer base. Outdoor signage may be considered advertising as well, or part of the initial fixturing. An advertising budget of more than 3% of sales would be extremely high for a restaurant. One half of 1% would be more realistic.

Restaurants and other service industries live or die on *word of mouth* advertising. A customer is either pleased or displeased with the quality of the service, and informs others that he or she recommends it or not. The customer enjoys the prestige of being a self-appointed restaurant critic; it is much like the blue collar worker watching Monday night football in a bar criticizing or applauding the abilities of the quarterback or the coach. He has not the slightest idea how to play football, but his knowledge as a regular viewer makes him an expert. He criticizes and applauds doctors, dentists, schools, movies, and a myriad of other services. He may not create a rush of customers to or away from a service provider, but a larger number of singers of praises or woe can spell success or failure for a stage play, movie, restaurant, podiatrist, travel agent, computer school, or pediatrician—and the best kind at that.

What can the venture capitalist learn from this extrapolation of Deweyian philosophy? The venture capitalist can observe that he should invest in products and services where (1) the customer will say: "Hey! This really works," and (2) others will believe him and try the product or service. Thus, productivity improving capital equipment sold to large corporations has been a popular investment area for venture capital, because a potential customer, when approached by the seller, can inquire of his counterpart at a referenced customer who is likely to say, "Yes, the product really works."

Health care delivery systems also have the "Hey! This really works" phenomena. Nobody ever complains about his dentist. He changes dentists, if unhappy. If a health care service is effective, the customer or patient expresses his or her joy with the product or service. This does not say much for the effectiveness of antacids, which advertise so heavily. But the surge of ambulatory and urgent care centers have been growing and prospering, with minimal advertising, because their health care services are equal to and less expensive than equivalent hospital services. It is the latter that are advertising heavily in order to attract more occupants. Health care delivery will continue to attract venture capital for several reasons, but word of mouth advertising is an important one.

There are some products and services that are quite effective, but the credibility of the users is inadequate to stimulate sales. A drug abuse program for production workers in automobile plants may be exceptional, but admitting to the problem, measuring effectiveness, and then talking openly of its effectiveness are all questionable. A program that improves prison conditions or lowers recidivism also presents the buyer with the risk of admitting the problem existed in the first place. Services to the handicapped fall into that category as do products and services for agencies that service the extremely poor and the handicapped. Products and services to people in third world countries suffer from the same buyers' credibility problem. Venture capitalists have typically not done well in these industries and there is a tendency to avoid them. If the John Dewey *point* cannot be made to identify the solution to a problem, venture capital is better off avoiding that particular marketplace.

Venture capitalists also tend to avoid companies whose products are targeted for mass consumer markets. These products usually fail to address the problem/solution equation. In fact, there is no problem; rather, the promoter believes that given enough advertising he or she can create the feeling of a problem and then offer the product as its solution. This marketing ploy has been accomplished several times, but it requires marketing genius. Venture capitalists achieve greater results when they avoid the requirement of marketing genius. Two examples of creating a problem in a mass consumer environment and then selling a solution to solve it include halitosis, cured by Listerine, and tired blood, cured by Geritol. Billions of dollars of sales have been created for these two products primarily because the image of the problem and the effectiveness of the solution have been so vividly created by brilliant marketing people.

Notwithstanding the rapid sales ramps and gross profit margins of consumer products such as Listerine, Geritol, and others, this is not a suitable arena for venture capital. There is no established $P$ to measure. The solution, or $S$, is available from dozens of the other sources. And the entrepreneurial team, or at least the marketing-experienced member of the team, must be more than competent. He must be sublimely gifted. This combination of factors all too frequently results in losses.

## Optimum Price/Cost Relationship

There are two aspects to the price of a product or service: the amount and the form of payment. Most venture capitalists will not begin to consider investment in a new manufacturer unless its product's gross profit margin is 60% or greater. This rule of thumb permits a considerable margin for error. Many entrepreneurial successes have occurred among companies with gross profit margins of 40% or better. The higher the venture capitalist sets as his minimum acceptable target gross profit margin, the fewer will be his losses. If one invests $1 million in a manufacturer whose product has a 60% gross profit margin, the venture capital will go twice as far toward financing a marketing program as it would for a product with a 30% gross profit margin. Or to state the converse, other things being equal, it would take $2 million of venture capital to attempt to capture equivalent market share for the 30% gross profit margin product.

In the rapidly emerging personal computer market, Apple Computer, Inc.'s IIE product, complete with a video monitor and dot matrix printer, was selling at retail in early 1982 for approximately $3300. Of that amount, the monitor and the printer represented approximately $1300 of the retail price, leaving $2000 for the Apple IIE computer. Assuming a 25% profit for the dealer, the Apple IIE had a factory price of about $1500.

Assume that the Apple IIE's cost of goods sold in 1982 was $300; thus, its gross profit margin was $1500−300/$1500, or 80%.

In the personal computer marketplace, before IBM's entry, Apple was the leader, with Tandy relatively close behind, and over 100 newcomers tagging along. Apple's 80% gross profit margin and rapid sales ramp permitted ample margin for errors—read Apple III and Lisa—plus new product development—read MacIntosh. One of the newcomers in the personal computer marketplace, Osborne Computer Corp., violated the 60% gross profit margin minimum requirement, and was carried out of the marketplace on its shield. The retail price of the Osborne portable computer (a monitor was built-in) was approximately $1600. Assuming a gross profit margin for the dealer of 25%, then the Osborne's factory price was approximately $1200.

Let's assume that the Osborne computer cost $400 more to manufacture than the Apple IIE, or $700. Monitors are difficult to manufacture for less than $300 and the Osborne had shorter product runs than the Apple. Further, Osborne added several hundred dollars of software as a bonus to attract customers. Assuming these unit price and cost numbers are accurate and that both companies were launched with $8 million of venture capital, is there any wonder that Osborne was bankrupt within 18 months?

|                     | Apple IIE | Osborne Computer |
|---------------------|-----------|------------------|
| Factory price       | $1500     | $1200            |
| Cost of goods sold  | 300       | 700              |
| Gross profit        | 1200      | 500              |
| Gross profit margin | 80%       | 42.7%            |

True, Osborne gained rapid entry into the marketplace, but it soon had to raise its price. It tested the $1800 retail level, but there was no validity for the higher price and the competition which had established itself at the higher price levels effectively barred Osborne from moving into their segments.

The issue of portability is quite another matter. The $P$ for which portable computers provide the $S$ was not clearly defined by Osborne. Had the company created an image as dramatic as "halitosis" for which its portable computer was the Listerine, its survival would have been accomplished easily. However, Osborne and the other portable computer manufacturers left it up to the customers to find problems for which portability offered solutions. To do so requires exceptional skills in marketing, which are not typically possessed by the new entrepreneurs and managers of the personal computer industry. Many of them all too frequently believe that marketing savvy means buying a page each month in the 20 or so computer industry trade journals.

Before leaving the subject of setting a high gross profit margin target, it bears reinforcement that a truly proprietary $S$ that effectively solves a large and growing $P$ will generate such attractive profits, that competition will rush into the marketplace within 18 months. The competition will have studied the pioneering company's products, advertisements, financial statements and, in some cases, it will have sorted through its garbage. Very little about the pioneering company's product, costs, marketing methods, and personnel will not be known to the competition. Further, if the marketplace is in the billions of dollars, the competition will be large companies with hundreds of millions of dollars of resources. They will be able to sustain a long price war if that is their intent. IBM entered the personal computer market in 1983 and wrested the leadership from Apple and Tandy. Without a large gross profit margin, Apple could not have stood its ground against IBM.

For venture capitalists who do not know it, IBM spends more on research and development each year than the entire venture capital industry invests in all its companies each year. Thus, if an entrepreneurial team intends to take a piece of IBM's market, it had better be well-funded and have an 80% gross profit margin, such as Apple has.

The second aspect of price is its form of payment. Entrepreneurs all too frequently pay too little attention to this area and venture capitalists all too frequently accept the form of payment set by the entrepreneur. A modest amount of study suggests that the price that one pays for a solution should bear some relationship to the cost of the problem and whether or not the solution eliminates or mitigates it. If the latter is the situation that obtains, and the problem needs repeated applications of the solution, many forms of pricing may be used. If the former—a one-shot solution—there are still other variables to the form of paying for the solution.

The principle forms of payment are as follows:

1. Direct sale
   a. Payment in cash, credit card
   b. Payment by third party (e.g., insurance)
2. Installment sale
   a. Credit must be arranged with a lender prior to sale.
   b. Ownership reverts to purchaser at time of sale with the product serving as collateral for the lender.
3. Lease or rental
   a. Customer pays for the privilege of using the product without owning it.
4. Metered or usage charge
   a. The customer pays an installation fee to obtain the product on its premises and then pays a monthly fee based on frequency of use.
5. Subscription
   a. Payment is made in advance for the right to receive a future product or service.
6. Facilities management contract
   a. The customer transfers the assets of a specified operation or facility—such as a data processing department—to the service provider who agrees to deliver the specified service for the amount of the annual budget.

The above forms of payment, with the exception of the facilities management contract, are frequently accompanied by add-on's. The more customary add-on's are:

Service contract

Handling charges

Related product purchases

Replacement parts

Coupons

It behooves the venture capitalist to give very serious attention to the form of payment. There is a tendency among entrepreneurs to under-price and to pass up opportunities to stack several add-on's onto the price in order to buy market share on the cheap. The unfortunate aspect of that logic is that, as Osborne Computer learned to its sorrow, it is difficult to move the price of the product up because other products have co-opted the higher price levels. You can lower a price much more easily than you can raise it.

The story may be apocryphal or absolutely based on fact; notwithstanding the point is worth making. When IBM introduces a new product, to test the possible price, its salesmen fan out in several directions to call on a number of potential customers. Upon having demonstrated the solutions offered by the new product to the potential customer's problem, the IBM salesman leads the discussion gradually to the subject of price.

"How much is this product?" asks the customer.

"Thirty thousand dollars," responds the IBM salesman.

Then, if the customer does not bat an eye, the IBM salesman continues:

Per month."

If still no eye is batted, nor leg crossed to indicate stiffening resistance, the IBM salesman continues:

"Plus a service contract of $1000 per month or $8000 for the first 12 months."

If still no resistance, the salesman adds:

"Plus two days training for $1500 for each employee trained; plus a parts warranty for $3600; plus some interesting peripherals and up-grades."

Facing no material resistance, the IBM salesman continues:

"Now let's talk about the software."

Whether or not this story is true is hardly the point. IBM did not get to be the dominant company in virtually every industry and industry segment that it has entered by dropping prices and poorboying its condition. When it enters an industry, it sets the price and the form of payment, which are relatively high, permitting others to sell under the IBM umbrella. Osborne Computer entered the market as a discounter without suggesting with add-on's that its product was in any way distinguished or special. Quite the contrary, it gave the appearance of not being serious.

Venture capitalists are well-advised to engage the services of a marketing consultant prior to investing to assist them and the entrepreneurial team in determining the most efficient price and form of payment. In several of the popular markets for venture capital investing, price and form of payment have become critically important. Hospitals, for example, can no longer say to equipment manufacturers: "I'll take the best." Now, under a Medicaid/Medicare enforced repayment policy, know as DRG, hospitals cannot pass along higher costs of medical services to Medicaid and Medicare. They may only charge the insurance carrier with the cost of the medical care.

If the entrepreneur makes it easier for people to pay, there will be less resistance to buying. Politicians have not learned this. They are bad entrepreneurs. They sell themselves exhaustively to a mass audience every 2, 4, or 6 years, using millions of dollars of other people's money. Yet, they make voting difficult and time consuming. Voting is like buying. If a politician were as competent as Ross Perot or Edwin Land (Polaroid), he would legislate for a simplification in the method of voting. For example, on November 3 of each year, all registered voters could dial a computer from their homes and register their votes by touching appropriate buttons.

Once the entrepreneur has settled on a price and form of payment for his new product or service, the price must be related to the cost of producing and marketing the product over time. The exercise is twofold: the first part is PERT chart analysis, and the second part is cash flow analysis.

PERT chart analysis is a time study of the flow of events in the company that create receipts and disbursements. For example, let's start, hypothetically, the ABC Paper Company that recycles and resells scrap paper. Assume that we rent a convenient and efficient paper mill. The intensely abbreviated time study of events will include:

1. Contract with large paper users to sell scrap paper to ABC Paper Company (1st to 90th day).
2. Hire indigents and unemployed people to pick up scrap paper from streets, refuse areas (7th to 21st day).
3. Contract with sources to purchase recycled paper from ABC (21st to 120th day).
4. Close on all contracts (180th day).

Thus, ABC Paper incurs 180 days of expenses, without offsetting receipts. In its cash flow projection, it must then account for a substantial initial cash deficit.

The principal purpose of the cash flow projection is to determine how much capital a new company requires in order to match its proposed deficit. Once having done this, the entrepreneur might tend to assume payment from his customer on the 181st day, upon having delivered the first roll of recycled paper to the first customer. However, new companies offering new products to old-line companies are not paid quickly. The product must be tested, and furthermore, the buyer knows that the seller needs him more than the buyer needs the seller. Thus, the cash flow projections must reflect delays in payment in order to raise additional funds to cover greater-than-planned-for deficits.

New companies are somewhat at the mercy of the buyer. Assume that the City Council in New York legislates an elevator tax to raise money from citizens who can afford to live on higher floors. Assume further that an entrepreneur has invented elevator toll machines to collect a new elevator tax from passengers. The Council passed the legislation on the theory that tall buildings are destructive to the ecological balance and that people who live in and work in tall buildings have more money than those who do not, and are destructive to the socio-economic balance. Hence, inhabitants of tall buildings will be taxed five cents per ride to pay for the expanded local services to those less fortunate.

The entrepreneur plans to manufacture, sell (or lease), install,

**EXHIBIT 20.   Unit Sales, Leases, and Service Calls**

| Receipts | Code | Month 1 | Month 2 | Month 3 |
|---|---|---|---|---|
| Unit sales | (#A) | — | 5 | 10 |
| Unit leases | (#A) | 10 | 20 | 30 |
| Service calls | (#A) | 5 | 10 | 20 |
| Unit sales | (#B) | 5 | 10 | 15 |
| Unit leases | (#B) | 20 | 40 | 60 |
| Service calls | (#B) | 10 | 20 | 30 |
| Unit sales | (#C) | 10 | 20 | 30 |
| Unit leases | (#C) | 30 | 60 | 90 |
| Service calls | (#C) | 20 | 30 | 40 |

and service the toll machines outside the elevators in high-rise apartment buildings. There are three sources of revenues—sales, leases, and service income—and most of the expense items of a manufacturing-distribution operation. Your task as a venture capitalist considering this deal is to run cash flow projections to reflect the various amounts and relationships of the several streams of cash flow. AAA, BBB, and CCC are the three different cash flow assumptions in Exhibit 20, each of which emphasizes a different strength: sales, leases, and service income.

Then, the three sources of receipts can be varied in order to see all of the possibilities, such as #A Sales with #B Leases and #C Service Calls. This exercise will produce 18 possible cash flow streams.

| AAA | BBB | CCC | CCB | AAC |
|---|---|---|---|---|
| AAB | BBA | CCA | CAB | ACA |
| ABA | BAB | CAC | CBB | ACC |
| ABB | BAA | CAA | | |

If a unit sales price is $500, unit cost is $200, a lease is $25 per month for 36 months, and a service charge is $10, the first 3 months cash flow of the new company could vary widely from AAA to CCC, as shown in Exhibit 21.

The CCC situation creates a greater cash deficit and a need for

EXHIBIT 21.   Range of Cash Flow Possibilities
(Amounts in $000's)

|                                 | Month 1    | Month 2    | Month 3    |
|---------------------------------|-----------|-----------|-----------|
| *AAA*                           |           |           |           |
| Cumulative units in the field   | 10        | 35        | 75        |
| Revenues                        | $    300  | $  3,100  | $  5,950  |
| Expenses:                       |           |           |           |
|    Cost of goods sold           | 2,000     | 5,000     | 8,000     |
|    SG & A expense               | 5,000     | 5,000     | 5,000     |
| Total expenses                  | $ 7,000   | $ 13,000  | $ 21,650  |
| Deficit                         | (6,700)   | (6,900)   | (7,050)   |
| Cumulative deficit              | $ (6,700) | $(13,600) | $(21,650) |
| *CCC*                           |           |           |           |
| Cumulative units in the field   | 40        | 120       | 75        |
| Revenues                        | $ 5,950   | $11,800   | $17,650   |
| Expenses:                       |           |           |           |
|    Cost of goods sold           | 8,000     | 16,000    | 24,000    |
|    SG & A expense               | 5,000     | 6,000     | 7,000     |
| Total expenses                  | $13,000   | $ 22,000  | $31,000   |
| Deficit                         | (7,050)   | (10,200)  | (13,350)  |
| Cumulative deficit              | $ (7,050) | $(17,950) | $(41,300) |

$41,300 to get through the first 90 days. The AAA model creates the smallest deficit.

The above example is embarrassingly simple, while in reality the process of arriving at the exact amount of a new company's cash deficit is a difficult and tedious process. It is the essence of the business plan, and venture capitalists should assume that, in most cases, entrepreneurs are not qualified to prepare cash flow projections and the venture capitalists should test the assumptions and redo the projections. More often than not, there will be errors of optimism in the area of form of customer payment.

## Invisibility of the New Company

It is axiomatic in the company launching business that *anything worth doing is worth duplicating.* An entrepreneur could have a patent on ice cream, but if it is selling well, dozens of competitors will come at him and risk patent infringement litigation. Their potential capital gains will cover legal fees and litigation costs several years into the future. Isn't that the Saran Wrap story?

For every successful new company, there will be many followers. Computer time sharing had over 400 entrants. Modular housing has had over 400 entrants. The portable computer had more than 100. Even disposable thermometers had a dozen new company formations.

To head off potential competition, the venture capitalist should encourage the entrepreneur to keep a low profile. Invisibility is the entrepreneur's friend. To reverse Zero Mostel's famous quotation: "When you got it, *don't* flaunt it."

Venture capitalists should avoid entrepreneurs who advertise before they can deliver. Someone may beat them to the delivery date. All publicity should be avoided until the product works and is ready for delivery.

It is important to have a good D&B rating. A good D&B is not only a healthy credit rating, but it is a description of the new business that can tell a good, concise story about a new company. Entrepreneurs should not treat D&B lightly. If they slam a door on D&B, their report on the new company may paint a less than complete picture.

Another reason for keeping a low profile is the law of breakage in new companies. When things fall apart in new companies, they fall into the most difficult to reach places and break into the greatest number of pieces and all at the same time.

## Summary of DEJ Factors

When a new company possesses all eight DEJ factors, two things are virtually certain:

1.  A major entrepreneurial fortune is about to be made and the venture capitalist should climb aboard.

2.  The entrepreneur probably doesn't need venture capital.

One of the best examples of a new company with all eight DEJ factors firmly in place was Electronic Data Systems Corp (EDS). It was launched by H. Ross Perot in 1964 with $20,000 and has never raised venture capital. EDS sold facilities management contracts to data processing departments of large corporations and government agencies in the mid-1960's when they had purchased millions of dollars of mainframe computers but were unable to process their data. In 5 years, EDS had its initial public offering at a price of 115 times earnings, which were approximately $9 million on revenues of $36 million. A few months thereafter, the market value for EDS exceeded $1.2 billion, of which Perot had more than 85%. General Motors acquired EDS in July, 1984 for $2.5 billion. Exhibit 22 examines the characteristics of a company that possessed all 8 DEJ factors.

### EXHIBIT 22.    EDS—The Model of a Perfect New Company

#### DEJ #1 Existence of Qualified Buyers

Corporate data processing inefficiency was a very real problem. Buyers did not have to be *educated*, that is, told they had a problem. Buyers knew they had a problem and knew they had to pay for a solution. Buyers were able to pay for a solution. A minimal amount of buyer education was required.

#### DEJ #2 Existence of Competent Sellers

Ross Perot, the EDS entrepreneur, hired managers who were skilled in providing solutions to the problems of the EDS customers. Mr. Perot was a skilled former IBM salesman and he hired personnel in his image. He was competitive and so were his employees.

#### DEJ #3 Homogeneity of Buyers

The problem that EDS solved was essentially the same for all buyers with minor differences in degree or severity. The solution did not have to be tailor-made or customized for each buyer. Selling off the racks is cheaper and provides more rapid cash flow than selling custom made.

EXHIBIT 22. (continued)

### DEJ #4 Large Number of Buyers

The number of potential buyers sharing essentially the same problem was in excess of 3000 corporations and institutions. Assuming each one had an annual data processing budget of $1 million per annum total potential, the market size for EDS's solution was $3 billion per annum and no other competitor was within 2 years of sharing a piece of the pie. (More than any other single factor, this explains why EDS's initial public offering was at a common stock price in excess of the then unheard of 115 times earnings.) Facilities management, 5 years after EDS began operations, became the fastest growing segment of the data processing industry.

### DEJ #5 Lack of Institutional Barriers to Selling

The buyers were not organized. They belonged to no association. There was no regulatory body to which they were responsible for their activities, such as the American Medical Association or Civil Aeronautics Board. Their buyers were new to their problem. Their purpose in seeking a solution was to save money, and for no other purpose for which they would have to seek permission or clarification from an outside or collective institution.

### DEJ #6 "Hey, It Really Works!"

EDS's solution was passed along from buyer to buyer by word-of-mouth advertising. Not only is word-of-mouth the cheapest form of advertising, it is also the most effective. A solution that really works is, of course, a necessity.

### DEJ #7 Optimum Cost/Price Relationship

The price of the solution was equal to the cost of the problem, that is, the buyer's data processing budget. EDS's price could not be questioned as being excessively high or unwarranted, because the buyer was paying the same price for his problem that he was asked to pay to have it solved. If the same $100 that brought him problems would now bring him solutions, he was $100 ahead. As they say in *The Godfather*, EDS made him an offer he couldn't refuse.

### DEJ #8 Invisibility of the New Company

EDS operated quietly and without fanfare. It did not advertise or promote heavily. It did not gain attention so that it could be copied by competitors. In 1973, 10 years after the formation of EDS, the first company larger than EDS (General Electric) entered the facilities management business. By that time Mr. Perot had banked hundreds of millions of dollars in capital gains.

## THE AUDIT OF E

There is no amount of instruction that can replace experience in judging potentially successful entrepreneurial teams. Every venture capitalist must develop his own set of antennae that filter in the winners and filter out the losers. The following characteristics are helpful as guideposts in the process. These characteristics of successful entrepreneurs are based on responses to questionnaires sent to several hundred successful entrepreneurs— primarily men who had made more than $5 million via the entrepreneurial process.

One's expectations of outstandingly successful entrepreneurial teams should be hydraulic, rather than permanently fixed at a vertical angle. The Intel Corp. team of Robert Noyce, Andrew Grove, and Gordon Moore is the apex to which all other teams aspire. This team was magnificently trained in company launching and managing rapidly-growing electronics companies at Shockley Transistor Corp. and Fairchild Semiconductor Corp. These three individuals made up an entrepreneurial team whose competence was the equal of Sloan-Mott-Brown of General Motors, and unrivalled since the formation of Intel in the late 1960's. An investment of less than $2 million, largely provided by the venture capitalist, Arthur Rock, built a company worth more than $800 million in less than 5 years.

To anticipate that the equal of this supremely gifted entrepreneurial team will cast their shadow on the door of a venture capitalist is to believe in the tooth fairy. Entrepreneurial teams are rarely one-half as competent as the Intel team at the time the business plan is submitted to the venture capitalist. One's ideals may be maintained at the Intel level, but it will require that the venture capitalist do some reshuffling of the team he is dealt in order to produce a competent team. Entrepreneurs do not select managers very well, as a rule. One of their indigenous problems is with delegation. Entrepreneurs do not delegate well for two reasons: first, they do not believe others can do things as well as they can; second, this belief is, in fact, true.

The potentially successful entrepreneurial team can be described, although "success" is not at EDS or Intel valuations but rather $50–$100 million in 5–10 years on an investment of $2–$5 million.

The venture capitalist must invest in a team, not merely an entrepreneur. If the entrepreneur has selected a manager partner but the person is not competent, it is up to the venture capitalist to replace him. If the entrepreneur has not selected a manager partner, it is up to the venture capitalist to locate and hire the most competent one he can find. Entrepreneurs by themselves, regardless of how high the values placed on the $P$ and the $S$ factors, cannot make successful companies. Entrepreneurial teams, made up of two or more qualified people, can make successful companies. Stated more bluntly, entrepreneurs deliver the opportunity to the managers and venture capitalists, who then create value from it. The entrepreneur is primarily important for the launch—without which, of course, there would be nothing—and the manager is primarily important to build a company that has value. The entrepreneur is extremely important to the venture during its formative years, when $P$ is being formulated and reformulated, and when $S$ is being designed, developed, produced, tested, and marketed to its first customers. This stage—call it the entrepreneurial stage—may last for several years, frequently to the point of maturity of the company's initial product or product line, and frequently to the point of profitability. The management stage takes over at that point and takes the company forward through its growth stage, including initial public offering and merger. Let us examine the characteristics that the venture capitalist should look for in order to invest in potentially successful entrepreneurs and managers.

## CHARACTERISTICS OF SUCCESSFUL ENTREPRENEURS

Interviews with over 400 successful entrepreneurs have produced the collage of superficial characteristics described in Exhibit 23.

These superficial characteristics can be explained, but it is the task herein to describe rather than explain. One may be unwilling to accept the notion than an investment is likely to result in a high valuation if the entrepreneur is 50 years of age, a committed bachelor, wears cologne, cuff links, laced shoes, a three-piece suit, and drives an American car, but based on the questionnaires answered by several hundred of the country's most successful entrepreneurs of the last decade, a venture capitalist is well-advised to decline an investment opportunity whose entrepreneur fails to meet

**EXHIBIT 23.    Superficial Characteristics of Successful Entrepreneurs***

| | |
|---|---|
| Age: | 27–33 years. |
| Sex: | 95% heterosexual male. |
| Facial: | Simple hair style, minimal upkeep required; frequently bearded. |
| Clothing: | Loafers, no jewelry or extra buttons; comfortable, simple. |
| Physical: | Thin, excellent health, no excesses, such as smoking, drinking or over-eating. |
| Marital: | 65% divorced, 35% married to first wife, zero bachelor. |
| Speech: | Speaks quickly, quick-witted, self-effacing. |
| Residence: | Lives in urban area. |
| Automobile: | 80% drive European cars, with minimal maintenance requirement. |
| Politics: | 80% vote liberal. |

*For greater details, see Silver, A. David, *The Entrepreneurial Life: How to Go for It and Get It*, Wiley, New York, 1983.

most of the superficial characteristics summarized in Exhibit 23. On the other hand, if the entrepreneur is 28 years of age, divorced, bearded, and drives a German car, and if the values of $P$ and $S$ are high, there can be greater assurance that the investment opportunity will result in a large capital gain. One may be reasonably certain, however, that the superficial characteristics of the entrepreneur are similar to those of many successful entrepreneurs.

In certain cases, some of the superficial characteristics must be overlooked. For instance, foreign born-and-raised entrepreneurs are frequently somewhat older when they begin their companies. Their entry into entrepreneurship has been delayed owing to origin of birth. They may observe different dress codes as well, as might be expected. Notwithstanding, an older entrepreneur has fewer years to enjoy the fruits of his achievement and may tend to become bitter if circumstances turn against him and he begins to lose control of the company's destiny. The simple dressing habits of entrepreneurs are to enable them to act with great speed and energy. There is precious little time for entrepreneurship and cologne, extra buttons, jewelry, and other amenities unnecessary for potentially successful entrepreneurs.

Far less is known about potentially successful female entrepreneurs, because the number has been too small to create statistically accurate samples. It is believed, however, that they are 6–8 years older than their male counterparts at the time they become entrepreneurs. Among other reasons one becomes an entrepreneur, there is the three-step process of *dissatisfaction insight,* and *energy.* The insight results in the formulation of a large problem and the design and development of its solution. The energy requirement is the indefatigable drive to do some one thing extremely well. And the entrepreneur must be dissatisfied that his or her employer, or some other similar agency for change, has ignored or overlooked the problem or has elected not to produce and market a solution for it. Because women have been denied access to vertical movement within their corporation, they have not experienced as many events about which to be dissatisfied. Thus, one might expect women entrepreneurs to be 20% older than men.

As for their marital status, it is more common for women entrepreneurs to be living with someone rather than married, which is, technically, bachelorhood and a negative indicator in the case of male entrepreneurs. However, for females it indicates commitment to another person, without taking on the responsibilities of bearing children. This is an acceptable condition for the entrepreneurial process.

Differences of skin color, religion, upbringing, homeland, or region are not material in determining the future success of an entrepreneur. All too frequently, venture capitalists select entrepreneurs who have similar backgrounds. Since venture capitalists are predominantly products of the middle class, 54% of whom have earned engineering baccalaureates and business administration masters degrees, whereas entrepreneurs have dropped out of college or graduate programs in many cases, the selection process proves fatal.* Venture capitalists should not seek friendships from entrepreneurs; rather, they should seek something more akin to jockeys.

Without suggesting that one prejudge an entrepreneur as he or she enters the room, there are a number of superficial

*For details, see Silver, A. David, *Who's Who in Venture Capital,* Wiley, New York, 1984.

**EXHIBIT 24   Substantive Characteristics
of Successful Entrepreneurs**

---

1.  Middle class background.
2.  Childhood deprivation.
3.  Absent father; dynamic mother.
4.  Guilt that mother has been disappointed.
5.  Dissatisfaction–Insight–Energy.
6.  Creativity.
7.  Honesty.
8.  Courage.
9.  Communications skills.
10. Happiness.

---

characteristics—one could say "first impressions"—that should be considered. Heavy, older, bejeweled, perfumed, committed bachelors are not characteristic of fanatically-driven, singlemindedly consumed, time and capital constrained entrepreneurs.

There are 10 substantive characteristics of successful entrepreneurs which must be investigated during the course of the audit of $E$. Several of these can be discovered quite rapidly, within the first 30 minutes of the initial interview. Bear in mind that in start-up situations, there may be only an entrepreneur and a handful of employees to interview. A manager partner must be located and hired. In first-stage companies, there is normally a manager partner—although he may have to be replaced—but some of the scrutiny applied to entrepreneurs in start-ups is less critical if the company has been shipping product for a year or so.

The venture capitalist should gain as much information as possible about the entrepreneur in the interviews. The 10 principal characteristics of entrepreneurs are listed in Exhibit 24, followed by a discussion of each and the areas of inquiry.

### Middle Class Background

Successful entrepreneurs were generally raised in homes that espoused middle class values. The children were encouraged by the parents to succeed for them. The ideal was to become a professional, such as a physician, lawyer, engineer, accountant, or the like, because to do so would bring praise to the parents. Success was applauded; failure was attributed to lethargy or slothfulness. The American Dream is alive and well in middle-class families— the belief that it is possible, through hard work and a good education, to rise to the top of any field. Entrepreneurs are raised in families that maintain the absolute feasibility of the American Dream.

Entrepreneurs rarely come from families that espouse upper-class values—the idea that change is probably for the worse; one should never invade one's capital; and achievement is something one's ancestors accomplished. Lower-class families that are concerned primarily with survival do not produce entrepreneurs either. There is rarely a mentor in this type of family to demonstrate how one climbs the ladder out of a woe-is-me world. Success and achievement are condemned as the result of being lucky or having cheated.

Occasionally one reads of an entrepreneur who cheats the investors and flees with their capital and the cash in the till. Clearly, in such cases, the venture capitalists failed to audit the entrepreneur's background in sufficient depth. Had they done so it is likely they would have found a childhood bereft of any positive parental guidance or setting of examples. The childhood would have included poverty and perhaps an unsettled household, such as a drunk and disorderly father. Whatever the precise conditions, they were so dreadful that the entrepreneur determined that, come hell or high water, he would never let circumstances return him to that sad state of affairs again. When his company gets into a financial jam, this kind of person will frequently become frightened and either direct a substantial amount of funds to his personal bank account or take all of the cash he can direct into his own account and flee.

Because entrepreneurs from more impoverished backgrounds generally enter the entrepreneurial period of their development later in life than entrepreneurs from middle class backgrounds, it is the older entrepreneurs who are frequently the most difficult to work with when their companies enter difficult times. These older entrepreneurs frequently get their backs up at the thought of losing control of their companies or having their ownership diluted by a percentage they had not planned for. On the one hand, they have a strong desire to place a great distance between their impoverished, bitter childhood and their present position in life; on the other hand, they have too few years ahead of them in which to launch another company if the present one does not succeed.

Children of statesmen, professors, or classical musicians rarely succeed at entrepreneurship. In homes such as these, middle class values are not espoused. The children are encouraged to select a profession that will provide inner joy and a sense of fulfillment. Teaching economics, archaeology, being in the State Department, or playing the harp are suitable goals for a child from this kind of family.

The venture capitalist can learn quite a lot about the entrepreneur's upbringing and family background by asking the question: "What did your parents do?" When that answer is noted, the venture capitalist can ask: "Tell me about the values of the family. Did your parents want a doctor or a lawyer?" In many instances, this question will evoke a lively response and the various branches that the conversation then takes can be followed. What the venture capitalist is seeking is a family background that took pride in the children, gave them the fundamentals to make something of themselves, and hoisted the American Dream of success before the children's eyes, then whispered in their ear every day: "Go do it, Son (Daughter), and make us proud of you!"

One should not confuse middle-class economic status with middle-class values. It is common for families with middle-class incomes and appurtenances of middling wealth to watch television all evening and eschew the values of hard working, success-motivated people. From these families, entrepreneurs simply are not launched. It is preferable that the mother operate a seamstress business in the family living room to make ends meet, to produce crackerjack entrepreneurs.

Order of birth in the entrepreneur's family is unimportant. There is a certain early maturity conveyed on the first-born child, but the second-born or the third-born might become more driven to succeed for reasons other than chronology. Further, early maturity or even late maturity has rarely correlated positively with successful entrepreneurship.

The bottom line is that the childhood of the entrepreneur was peopled with mentors who told the child he could go straight to the top in the sciences, the professions, or industry, so long as he studied vigorously in school, put his shoulder to the wheel at work, and wore clean clothes and shoes. This message is repeated again and again in interviews with the country's most successful entrepreneurs, such as T. Boone Pickens (Mesa Petroleum), Kemmons Wilson (Holiday Inns), H. Ross Perot (EDS), W. Clement Stone (Combined Insurance), and many other modern entrepreneurs, all of whom sing from the same choir book on the critical issue of middle-class values.

### Childhood Deprivation

It is critical in the initial interview with the entrepreneur to locate his "pain." The venture capitalist should ask: "What made you start this company, risking so much and sacrificing so much?" Entrepreneurs are generally pleased with the opportunity to discuss their pain, particularly if they are in a conversation with someone whom they believe understands the pain.

The pain must be deep and serious. Successful entrepreneurs do not take their companies lightly. They do not take capital lightly, either. If their pain—the thing that happened to them in their childhood which they are now trying to overcome—is deeply important to them, then nothing will stop them from succeeding. "Break my arm" the outstanding entrepreneurs shout at competitors and detractors, "I'm going to beat your company to the top."

Childhood deprivations take many forms. The most typical are physical, ethnic, and economic deprivations. The deprivations are eventually overcome, but when the entrepreneur was young and his or her friends were completely happy, he or she was in torment. A promise was made at the time by the deprived child to himself that someday he would show his playmates, or whomever, that he would excel far beyond their imaginations and the last laugh would be his. It is the memory of this intense pain that provides the entrepreneur with his unflagging drive, particularly when random events have conspired to crush his new company.

Physical deprivations are primarily those illnesses that keep the child from somersaulting, running, and playing outdoors with children his age. Rather, he is confined in bed, in the house, or on crutches. For example, Fred Smith, the entrepreneur of Federal Express, had a form of cystic fibrosis that kept him on crutches for the first 4 year of his life. Francis Coppola, the entrepreneur of the films *Godfather*, *Apocalypse Now*, and others, spent much of his childhood in bed with polio.

Lack of height or physical stature is a frequent stimulant—although not a primary driver—of entrepreneurs. In a society that worships the National Football League, smaller people are disadvantaged. Tall people are considered superior salesmen, for example. Short entrepreneurs compensate in unusual ways for their size. Diminutive David Sarnoff, the entrepreneur of RCA Corporation, furnished his office with undersized furniture, covered the windows with heavy drapes, and raised his desk on a small platform in order to make the visitor feel that he was in the presence of a man of above-average height.

Gino Paolucci, the undersized entrepreneur of Chun King Corporation, seated his management team around a long conference room table. Rather than take his place at the head of the table to conduct management meetings, Mr. Paolucci stood on top of the table and shot questions at his managers. Another small entrepreneur, Charles Revson, who built Revlon, Inc., into a large cosmetics and health care delivery company, also walked on the top of his conference room table, along with other antics.

Entrepreneurs would not win any beauty contests. They are frequently poorly informed about how to maximize their appearance. Entrepreneurs are more interested in maximizing their time. Their physical appearance is not a consideration. Women entrepreneurs are as unconcerned with their appearance as are men entrepreneurs. Thus, if the entrepreneur's deprivation is physical, the drive to overcome it is not by plastic surgery or elevator shoes, but rather by forming a company to do one thing extremely well.

Ethnic deprivation is a frequent driver for entrepreneurs. "Hey, there's that little Greek kid." A derogatory term has burned into the soul of many entrepreneurs, although the word "Greek" was substituted with other ethnic slurs. Frequently, one hears from entrepreneurs that their childhood was spent helping their mother in her store or with her business in the home. They were unable to play with their childhood friends for several reasons, including (1) their family was different, (2) their language was different, (3) their clothes or customs were different, or (4) they were busy with family obligations. The derogatory remarks are frequently uttered by grocers, teachers, and shopkeepers in front of the child and members of his peer group. "Hi, Boys, I see you have the little Roosky kid with you today." That type of remark, although seemingly harmless, burns into the soul and memory of the child. It sets him apart from the members of his peer group in a negative manner. This occurs at a time when his gut values are being formed and it crushes him emotionally. He pledges at the moment to develop the strength and skills to rise above the plane of being different. The child determines to make something very important of himself.

Economic deprivation is reported by many entrepreneurs. W. Clement Stone and his mother got on their knees together every night and prayed that she would sell an insurance policy the next day. The economic deprivation is particularly fruitful to the child with pride. His family is poorer than others because their is no father, they haven't learned English too well, or other factors. Once again, here is a case of the child being persecuted by events beyond his control. Ecomonic deprivation burns into his heart and makes him feel terrible and different. He promises himself that someday he will show his peer group that his family was better than they could ever have imagined. Economic deprivation, coupled with middle-class values, can be a powerful driver for the entrepreneur.

The venture capitalist must locate the pain. If there has been no pain, then the entrepreneur's drive must be questioned. Does he have what it takes to get through the tough times? No pain. No gain.

## Absent Father, Dynamic Mother

In the questionnaire as submitted to over 400 successful entrepreneurs, more than three-fourths of them responded that their mothers were the dominant influence in their early lives. This is not the case with female entrepreneurs, who frequently acknowledge the importance of their fathers who instilled in them a fierce competitive spirit. In addition to the young entrepreneur's value systems being positively affected by their mothers, the majority of them were raised in homes where their fathers were absent.

The absent father criteria in the backgrounds of so many successful entrepreneurs requires further explanation. In many instances, the father died when the child was quite young, or even earlier. This was the circumstance of such entrepreneurs as Fred Smith (Federal Express), William Benton (Benton & Bowles,

Muzak, Encyclopedia Brittanica), Kemmons Wilson (Holiday Inn), and T. Boone Pickens (Mesa Petroleum). The father is praised in death, but the son becomes "mother's big man" at an early age. He develops a maturity and a sense of purpose very early in life. More important, he learns that his life has no safety nets. This encourages him to be a more careful planner, even a double-failsafe planner, early in life.

When you are the only fatherless child on the Little League Team, the pain can be as deep as that of the bedridden child who cannot join the Little League Team. Sliding into homeplate and scratching your knee is a trophy if your father comes over to the dugout to wipe the blood away. If you wipe your own blood off your knee, it's not a trophy—it's a pain, and you learn to treat your own wounds. Entrepreneurship is a lonely experience with many bloody knees that nobody except the entrepreneur will tend to.

The absence of the father might be the result of a divorce or the father's business requiring extensive travel. As in the case with father's early death, the mother positively strokes the future entrepreneur. She creates a value system for the child based on studying hard, working hard to help mother, and succeeding in a profession or in business to make mother proud. The stories of the bond between young men and their mothers, written by biographers of General Douglas MacArthur, W. Clement Stone, Ray Kroc, David Geffen, William Benton, and Leslie Wexner, founder of The Limited Chain (whose mother is a member of his board of directors), and other captains of government and entrepreneurship are legion.

It is incumbent upon the venture capitalist to determine the role of the father and the mother in the early life of the entrepreneur. If the father was alive, available, and served as a mentor to the son, then the entrepreneur's drive probably comes from deprivation or perhaps guilt. If there was a father present, a non-stroking mother, and no deprivation, the likelihood of the entrepreneur's future success must be measured even more carefully than if the pain is right out front.

### Guilt That Mother Has Been Disappointed

A simple question of the entrepreneur, such as the following, typically evokes a jovial grin and an interesting answer: "Is your mother disappointed that you are an entrepreneur and not a scientist or professional?" It is almost always the case that entrepreneurs drop out of school or leave a career path in order to start a new company. Professor An Wang left a tenured faculty position at Massachusetts Institute of Technology to launch Wang Laboratories. Dr. Edwin H. Land dropped out of Harvard College in his freshman year to research the question of polarizing light. He formed Polaroid Corporation a few years later and his doctorate is honorary. Walter Heinze, the co-founder of STP Corporation, dropped out of high school, as did Robert Sikora, the founder and chief executive officer of Bobby McGee's Conglomeration, Inc., perhaps the most successful dinnerhouse and entertainment chain in the country. The numbers of physicians, lawyers, and physicists who have found greater satisfaction as entrepreneurs probably number in the tens of thousands. Those who have created valuable companies probably number in the hundreds.

It is essential that the entrepreneur feels guilty about dropping out of his profession to start his company. Whereas entrepreneurs regard their mission as equal to that of medical researchers, public opinion is not, at least thus far, on their side. The press normally treats entrepreneurs with as much respect as they treat New Jersey mayors. Entrepreneurs are portrayed as money-grabbers, promoters, and carnival show barkers by most newspapers. Thus, leaving college, graduate school, or a profession to start a computer company or its equivalent is generally horrifying to the mother. The determined son, however, vows to make a success of his new company and to make the mother proud. Venture capitalists want to back guilty entrepreneurs. Successful entrepreneurs are more frequently drop-outs from universities with middling reputations than they are graduates of Ivy League or equivalent schools. It is difficult to name, for example, three successful entrepreneurs who received their degrees from Princeton University.

A doubly guilty entrepreneur is one who has recently selected his company in a choice between his company and his wife. The divorced entrepreneur is terribly guilty that he could not hold his marriage together while launching his company. The entrepreneur whose marriage remains intact during the launch period can thank his spouse, through whose efforts the marriage was held together. But for the divorced entrepreneur, there is new energy. This comes from the divorced entrepreneur's desire to "show her that she gave up on me too soon." Guilt connected to energy can drive the entrepreneur to new heights, to get a second wind that brings an accelerated ramp-up to the new company's sales.

The venture capital process by no means takes the posture of encouraging divorce. In fact, the married entrepreneur is in many instances as guilt-ridden as the divorced entrepreneur. He is guilty that he is away from the family so much. And even when he is not away, his thoughts are. The supportive spouse understands this and encourages the entrepreneur to work "smarter" in order to accomplish his goals more quickly.

### Dissatisfaction-Insight-Energy

One might say that there are many non-entrepreneurs throughout society who came from middle-class value systems, experienced a deprivation in their childhood, whose fathers were absent, who dropped out of school, married, and got divorced. Why are these experiential characteristics unique to entrepreneurs? They are not the exclusive property of entrepreneurs. Artists, writers, musicians, and others carry burdens similar to those of entrepreneurs. They have many of the same experiential characteristics as entrepreneurs, to be sure, and the result is a beautiful articulation of the world's problems flowing from their pens, a representation of the world's problems that decorate their canvasses, and a cacophonous description of the world's problems through melodies and related sounds. Entrepreneurs and classical artists are cut out from the same cloth and generally get along wonderfully, but the relationship stops there.

The artist possesses enough dissatisfaction to understand the problem and the skill to represent it on canvas or in music. Writers see the problem and have the insight, frequently, to develop a solution, if only on paper. But writers lack the energy to solve the problems they identify. A third group is dissatisfied and energetic, but lacks the insight to identify the problem and develop its solution. This group is called *consultants*. Frequently consultants leave industry with great distaste for several aspects of it and make a living selling information about the industry to those who need to be informed. Entrepreneurs will occasionally leave the industry and become consultants while formulating the problem or potential market, and a means of solving it. It is not uncommon for entrepreneurs to consult for up to 2 years before taking the leap.

The venture capitalist must locate the dissatisfaction-insight-energy linkup, because without it the person he may back financially could be merely a dissatisfied person with brilliant insight. In other words, an artist. Questions should be put to the venture capitalist such as: "Did you come up with this idea while at XYZ Corporation?" "Did you offer the idea to XYZ Corporation?" "Had you offered similar ideas to them in the past?" "Did you discuss their refusal to accept the idea and run with it with your immediate superior?" It is important, if the entrepreneur's idea was refused by his employer, that he wants more than anything to show them how wrong they were to turn him down. Itek Corporation, formed by former Eastman Kodak engineers, stands for "I'll Topple Eastman Kodak." LTX Corporation, formed by ex-Xerox personnel, stands for "Let's Take Xerox." The dissatisfaction and desire to prove the former employer wrong is an important drive.

The insight is the ability of the entrepreneur to see all aspects of the problem that he intends to solve. This characteristic blends into the characteristic of *creativity* as the product or service passes through the design and development stage. However, what is relevant to the venture capitalist is how deep and how broad is the entrepreneur's insight into the problem. For example, does he or she see a problem as straightforward, in need of a one-shot product or service? Or has the entrepreneur seen the various aspects of the problem and converted these differences into market segments that need to be addressed in different ways, with different marketing organizations? The latter is, of course, the more thorough, indeed entrepreneurial, approach. It is one thing for an entrepreneur to leave an oil giant through dissatisfaction with its inability to invest in additional proven reserves with greater facility. It is quite another thing for an entrepreneur, such as T. Boone Pickens, Jr., to start a trend of acquiring major oil companies in order to get to their reserves. It is the task of the venture capitalist to separate the Pickenses from the insightful critics of the status quo.

The energy factor cannot be underestimated. Entrepreneurs typically have very little capital when they set out to solve their problem. But they have a heart bursting with the insatiable drive to succeed and their proprietary (or non-proprietary) idea for a solution to a large problem. Understanding leverage, the key to making things happen, is to move quickly. They set several balls in motion simultaneously and run at a sprint to keep them in the air.

Thus, entrepreneurs move quickly, speak quickly, and think quickly. They wear loafers, because lacing shoes takes too long. They frequently wear untrimmed beards, because to do so eliminates the need to shave. They drive fast, reliable European cars, because maintenance problems are a time-eater. On airplanes, entrepreneurs take aisle seats near the front in order to disembark quickly. The better ones never check baggage. When they turn in rental cars, it is frequently by giving the key and rental agreement to the airline attendant and telling her that the car is out in front. There are other shortcuts that the high energy entrepreneur knows about. The venture capitalist should interview the entrepreneur along the lines of how he maximizes his time. What are his hobbies? Entrepreneurs have few. What does he read? Entrepreneurs read very little more than trade journals. How does he spend his weekends? Usually on quiet aspects of the business, such as planning. Without a high-energy entrepreneur, the venture capitalist will find that the operating statement projections will not be met on schedule, but the company will run out of capital ahead of schedule.

Entrepreneurs involved in their second start-up frequently lack the energy they had the first time around. They are often a greater risk for this reason.

These five experiential characteristics of successful entrepreneurs are inevitable. The entrepreneur picked them up along the way by reason of birth, circumstance, and career choice. The venture capitalist can inquire about them and receive declarative "Yes" or "no" answers. The second five characteristics shared by the better entrepreneurs are more subjective. The venture capitalist cannot ask the entrepreneur: "Are you creative?" "Do you have courage?" He must observe the full and complete personality of the entrepreneur to see if these second five characteristics exist, and moreover, if they exist in sufficient quantities to mark the entrepreneur for success. These five characteristics which must be measured and evaluated by interviews and reference checks are the following:

Creativity
Honesty
Courage
Communications skills
Happiness

## Creativity

The principal test for this critical characteristic is to determine how thoroughly the entrepreneur has problem-formulated. An immature problem-formulation process results in the building of a black box solution for a problem that very few people feel as strongly about as does the entrepreneur. Far too much technology has been thrust on customers who were unaware of the problem they were supposed to be purchasing the solution to solve.

In order to pass through a venture capitalist's screening process, the entrepreneur should see his potential market as multi-tiered, with some people requiring more information about the problem while others are ready to purchase the solution. If the entrepreneur has a more simplistic view of his potential market, the result will likely be funds wasted on a marketing effort of a solution to a non-problem. Established consumer products marketing companies do this each year with some forgotten names, such as Real Cigarettes, FDS Feminine Deodorant Spray, and Earth Shoes.

To successful entrepreneurs, generating demand for their product with advertising is not a consideration. A promoter thinks of advertising, but an entrepreneur assumes that a careful review and understanding of the needs of the marketplace will dictate the method of conveying products to the various tiers of the marketplace. A quality entrepreneur will describe his potential market to the venture capitalist as multi-tiered, with certain customers seeking more information about the problem, others with a need to come together in a seminar or conference to discuss the problem with other sufferers, a third tier of customers requiring hands-on advice prior to purchasing the solution, and others ready to pay for the solution. To see the potential market as anything less usually suggests that this particular entrepreneur is not a problem formulator. He or she has not prepared the canvas and arranged the objects to be painted, yet he has three brushes dipped into the paint and he is asking for funds to buy more paint and brushes. The launch has been too hasty. It has more form than substance. The $E$ factor lacks creativity.

In helping the entrepreneur think of his potential market, it is helpful for the venture capitalist to suggest that the problem might take the shape of a pyramid. The largest number of potential customers are at the base and need more information about the problem. The smallest number of potential customers are at the top and aware of the problem and are willing to pay for its solution. The pyramid method of looking at potential markets is known to some entrepreneurs; sometimes it is described as a funnel, arrow, or some other abstraction. The classical problem formulation pyramid appears in Exhibit 25.

The classical form of selling information about $P$ is the newsletter. In fact, to identify the formation of a new market, one need only become aware of new newsletters. For example, in 1980–1982, there were dozens of newsletters created to sell information about

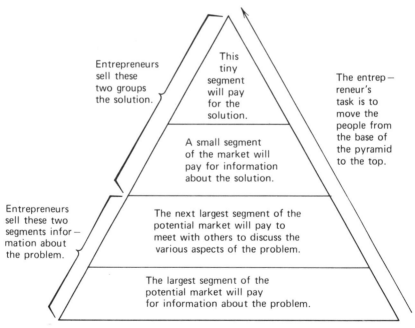

**EXHIBIT 25. Problem Formulations: The Entrepreneur's Creativity**

the dozens of new vertical market, computer software industries. The personal computer was becoming sufficiently cost-effective to attract programmers to develop software for a broad range of vertical markets. The newsletters were called by similar names: Computers in Medicine, Computers in Politics, Computers in Archaeology, ad nauseum. Naturally some of these newsletters became magazines, particularly where the venture capital-rich hardware companies saw an opportunity to advertise directly to doctors, government officials, and archaeologists. In this manner, the entrepreneur can make money two ways rather than one at the base of the pyramid: subscriptions and advertisements.

When interviewing entrepreneurs on the subject of evaluating the $P$ that they have formulated, the venture capitalist should anticipate an understanding on their part of the pyramid structure of the formation of new markets. Entrepreneurs are developing a surprising level of sophistication about the launch process as a result of a number of factors, not least of which is desperation. When an entrepreneur has no resources for advertising and cannot attract start-up venture capital because no one else sees the $P$ that the entrepreneur sees, there remains one source of capital: the customer. But if the customer is not ready to purchase the solution, what can he be sold? The problem. How does one package the problem—in the form of information. In so doing, entrepreneurial companies rip holes in the marketing plans of large well-financed competitors whose competitive weapon is advertising. Information that we pay for has more credibility than advertising, which is free. It is the conceit of the advertiser that costs him market share when competing with the well-packaged newsletter.

As the personal computer, cable television, and satellite transmission becomes more ubiquitous, the newsletter is likely to be transmitted electronically or digitally (along with lots of other things) into homes and offices. Entrepreneurs will be able to reach the people at the base of the pyramid even more quickly.

Experienced venture capitalists seek entrepreneurs who have peripheral vision or a pyramid view of their developing markets. One is well-advised to decline entrepreneurs who simplistically say, "With your money I can advertise my product to those most likely to buy it, and every year thereafter we will plow back a percentage of revenues into advertising to grow sales rapidly." Interviews with a broad variety of entrepreneurs have shown that an entrepreneur who makes this statement suffers from excessive corporate exposure and has failed to problem-formulate creatively.

The venture capitalist should expect the entrepreneur to have quantified $P$. Most entrepreneurs can get a fix on the number of potential customers in their developing market. There are many sources of information, but the entrepreneur must show that he has taken the time to dig them up. The U.S. Department of Commerce gathers information from the U.S. Bureau of the Census, plus annual industry-generated information. Investment bank research departments collect market share data on the industries they follow. *Thomas Register of Manufacturers* is a complete list of manufacturers by city. *The Encyclopedia of Associations* provides membership numbers, as well as telephone numbers and addresses of association headquarters that make gathering the numbers of mechanical engineers, lawyers, dentists, veterinarians, and so forth quite easy. Dun & Bradstreet gathers information on all sorts of companies and sells it in various packages. Finally, the *Yellow Pages* are free for the asking, and many entrepreneurs keep the *Yellow Pages* of the 50 largest cities near at hand for a bird's eye view of their marketplace. With these multitudinous source books easily available, one should expect an entrepreneur during the audit of $P$ to quantify the potential market. Tossing out numbers will not do. Giving a total market size and adding, "and we anticipate capturing a 10% market share," also will not do. The entrepreneur should overwhelm the venture capitalist with information about the number of potential customers in the market. To do less is to inadequately formulate $P$.

## Honesty

This is tested for in several ways. The principal method is to contact people who have known and worked with the entrepreneur over a period of time. Venture capitalists are well-advised to telephone at least six former co-workers, six former superiors, and six people who worked for the entrepreneur. One should also call the entrepreneur's schools to validate his degrees; plus people he has borrowed money from or purchased goods and services from.

After 30 calls, one will know the entrepreneur's level of honesty pretty well. Because older entrepreneurs become bitter and tend to bend rules when their companies get into trouble, blame others for their problems and consider the venture capitalists as adversaries, they should be put through a more detailed audit than those in the preferred age range, 27–33.

In addition to the names and telephone numbers of references provided by the entrepreneur, the venture capitalist should telephone people whose names were not provided by the entrepreneur. To obtain these names, it is necessary to ask the entrepreneur's references for names of other people whom they could recommend to call. A useful question is the following (assume the entrepreneur's name is "Joe"). "Was there someone at work who was Joe's competitor; perhaps someone whose star diminished as Joe's ascended; someone who might think Joe did not perform all that well?" A question that dramatic puts the respondent in a powerful position, like J. R. Ewing in the TV soap opera "Dallas." It usually results in several additional references not provided by the entrepreneur.

The venture capitalist should attempt to verify several of the entrepreneur's more optimistic statements. These usually include some of the following: "Our counsel thinks the product is patentable." "The unit manufacturing cost of the product in runs of 1000 is around $500." "ABC Manufacturing Company wants to become the beta site to test the product." At some point, these statements should be verified, with the entrepreneur's permission, by telephoning the patent counsel, the contract manufacturing firm, and the potential beta site. The entrepreneur may be guilty of lack of honesty, in which event his business plan should be declined. In most cases, however, entrepreneurs are optimistic and have faith in their optimistic statements; but they are not dishonest. Many of the private telephone long distance carriers and interconnect equipment companies, prior to the dismantling of AT&T in early 1984, firmly believed that they would cause the breakup of AT&T. Many in their audience politely turned their heads and laughed. A few years later, AT&T was broken up. Were the telecommunications entrepreneurs dishonest—certainly not. But their optimism was interlaced with reality and it was difficult for them to see the future in any other way.

An entrepreneur is quite capable of believing that accounts receivable are amounts equal to the orders that are likely to result from a sales trip he is planning. If, when the venture capitalist reviews the financial statements, he does not find accounts receivable of that amount, has the entrepreneur been dishonest? Probably not, but a strong, thorough manager partner should be found for the entrepreneur rather quickly.

If after thoroughly investigating a sufficiently large number of references the venture capitalist feels uncomfortable about the entrepreneur's honesty, the project should be abandoned. The two individuals must live together for about 5 years, and the marriage will not work if one constantly questions the honesty of the other. Successful entrepreneurs are intellectually honest, primarily because their motivations are relatively pure: to convey a solution to a problem shared by a large number of people.

### Courage

This characteristic of entrepreneurs is similar in many respects to that seen in world class athletes. Quality entrepreneurs will not stop trying until they win. Nothing can deter them. Not lack of capital—they will find it somewhere. Not lack of customers—they will make more sales calls until the orders begin to stack up. Not lack of credit from suppliers—they will visit all the suppliers personally in order to obtain larger credit lines.

Entrepreneurial courage is portrayed by the manner in which the entrepreneur does his planning. Because he was raised without safety nets and developed a sense of purpose to his life at an early age, the entrepreneur understands that failure is a likely possibility. He hears footsteps and looks for exit routes. He hears 50 "no's" every day and expects to hear 50 more the next day. He anticipates that the work he delegates to others will not get done as well as he could have done it, and he is frequently correct. Because the entrepreneur understands that most plans do not work out satisfactorily, particularly in the case of new, small, and unstructured companies, he sets up fail-safe plans. The better entrepreneurs have alternative plans and strategies for most of their primary plans.

One way for the venture capitalist to measure the courage factor is to see how well the entrepreneur has planned in order to avoid failure. The venture capitalist can ask the entrepreneur: "It says in the business plan that you need $2 million to get you to $15 million in third-year sales. What are your plans for raising the $2 million?"

If the entrepreneur says something like, "Why, with venture capital, of course," he is not exhibiting the market of a good fail-safe planner. A courageous entrepreneur is more likely to say something like the following:

> "It would be nice to raise all $2 million quickly via a venture capital financing. However, because that might not happen in time, we are talking to a German manufacturer about licensing the European rights to our first product for $750,000. We have expressions of interest from a U.S. manufacturer for a license at a suggested price of $250,000. My secretary's brother has offered to invest $100,000, and we intend to put an SBA 502 loan on top of that for an additional $500,000. And my lawyer wants to put together an R&D tax shelter financing for $1,000,000."

An answer such as that indicates that the entrepreneur is aware of the possibility of everything going wrong and he has planned accordingly with numerous alternative financing methods. Like the Marines landing on a beach, the entrepreneur fires in all directions and when he sees something fall, he runs in that direction. First-class entrepreneurs simply will not permit failure and they plan many fail-safe strategies and keep side and back doors open in case they have to beat a hasty retreat to higher ground. It is the duty of the venture capitalist to take the measure of the entrepreneur's courage by examining his fail-safe plans.

## Communications Skills

Quality entrepreneurs are excellent speakers. They have the ability to convince people to do things for them that the people had no intention of doing. They leverage time and people, and use both to obtain capital which they, in turn, leverage. In order to accomplish these multipliers, entrepreneurs must be good communicators. They must have persuasive abilities. Some of them, like

Fred Smith of Federal Express, can speak as well as the top evan-
gelists. Others speak in a machine gun fashion, like Tom Kelly of
TIE/Communications. Still others, like Bill von Meister, founder of
Source Telecomputing Corporation, and David Padwa of Agrigenetics, persuade through the vast storehouse of their knowledge.

Even quiet, reserved, science-backgrounded entrepreneurs develop an ability to persuade people to do things for them. If they
cannot develop strong communications skills, the entrepreneurs
do not attract a group of employees, suppliers, customers, and investors willing to walk through the fires of hell for them.

The venture capitalist can tell very quickly in the initial interview whether or not the entrepreneur is a good communicator. If
the venture capitalist must pull information piece by piece from
the entrepreneur, it is best to decline the deal. Raising money is
communication. Selling a product is communication. Hiring and
training personnel is communication. If the entrepreneur is
unable to speak clearly and persuasively, he may have difficulty
during the launch.

### Happiness

The final characteristic of successful entrepreneurs is their happiness. They laugh quite a bit and are the least bitter of practically all
people. They receive joy from small victories during the day.
Getting a seat on a sold-out airplane. Collecting a long overdue accounts receivable. Talking a credit manager of a supplier into shipping a component needed to complete a product, which when
shipped will generate a payment from the customer that will be
used to cover a like amount of checks that were written that day.
Accomplishments like that produce a happy entrepreneur.

A test that the venture capitalist can use to determine the happiness factor of the entrepreneur is to listen carefully for bitter-
ness. Successful entrepreneurs never speak derogatorily about
other ethnic groups, nor do they tell ethnic jokes. They are generally too busy to know any new jokes. And they regard themselves
as fairly low on the ladder of success, thus derogatory jokes and
remarks would be inappropriate. People do not put others down
when they are happy with their particular chase. And it is the
chase, more than any other single factor, that makes entrepreneurs blissfully happy.

## THE MANAGER PARTNER

The characteristics of the entrepreneur's business partner are quite a bit different than those of the entrepreneur. Whereas the entrepreneur is energetic, the manager partner is thorough. Whereas the entrepreneur is creative, the manager partner is a careful implementer. Whereas the entrepreneur has a heart full of pain that drives him to overcome a variety of obstacles—some of them self-imposed—the manager partner has industry experience that dictates the business moves to be made, when and how.

In start-up companies, the venture capitalist must usually assist the entrepreneur in finding a manager partner. In first-stage companies, the entrepreneur has hired a partner, but in many instances he must be replaced. In either case, it is the function of the venture capitalist to interview manager partners, help negotiate their salary and equity incentive, and give them to the entrepreneur. It is the manager partner who likely will make a successful business out of the new company. Thus, his hiring is critical.

In successful entrepreneurial teams, the manager partner has many of the following superficial characteristics:

| | |
|---|---|
| Age: | Approximately 16 years older than the entrepreneur; mid-to-late 40s. |
| Residence: | Well-kept suburb; owns home. |
| Marital status: | Approximately 82% married. |
| Has assets: | Yes. |
| Voting preference: | Conservative |
| Typical car: | American-made sedan. |
| Shoes: | Lace-up. |
| Hair: | Conservative; styled. |

It is necessary that the manager partner be somewhat older than the entrepreneur in order to have been in the corporate world longer. The key to success for many new companies is surviving against competition from large corporations. The manager partner will usually know how the "enemy" thinks, plans, and then strikes. A manager partner from a non-related corporation background, such as industrial consultant, accountant, lawyer (although many do well as entrepreneurs), university department head, or from the U.S. Armed Forces, simply will not be as satisfactory as a "corporate achiever."

## Corporate Achiever

It is the corporate achiever whom the venture capitalist should be seeking to manage *all* of his portfolio companies. The time to bring them in is as early as possible in the company's growth, but in any event not after the company has grown through its entrepreneurial stage. Many venture capitalists spend nearly 40% of their time locating, interviewing, and hiring corporate achievers for their entrepreneurial companies. It is a time consuming, tedious, but absolutely essential part of the venture capital business.

The entrepreneurs in this country who have matured into successful managers represent a small percentage of all managers. *Venture* magazine in 1982 listed 50 entrepreneurs who were still at the head of their large publicly-held companies. When private companies are included in the study, the number probably increases by 5 to 10 times. And when the measurement of success is lowered to say, $20 million in sales, the number probably increases another 5 to 10 times. However, to a venture capitalist, the goal is revenues well in excess of $100 million in 5 years and a public market, or sales to a public company. Thus, to grow the company rapidly, a corporate achiever is needed.

What are their characteristics? They have the corporate jungle fighter characteristics listed by Maccoby in *The Gamesman*.

They can pick a product out of a line, build a team around it, set up a marketing plan, implement the plan, and generate sales for the product of $10 million, $30 million, and $60 million over 3 years. When the venture capitalist reference checks these claims, he finds that the large corporation says that the person, in fact, was the head of the team that achieved them.

He is not timid and he does not come cheap; but the venture capitalist's leverage in negotiating salary and equity incentives with the corporate achiever is that *he desperately wants out of the corporate world*. His dissatisfaction and energy are very much like that of the young entrepreneur at the time he bolted from the corporation. But the corporate achiever lacks the insight and the creativity to go out on his own. His heart has gone into his job and his heart has been taken from him, so that he dissolves into the corporation and the corporation into him. His identity is so misplaced that sometimes he thinks corporately during tender family moments. His sex life, according to Maccoby, begins to dwindle. He has to get out of the corporation and get his heart back.

Generally, the more careful ones will speak with executive recruiters and make their wishes known: entrepreneurial company in a related industry, comparable salary, plus stock incentives. Some send out resumes to venture capitalists, but the number of corporate achievers in a stack of 200 managers' resumes that come to the typical venture capital firm in a given month are probably fewer than 1%. The very-much-in-a-hurry group resign and contact the venture capitalists directly, or speak up at venture capital club meetings and make their availability known. To attend a venture capital club meeting in most cities that have them, one need contact a member and attend as his guest or seek a special invitation from the club secretary.

The glue that bonds the corporate achiever to the entrepreneur is the desire to build a major company. If the potential manager partner is not oriented toward building a major company, he is not a corporate achiever. The venture capitalist can detect the difference during the interview. One of the key questions is, "What is your fantasy (substitute 'goal,' 'objective') over the next few years for yourself and this company?" The correct answer is, "To help build this company into the industry leader, with sales of $100 million on their way to $200 million and a stock price high enough to make everybody rich." Some corporate achievers continue their response with, "Then I am going to become a venture capitalist." Indeed, there are many former corporate achievers who helped to successfully build a small company, and then became venture capitalists. Their success is not guarateed.

The venture capitalist's ear should be cocked and carefully tuned to hear phrases such as "create something of value," "build value," "build a leading company," and "be on a winning entrepreneurial team." Some potential manager partners have not achieved anything spectacular at their former corporation. They have not been through a rapid build-up situation. Unlike West in Tracy Kidder's *Soul of a New Machine*, the archetypal corporate achiever desires to leave the corporation after demonstrating his ability to bring out a new product on time and under budget, and to do it for an entrepreneurial company where his reward will be direct and tangible.

## Terms of Employment

The corporate achiever once selected frequently must be relocated and housed, paid a salary, and provided with an equity incentive. Depending on the competition for the services of the person in question, it is possible to seek a 20–25% salary reduction to join the new company. The corporate achiever may have been earning $150,000 per annum as sales vice president for a leading time sharing company in the San Francisco Bay Area. But the company he will be joining has sales of $1 million per annum, pays its founder and chief executive officer $60,000, its chief financial officer $42,000, and its chief engineer $36,000. The new person is coming aboard as chief marketing officer, and will report directly to the board, but he will have to be paid more than the founder and chief executive officer. However, a salary in excess of $90,000 would be exorbitant. A new injection of venture capital will provide capital for his salary and his marketing plan. Yet, one person's salary in a tiny company must be as small as possible. Typical salary ranges to attract corporate achievers, using 1984 as a benchmark, are as follows:

| Stage and Size of Company | Corporate Achievers' Salary Range |
|---|---|
| Start-up (no revenues) | $60,000–$75,000 |
| First-Stage (revenues of $500,000 to $5 million p.a. for manufacturing; $5 million to $15 million for distribution company). | $75,000–$90,000 |
| Second-Stage (revenues of $5 million to $15 million for manufacturing; $15 million to $30 million for distribution company). | $90,000–$150,000 |

If the potential manager partner asks for a sales or earnings bonus, he is probably not a corporate achiever. He lacks knowledge of the process of creating value via building something very special, but rather prefers the easier money.

The corporate achiever normally fills the role of chief marketing officer. He may request a great title, which is not a positive sign, but it should not necessarily be offered. Even Executive Vice President-Marketing is too much title in a first-stage company. It is possible to offer that title in a larger company. The rule in offering titles is that you can always go up, but you can never come down.

Depending on the competition for the person in question, moving expenses, rental of a home in the company's city, and other perks must be offered. If the person's children must go to a private school in the new city to equal the quality of the prior public school education, the venture capitalist may have to add tuition payments. Conversely, the tuition could be factored into the salary. Moving expenses are generally covered. Paying the mortgage on the previous home, until it is sold, is fairly common as well. The list of perks can go on and on, but many corporate achievers realize that there will be down the road plenty of cars, tuition payments, jobs for the spouses, and so forth, if he does the job he is being hired to do.

The stock incentive for a corporate achiever is typically between 5 and 10% of the company's stock. The stock is greater the smaller the company, given equally qualified managers.

The manner of issuing the stock is usually via a 5-year stock option plan, in order to assure that the person will remain at the company for 5 years and to keep the price of the stock as inexpensive as possible. Thus, the corporate achiever who has negotiated 10% of the company's stock would receive 2% for his first year's services, and 2% per annum thereafter, assuming his services were continually desirable. If terminated within 5 years by the board for cause, the person must sell his stock back at cost. "Cause" would include non-performance, interfering with other departments, misfeasance, or other horrors. If the person leaves in the middle of the 5-year program to seek his fortunes elsewhere, he may sell his stock back to the company for the greater of his cost or book value. Further, if the company is acquired or goes public within the 5-year period, the full amount of the person's stock is immediately issued.

The investigation of the background of the corporate achiever involves contacting his former (if he has left his current position) co-workers, particularly peer level and below. Superiors, co-workers, and people who worked for him at his immediately previous company are useful, as well. The venture capitalist is looking for leadership, ability, business acumen, intelligence, honesty, and work ethic. The venture capitalist is not looking for a dreamer or someone who plans but has never implemented a plan. The responses should include: "He took our sales from $500,000 to $10 million in one year." "He knows the key customers, how they think and what they eat for breakfast." "He anticipated a competitor's moves and shut them out of the marketplace." From a subordinate: "He clearly outlined my assignment, showed me how to do it, and rewarded me when I did it." From an employer: "If I ever wanted a job done, I would go to him first." From a peer: "He doesn't have a neutral gear."

If an executive search firm is used to find the corporate achiever, it must be paid. The typical fee is 30% of the person's first year salary. The fee is difficult to reduce and impossible to eliminate. Several large venture capital firms have either added executive search consultants to their staffs or placed them on retainers, in order to get their constant attention and continual service and help to mitigate the high fees which their portfolio companies pay. If a search firm is used it should do some independent reference checking, including obtaining a copy of the person's university transcript.

### Summary of the Audit of the Entrepreneurial Team

The above constitutes the characteristics of the successful entrepreneurial team and how to audit to discover if they exist. It is the most critical of the five audits, because building a company is a people-motivating-people task. The best technologies addressed at the largest markets will fail if the entrepreneurial team is weak. Qume may not produce the best printer for computers, but its entrepreneurial team was perhaps the best in the printer industry. Apple may not produce the best personal computers, but its entrepreneurial team has continually been one of the best.

The venture capitalist must also audit the key functional people, such as chief financial officer, chief production officer, and chief engineer. Investigation should include reference checking, including transcripts. The objective is to determine if they do their job as outlined and on time, if they are very loyal, and if they have the capacity to manage in a growth environment. Ideally, one or two of the people will have been in a growth situation before and will have managed a group of people before. Entrepreneurs do not hire well in the beginning—it is an acquired skill—so these qualities would be more of a surprise than a given.

It is frequently the case that one of the middle managers has unusually strong abilities but very little equity, whereas another member of the team, or perhaps several, has fewer abilities than originally believed, but a substantial piece of the action. It is difficult for the venture capitalist to reshuffle the equity, but what usually happens is that an exit method is established to enable the manager who leaves to sell back his or her stock to the company at the greater of cost or book value.

The venture capitalist also wants to hear that communication within the company is clear and frequent. He should also look for a sense of ethics or code of ethical conduct that is above reproach. A positive response from the chief financial officer to a critical question is that he pays all the bills as soon as they are due, but if he can't: "I get right on the telephone and call the supplier and ask him to work with me for a few days or weeks." Music to a venture capitalist's ears. A controller who knows how to keep the ship afloat without any money.

The chief production officer should also be someone who can work minor miracles on a daily basis. Find a good buy on copper wire here, barter for some high-quality rectifiers there, cottage out a lot of the work that can be done more cheaply on the outside. It is reassuring to hear that the chief production officer has been in a small company before and knows how to operate without money.

The sales personnel are a different breed. Normally, they smile and say optimistic, pleasing words. The turnover among sales personnel in early-stage companies is very high, because the people do not take the time to study the product they are selling and the market they are selling to. The most deadly thing they can tell a venture capitalist is that they need money in order to increase sales. First of all, that is obvious, for what other reason would the venture capitalist be visiting. Second, money may buy advertising to create product identity, which generates leads for the sales-person, but it does not necessarily increase sales. Senior sales personnel should be prepared to discuss OEM sales, cross-licen-sing, foreign joint-ventures, dealer sales, the decision to use repre-sentatives rather than a direct sales force, pricing, and how the three top competitors deal with all of the above. The senior sales personnel should also be prepared to discuss the company's product line in depth. If they do not know its strengths and weak-nesses in an interview with a venture capitalist, they probably can-not convince a customer to buy the product in the field.

Most venture capitalists do a modest amount of reference checking on junior members of the entrepreneurial team, including the senior officers. It is important that their honesty be impeccable, and this can be established with a few telephone calls to check facts in their resumes. While doing so, the venture capi-talist can look for examples of over-achievement in the person's background and perhaps a drive to be in a smaller, less-structured company.

Should discrepancies arise during the reference checking on key personnel, an experienced venture capitalist will usually re-view it with the entrepreneur. For example, assume a key person had previously filed personal bankruptcy when he had started a company on his own. The fact had escaped mention in his re-sume. Did the entrepreneur know about it? Could the bankruptcy bring injury to the company in the future? Did the key personnel adjudicate the petition completely and, if not, why not? Failure on the part of a key person to present his background, warts and all, is a red flag that will cause the venture capitalist to dig more deeply for facts to see if there are other errors and omissions of fact. The financing can be delayed and perhaps derailed as a result.

Venture capitalists generally should construct a board of direct-ors for the new company unless the entrepreneur has done a good job of it. Normally, in a start-up, the entrepreneur has done very little about building an efficient, helpful local team—calling in consultants, directors or advisors. Thus, all too frequently entre-preneurs face venture capitalists alone; and because entrepre-neurs don't have other experienced people to help, the venture capitalists turn down a good $E$, big $P$, terrific $S$ start-up for the same reason: it looks labor-intensive. A strong local board, made up of serious businesspeople capable of being helpful with their knowledge, contacts, and wallets, is a welcome sight to a venture capitalist. Relatives, accountants, doctors, and people who could not possibly help launch a small company should be weeded off the board.

## The Financial Audit

The entrepreneur must be prepared to account for every dollar spent up to the point of the venture capital financing, as well as every dollar in the financial statement projections. Many entrepreneurs move so quickly and spontaneously that it is impossible and impractical for them to maintain clear and accurate books and records. Some observers of entrepreneurs say that a typical entrepreneur can create enough activity on a Monday morning to keep his manager partner busy straightening up for a week, and then change his mind by mid-afternoon and redo everything. Venture capitalists are aware of this piccadillo of entrepreneurs, but they should not forgive it. Financial statements are how the score is kept in the venture capital business, and every company must maintain the most accurate and complete records possible. This duty falls on the shoulders of the controller, or in the case of a start-up, an inexpensive bookkeeping service.

Large and small accounting firms have started to look to entrepreneurs as a source of new business. They have created small-business departments to prepare the monthly general ledger for start-ups at costs as low as $300 per day. That is approximately the cost of buying a personal computer and paying for it over 12 months. But the personalized relationship of dealing with a professional accountant once a month may have benefits unrelated to the maintenance of accurate financial statements.

The respect that the entrepreneur in a start-up pays to this area of his business should be carefully observed by the venture capitalist. If the controls aren't there, they must be developed. A chief financial officer must be hired prior to closing.

Although it is not necessary to have audited financial statements prior to receiving venture capital, in certain cases, experienced venture capitalists will ask that an audit be done. These instances are as follows:

1. A relatively short operating history (less than 6 months) such that an audit would not be very time consuming.

2. Relatively poor record-keeping, where the financial statements have questionable and perhaps disputed entries. An experienced bookkeeper, or someone not trained in bookkeeping at all, attempted to keep the records but was inadequate to the task.

3. A financing out of bankruptcy or insolvency. The audit permits a clean, fresh beginning.

4. A financing that involves the buy-out of one of the early investors. There is a need to document his or her investment to determine that it was all cash, rather than cash plus services, and to determine that it was an investment in equity, rather part investment and part loan.

5. Venture capital financing that appears to be substantially in excess of revenues or other measures of the company's size. For example, a first-stage company with annualized revenues of $750,000 that is receiving $2,000,000 in venture capital for 33% of its common stock ownership.

There are other circumstances as well where an audit is useful or necessary, but they occur with less frequency than the five cited here. When an audit is not required before the venture capital financing, it will certainly be required sometime after the closing. In fact, if the post-financing audit discloses a financial condition materially different than, and not as positive as, the financial condition presented by the company to the venture capitalist, the company is possibly liable to charges of fraud, even though the differences occurred unintentionally. Were this to happen, the venture capitalist could demand the return of the full amount of his investment, plus legal fees and damages. An entrepreneur is well-advised to present original audited financial statements to venture capitalists and not photostats of the accounting firm's work. Venture capitalists should not accept copies of auditor's reports. They could have been modified by a desperate entrepreneur.

In some instances an accounting firm is unable to give an unqualified audit, which is what most people mean when they use the word "audit." For example, if the prior period—say the previous year—had not been audited in a manner acceptable to the auditor, then the beginning inventory figure, among others, would be suspect. In this case they would only be able to give a "qualified audit" for which they would have counted ending inventory, but would not have counted inventory at the beginning of the period.

If inventory is the only qualification, the venture capitalist will not be too disturbed. However, if the qualification has to do with insolvency or fraudulent entries, the venture capitalist might end his due diligence process upon receipt of the accountant's qualified audit.

The weakest financial statement that an accountant can provide a company is a "review statement." Here the accountant merely reviews the books and records gathered by the company, but does not verify the numbers. Normally, verification involves calling customers to see if their invoice jibes with the company's accounts receivable and calling suppliers to see if their accounts receivable jibes with the company's accounts payable. Banks are called to verify notes payable and interest received. Invoices for equipment are reviewed to see if they have been carried correctly on the company's books. In a review statement these things simply are not done. Most venture capitalists place very little stock in review statements.

The due diligence process, in summary, will require an audited financial statement prior to or soon after the closing of the venture capital financing. The audit will take time and will cost more than the company would like. If there is a financing, the bill will be paid out of the proceeds. If there is no financing, the bill will be like a lead weight. A competent entrepreneur keeps careful books and records that the accounting firm can then use to frame its audit. If the accounting firm must begin with a blank page or sloppy records, the financial audit might take more than the usual 30–45 days.

Does there exist a financial condition in a start-up or first-stage company so terrible that it should cause a venture capitalist to turn it down? The answer is "no." A balance sheet so loaded with debt, all of it on demand, might appear frightening. But the venture capitalist interested in investing has quite a lot of leverage in negotiating the debt down, converting some of it to stock and paying some of it off. However, until the debt is renegotiated satisfactorily, the venture capitalist should avoid investing. As he invests, his leverage begins to diminish.

On the asset side of the ledger, entrepreneurs are from time to time capable of doing strange things, all of which must be removed prior to funding. The most common is capitalizing research and development expenses, rather than expensing them as incurred through the operating statement. R&D expenses should never be capitalized, because there is no assurance that anything of value has been developed. The accounting profession does not prefer capitalization. Most securities analysts discount capitalized R&D whenever they see it on a financial statement.

Occasionally there will appear among the assets a large (more than 10% of total assets) unrelated asset, such as piece of real estate. Glancing over at the operating statement, the venture capitalist sees rental expenses, and wonders how real estate got into the statement of an entrepreneurial company selling a non-real estate product or service. The usual answer is that an investor contributed property that he claims is worth, say, $100,000, for a like amount of shares in the company's common stock, and the company now has $100,000 of collateral to borrow against. What does the company's commercial banker think about the $100,000 value? A look at the Notes Payable-Banks line shows a $75,000 loan and a footnote. A 75% advance against the $100,000 of real estate would mean that the investor got $100,000 of stock for $75,000 cash. Unless he has provided $25,000 of services, the investor took advantage of the entrepreneur. Not an uncommon thing.

The footnote is more revealing. It says, "National American Bank has provided a 90-day loan to the company, secured by the company's accounts receivable, inventory, real estate, and personally guaranteed by its president." The company's accounts receivable, which appear collectible, are $60,000 and its inventory is $60,000. So, how much good is the real estate doing? A call to the bank, or to a qualified appraiser, may reveal market value of $100,000, just as the investor said. However, banks loan against liquidation value—the price that the property would bring if it *had* to be sold in 90 days. The banker informs the venture capitalist that his appraiser placed a liquidation value of $60,000 on the property. Thus, it might have cash value to the company, assuming a 75% loan ratio, of $45,000. Thus, the investor may have pulled a fast one on the entrepreneur and he probably should be bought out, or better yet, he gets his property back, a small amount of shares for assisting the company in obtaining the loan, but he returns his $100,000 worth of stock. The banker's agreement will be required. But if it means $1 million or so is coming in underneath his $75,000, he should agree to less collateral for his loan.

It is during the financial audit that the venture capitalist should determine the ownership of the company's common stock, what price they paid for it and what consideration they gave the company for the stock. There are frequently many surprises. First, the company may be treated as an 80%, or largely owned subsidiary of another company that has been providing the financing. Second, an individual may be advancing the company capital and deducting its losses personally, but holds most of the common stock. Third, the company may be a general partner or contractor to an R&D partnership put together by an attorney, and the company owes a 10%, or large number, sales royalty to the limited partners who provided the capital, plus the limited partners have the right to purchase 20% or more of the company's common stock at a nominal price.

These three surprises are unacceptable to the venture capitalist. Control of the company's destiny is in the hands of a third party, even after the venture capital financing in the first two cases. In the third case, giving 10% of the future sales is intolerable. Assume the company generates sales and that its net profits before taxes are 20%, a 10% sales royalty would reduce profitability by 10%. That amounts to a permanent dilution for all other stockholders. That is, at every round of financing, even though all other stockholder's percentage ownerships decline, the 10% of earnings is a permanent fixture. In a cohesive new company, where all hands are pulling together, no single entity should hold non-diluting stock.

The venture capitalist, assuming he wishes to pursue the investment, should roll-up the limited partnership. The parties should exchange their partnership interests for common stock and roll-up the partnership with its odious royalty feature. In the first two cases, the entrepreneur has gotten himself caught in a crack. He cannot get new capital to grow with because he is chattel in the eyes of his first-round investor. Without the consent of the first-round investor to reduce his ownership to a reasonable percentage in relation to the new capital, perhaps one-third of its ownership, a financing will not occur.

There are other conditions in the stockholders' equity section of the balance sheet that are frequently out of line, but can more easily be set right prior to the closing. These topics will be covered in the Legal Audit section.

Turning to the operating statement, the venture capitalist is looking for ratios and expenses that seem out of line. If the company has been making shipments, what has been the historical cost of goods sold as a ratio to sales? What factors make up cost of goods sold? Has an auditor approved the number? Is it in line with the projected ratio of cost of goods sold to sales? Frequently, entrepreneurs will withhold some expense components of costs of goods and put them below the gross profit margin line. In the software industry, the package is an item frequently carried in advertising. That is bad accounting. Further, post-financing, the packaging may have to be redesigned and improved. Cost of goods sold will increase in an industry where there is intense pressure on price. Knowing one's true costs is critical. Let's look at an example, Exhibit 26 following, from the software industry, where there is continual upward pressure on costs and downward pressure on price. The principal task of the venture capitalist is to pick the company with the best software, so that rapid sales growth will offset the inevitable squeeze.

In Situation A, the venture capitalist sees the enticing nearly 80% gross profit margin, common in the computer software market. Does the venture capitalist remember to ask if the company owns its software, or if it was written by an outside author? The royalty payments could be delayed and not show up in the operating statement. The entrepreneur may have forgotten to give the royalty agreement to his controller to enter it as an accounts payable. Situation B shows what happens to gross profit margin if the company has the additional costs of paying royalties to a software author. It declines to nearly 60% of sales.

When the venture capitalist puts his dollars in the company in Situation C and the first assignment undertaken by the corporate achiever brought aboard by the venture capitalist is to repackage the products. He takes them out of thin blister packs that hang on

EXHIBIT 26. Home Computer Software Company: Effect of Price Squeeze

| | Situation A | % | Situation B | % | Situation C | % | Situation D | % | Situation E | % |
|---|---|---|---|---|---|---|---|---|---|---|
| $ Sales price/unit | $15.95 | | $15.95 | | $15.95 | | $9.95 | | $9.95 | |
| Cost of goods sold: | | | | | | | | | | |
| Diskette encoding | .25 | | .25 | | .25 | | .25 | | .25 | |
| Documentation | .75 | | .75 | | .75 | | .75 | | .75 | |
| Packaging | 2.50 | | 2.50 | | 5.50 | | 5.50 | | 5.50 | |
| Royalty | — | | 3.20 | | — | | — | | 2.00 | |
| Total cost of goods sold | 3.50 | | 6.70 | | 6.50 | | 6.50 | | 8.50 | |
| Gross profit | 12.35 | .79 | 9.25 | .59 | 9.95 | .63 | 3.40 | .34 | 1.45 | .15 |
| Funds available for reinvesting or advertising | $12.35 | | $ 9.25 | | $ 9.95 | | $3.40 | | $1.45 | |

hooks and puts them into bright happy boxes like cereal boxes, or whatever industry the corporate achiever comes from. Gross profit margin declines to 63%.

In Situation D, an industry leader announces henceforth that all 500 products in its line of home computer software would be sold at retail at $19.95 per unit, rather than $29.95. Bingo!

All small software companies, having no justifiable reason for a higher price, must bring their wholesale unit price down to 50% of $19.95, or $9.95. The company's gross profit margin declines another giant step to 34%. The venture capitalist may have chosen poorly on this particular industry. And, for the venture capitalist who bet on the company that did not own its software, Situation E gross profit margin is all but eliminated by the author's royalty.

There are many ways to create horror stories involving investments that go sour because the cost of goods sold of the principal products was not well understood. Home computer software is a good one, because diskettes arguably may (some say should) sell at retail nearer the prices of audio cassettes. At least it would eliminate pirating. Thus, a package redesign and a 20% royalty would be intolerable additional burdens to cost of goods sold. Dividing the cost of goods sold in Situation A, $3.60 per unit, by the revenues in Situation D, $9.95, the company has a 36% cost/sales ratio and a still attractive 64% gross profit margin. That is the software company to back. When the venture capitalist shoots an arrow at the target painted on the barn, he hits the bullseye. In the other situations, the less thorough venture capitalist shoots an arrow at the barn and then paints a bullseye around it. There is knowing one's cost of goods sold prior to investing. Then there is learning it later, when it is too late.

Other items on the operating statement bear scrutiny. The ratio of advertising expenses to sales. The object is to have very little advertising. Salaries. Who gets paid what? Benefits. What are they? There will have to be key man life insurance post-financing. Is everyone who is key insurable? Does the company own any vehicles, or lease any? If so, who uses them. Does the company lease any capital equipment, or is it all owned? Is the company's rent in line with the other tenants in the area? Is this the best area? Is there a good labor pool? What are the wage rates for all classes of labor? Questions, questions, questions. If the company goes under, remember, it will probably be due to a factor that was not sufficiently understood prior to the investment.

If the financial statements have been prepared by an auditor, there will be footnotes. They must be reviewed as carefully as the numbers, because they hold a great deal of information. Bad debts, depreciation, amortization of start-up costs, funded indebtedness, deferred credits, and taxes and transactions with stockholders are the most frequently covered areas in the footnotes. There could be lots of bad news in the footnotes: high bad debts, a stockholder fight, accounts payables to key suppliers converted to funded debt due to inability to pay.

And still, with all this investigation, there frequently seems to exist in small companies receiving their sizeable injection of venture capital, an ability to spend more than the business plan said they were going to. Let's look at how the business plan audit proceeds.

## THE BUSINESS PLAN AUDIT

In every business plan there are financial statement projections. These projections are referred to as "hockey sticks" because that is the shape they take, as Exhibit 27 illustrates.

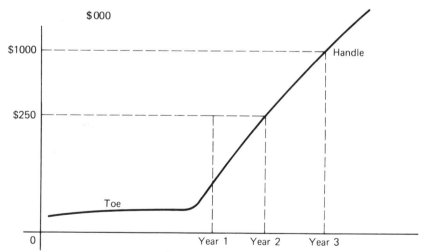

EXHIBIT 27.  The Entrepreneur's Hockey Stick

The projections say to the venture capitalist, "I am at the toe of the hockey stick now, but if I can raise some capital, I'll get up to the top of the handle in three years." The process of raising venture capital is one of giving credibility to the hockey stick. If the due diligence process results in a favorable audit of $P$, $S$, and $E$, and financial statements so concise and accurate that the accountant gives an unqualified opinion, then most venture capitalists will accept the hockey stick as highly credible. Venture capitalists are optimistic about these kinds of companies, because it gives them deals to invest in and they want to believe that the projections will be achieved. Of course, this has practically never occurred in the history of entrepreneurship. Few entrepreneurs recently backed by the venture capital community have missed the mark as widely as did the Genoan explorer backed by Queen Isabella in 1492 but, in fact, projections are practically never realized. If the due diligence process produces outstanding audits of $P$, $S$, and $E$, with carefully derived financial statements, the hockey stick is generally saluted.

However, in most cases $P$, $S$, and $E$ do not get perfect report cards and the hockey stick is reexamined. This should result in the following dialogue:

*Venture Capitalist*: "Our checking suggests some slowness in the reorder rate that you project and a longer time to introduce Project No. 3. We see other delays in collections and a possible need for bank financing in Quarter 6, rather than in Quarter 8. Given this, we would like to recast the cash flow statement projections as follows: monthly for the first 12 months after the closing and quarterly for Years 2 and 3."

*Entrepreneur*: "Why do I need to recast the projections? Why don't you merely make the adjustments?"

*Venture Capitalist:* "We think the exercise will prove constructive for you."

The points of the dialogue are essentially two: (1) The venture capitalist has learned quite a few things about the company during his audits of $P$, $S$, and $E$ that cause him to see a need to change some of the assumptions in the projections. The hockey stick will be more credible at a lower, longer ramp. More capital will be needed, because there are more costs than the entrepreneur had projected and so forth. (2) Business plans get old during the due diligence process. What was projected as Quarter 1 Post-Financing, for example, has now occurred in an actual quarter. New costs have been added; new sources of revenue from existing products, new schedules for product development have been changed. Because the business plan, amended, becomes part of the closing papers, the entrepreneurial team and the venture capitalist must agree to a business plan, and in almost every case it must be amended, because the original business plan is stale.

## THE LEGAL AUDIT

The items to be reviewed are contracts with customers, supplies, lenders, lessors, employees, consultants, former employees, and any other person or company that the venture capitalist locates during the due diligence process. Contracts with international distributors are frequently overlooked. Patent applications may have been mentioned by the entrepreneur. Do they exist? If patents are important to the company, a validity opinion will have to be obtained from a separate, patent counsel to see if the company's claims are valid.

Employment agreements frequently hold surprises. Certain people are to receive substantial bonuses tied to sales or earnings. If not discounted, these bonuses could be like the percentage royalty that acts like non-diluting stock. It is unacceptable.

The company's bank should be visited prior to closing to measure its enthusiasm for the company. Does it wish to have a continuing relationship? Would it like to rewrite a new note and remove the entrepreneur's personal guarantee now that $1 million or so is being invested? If not, the banker could be offered his money back (by increasing the investment) and the company will place the proceeds of the funding with a competitor.

The visit to the bank could lead to signature card changes. The venture capitalist may have found someone within the company to co-sign along with the entrepreneur. Perhaps a new chief financial officer is hired and he signs all checks up to $5000 or $10,000, at which point the entrepreneur must co-sign. Further, the venture capitalist may wish to be a signer on the account if the company is quite young and has never had capital of more than $50,000 or so. Too much money, all of a sudden, could shock the entrepreneur and co-signing the larger checks with the venture capitalist might be comforting to both parties.

The venture capitalist should hire an attorney with securities experience, because he or she will be aware of the legal audit process. This part of the due diligence process does not help the investment succeed. But it helps to avoid losses through oversights.

## SUMMARY OF THE DUE DILIGENCE PROCESS

The due diligence process is neither short nor sweet. It is where the venture capitalist makes it or loses it. Other parts of the venture capital process to follow either protect against losses or enhance the investment. However, it is the due diligence process in which, in a Platonic sense, truth is found, or something that looks like truth is found. In Plato's *Republic* the artisans are chained in place in caves. They are told to look at shadows cast on walls by objects that move behind them. The artisans cannot turn around to see who or what is casting the shadows. The artisans' job: To define the shadow casters by the shadows they cast.

Venture capitalists are the nearest thing to Plato's artisans in modern industry. They are asked to determine the credibility of a company's projections—its shadows—without any more information than what the projection casters give them, plus what they find on their own.

The due diligence process described herein is meant to be thorough. However, it is impossible to cover every item or action that should be investigated. Each company that a venture capitalist audits will bring several brand new problems to work on. That is the nature of the business. Ever changing. Always new.

# 4

# VALUATION, TERMS, AND CONDITIONS

Venture capitalists over the last several decades have attempted to develop fixed formulas for valuing companies. One West Coast SBIC used the following formula unbendingly for many years: take the ratio of the entrepreneur's contribution, expressed as beginning net worth, divide it by the venture capitalist's new investment, and divide that number by two. The resulting ratio would be the venture capitalist's ownership. For example:

Situation A

$$\frac{\text{Beginning net worth}}{\text{New capital}} = \frac{\text{Dividend}}{2} = \text{V.C. ownership}$$

$$\frac{\$25,000}{\$100,000} = \frac{.25}{2} = .125$$

This SBIC loaned its funds to going concerns, otherwise, as is evident by the equation, it would receive less ownership, the smaller the company's net worth.

Other venture capitalists have asked what the entrepreneur's terms were as he entered the room for the first interview. When the entrepreneur responded, "$1.5 million for 25% ownership," or some other terms, the venture capitalist would say immediately: "After reading your plan, I'm sure we wouldn't be interested in less than 40% ownership. But, if you wish to try to persuade me otherwise, please have a seat." That style, frequently seen in the East, is very effective, because it sets the tone of the discussions as the entrepreneur has to prove the company is worth more than $3,750,000, post-financing ($1,500,000/.40).

Another means of negotiating valuation is to tell the entrepreneur that his terms are acceptable if every statement made in the business plan and every piece of information turned up during due diligence positively reinforces the operating statement projections. But if negatives are found, the valuation will come down. Then, during the diligence process, the valuation does come down as some of the absolutes become relatives and some of the contracts become merely serious discussions.

Yet another rule of thumb is that the venture capitalist will not pay more than 400%, or some other multiple, over the last price paid or over the entrepreneur's price. There is no logic to this, except that the venture capitalist seeks a low price.

The importance of a low price to the venture capitalist is essentially defensive. If the investment sours, it can possibly be sold to another company and the venture capitalist gotten out whole—if the price is low enough. If the venture capitalist pays too high a price, he may sell the company, but only be partially made whole. Buyers at liquidation sales do not care whose ox they gore. It is easy to buy, much harder to sell.

In addition to the first axiom, *pay as little as you can*, the next most important law of pricing is *hold the line on your offer.* Clever entrepreneurs will try to tough out a better price from you, but price is more important to the venture capitalist than to the entrepreneur. The latter can propose and devise means of obtaining more stock over time through stock incentives, stock options, and other means. The venture capitalist suffers dilution from the first moment he invests.

There are several means of establishing pricing formulas or, at a minimum, a framework for thinking about valuation in an orderly, consistent manner. One useful method is to assign quantities to the factors $P$, $S$, and $E$ utilizing analytical techniques common for all deals and in a manner discussed in the Due Diligence Section.

Assume that the values of $P$, $S$, and $E$, for any single investment opportunity cannot exceed 3, nor be less than 0. An outstanding start-up, such as Intel Corp., would receive values for $P$, $S$, and $E$, of

3, 3, and 3. A weak investment opportunity might beckon values as low as $P = .5$, $S = .3$, and $E = .1$. When multiplied together, the value of $V$ is $.5 \times .3 \times .1$, or $.015$. The maximum score that a start-up can achieve in the mental calculator of a venture capitalist is 27, computed as follows:

$$(P) \times (S) \times (E) = V$$
$$3 \times 3 \times 3 = V$$
$$3 \times 9 = 27$$

Let's carry the $P \times S \times E = V$ equation one step further. Daisy Systems, a start-up CAD/CAM company, for example, was valued privately by its lead venture capitalist in 1982 at more than $35 million, notwithstanding practically negligible revenues. Six months later, at its initial public offering, the public increased Daisy's valuation to more than $100 million without material increases in revenues. CAD/CAM—or Computer Assisted Design/Computer Assisted Manufacturing—has been designated by *Fortune* and other sources to be a new technological solution to industrial problems as important to American industry as was the Industrial Revolution. That statement alone, one could argue, warrants a value for $S$ of a full 3 points, assuming that the Daisy Systems CAD/CAM solution actually works. The problem, or $P$ value, addressed by Daisy Systems has to do with the rising cost of manufacturing integrated circuits. As hundreds of thousands of transistors are placed on a tiny piece of silicon, the time and cost to design the circuitry skyrockets. CAD/CAM is capable of mitigating that problem. There are approximately 900 world-wide selling sites—plants that manufacture integrated circuits—willing to purchase software to help them avoid costly design errors. At $100,000 per system, the market is $90 million in size. Let's assign a value of 1.4 to that problem.

At this point, if Daisy's entrepreneurial team, self-appointed to deliver $S$ to $P$, were a zero, Daisy's value to venture capitalists would be zero; that is, $3 \times 1.4 \times 0 = 0$. If the Daisy team coupled brilliant CAD/CAM design engineers with an achiever from industry who knew how to manage scientists and market their products, the $E$ factor might warrant a 2, thus giving a value of 8.4 to the start-up. If the amount of capital needed for the launch is $5 million and the venture capitalists obtain 70% of the ownership, then the valuation of Daisy would be approximately $36 million, computed as follows:

$$P \times S \times E = V \times \$ \text{ invested/investors' } \% \text{ ownership}$$
$$= \text{Post-financing valuation}$$
$$1.4 \times 2 \times 3 = 8.4 \times \$3 \text{ million}/.70 = \$36 \text{ million}$$

This valuation method may not have been used by the lead venture capitalist in pricing the deal, but it works out fairly closely to the $35 million start-up valuation accorded Daisy Systems.

As venture capitalists gain more experience in taking deals from dreams to business plans, to launch, staffing, production, marketing, miscalculating and adding more capital, sales ramp-up, and finally public offering, they begin to develop a feeling for price. The formula $V = P \times S \times E$ is extremely useful as a beginning tool, because it can serve as a framework for comparative valuations. It can be used to measure a cancer therapy deal against a chain of computer classrooms. Whereas the cancer therapy deal may address a $P$ of 2.8 and the audit of $S$ reveals that it works very efficiently and is worth a 2.6; yet, the entrepreneurial team is made up of three scientists who insist on 51% ownership post-financing and will not allow a corporate achiever to manage the company's launch. The $E$ factor is about .5. The value for V of the cancer therapy deal is:

$$V = P \times S \times E$$
$$V = P \ 2.8 \times 2.5 \times .5$$
$$V = 3.5$$

On the other hand, an experienced designer of industrial material for teaching programming and an operator of a retail chain of sporting goods stores join together to launch a chain of computer programming classrooms. The $P$ might warrant a 2, the $S$ a 1.5, and the $E$ a 2, for a value of V of 6. A more attractive deal than the one in cancer therapy, using the same yardstick for both.

Another rule of thumb applied by venture capitalists, primarily in the Northeast, is that the venture capitalists should not pay for his stock a price greater than 400% of the price paid by the entrepreneur for his or her stock. This may sound like a stiff, inflexible rule, but one should turn it around and examine it. Why should a venture capitalist be unduly leveraged by an entrepreneur? Particularly in an age of "value-added venture capital," when the investor becomes a free, hard-working, and experienced *employee* of the entrepreneur. Indeed, why shouldn't the venture capitalist pay a price much closer to that which the entrepreneur paid for his stock?

Venture capitalists who fight vigorously for the price they want are quick to make the argument to the entrepreneur: "Don't try to leverage venture capitalists. Use them as your financial partner to leverage others." If the entrepreneur cannot understand this logic of adding a hard-working partner to his team when he adds venture capital, then he deserves the disinterested smorgasbord of individual investors that he is likely to get.

## HOCKEY STICK METHOD

To determine the amount of ownership that the venture capitalist requires in order to make a given investment—which is another way of measuring valuation—many venture capitalists rely on the Hockey Stick Method. It derives its name from the observation that all financial statements look like hockey sticks. The present under-capitalized company is at the toe and the rosey future is up at the handle.

The venture capitalist completes his due diligence and accepts the credibility of a given set of 3-year operating statement projections. He multiplies third-year projected net profits after taxes by a conservative price/earnings ratio, normally 10–15, or the price/earnings ratio of the composite DJIA stocks, which has hovered around 12 for the last decade. The venture capitalist, in so doing, says: "I believe that this company should earn $1 million (or whatever the number is) after 3 years and have a value of at least 12 times $1 million, or $12 million."

The venture capitalist's target return on investment is approximately 5 times in 3 years to 10 times in 5 years, which translates logarithmically into a compound return on investment of between 60 and 70% per annum. See Exhibit 28 for a logarithmic scale that connects ratios of final to initial values over time to compound annual returns on investment.

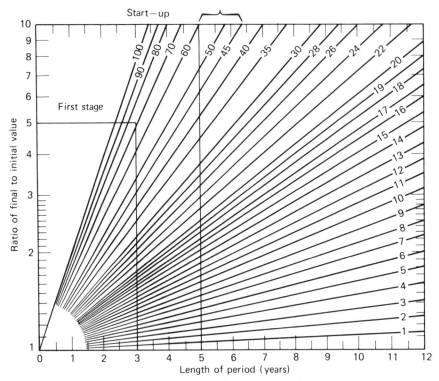

**EXHIBIT 28.** Logarithmic Scale of Ratios: Final to Initial Values Over Time

The amount of venture capital that must be invested is then multiplied by the ratio of final to initial value: say 5, because in this example the projections were only for 3 years. Assume the company requires $800,000. That amount is multiplied by 5, and the multiplicand of $4 million is the amount the venture capitalist expects to make on his investment.

The target of $4 million is then divided by the company's projected third-year value, which in this example is $12 million. The result, or 33% ($4 million/$12 million) is the percentage ownership that the investor requires. He may ask the entrepreneur for 37.5% or 40%, but his required ownership level is 33%. If .33 is divided into $800,000, one can see that the company's post-financing valuation is $2.4 million. It was worth, in the eyes of the investor, $1.6 million before the venture capital, and $2.4 million post-financing.

In an article that I wrote for *Venture* magazine in August 1981, a descriptive drawing was created that amplifies the hockey stick method of pricing early-stage investment opportunities. In this diagram, the need for venture capital is $1.5 million and third-year projected net profits after taxes are $2 million. The formula is

$$\frac{\text{Amount of Venture Capital} \times 5}{\substack{\text{Third year net profit} \\ \text{after taxes} \times 10 \text{ or } 12}} = \substack{\text{Percentage ownership required by} \\ \text{the venture capitalist to meet a} \\ \text{conventional ROI goal}}$$

The illustrative diagram from *Venture* is reprinted in Exhibit 29.

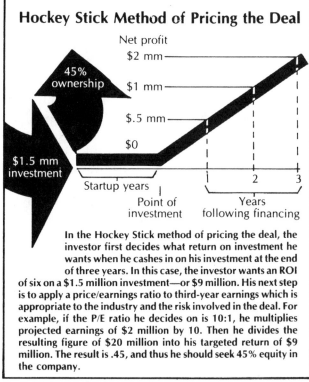

**Hockey Stick Method of Pricing the Deal**

In the Hockey Stick method of pricing the deal, the investor first decides what return on investment he wants when he cashes in on his investment at the end of three years. In this case, the investor wants an ROI of six on a $1.5 million investment—or $9 million. His next step is to apply a price/earnings ratio to third-year earnings which is appropriate to the industry and the risk involved in the deal. For example, if the P/E ratio he decides on is 10:1, he multiplies projected earnings of $2 million by 10. Then he divides the resulting figure of $20 million into his targeted return of $9 million. The result is .45, and thus he should seek 45% equity in the company.

EXHIBIT 29. Compound Growth Rates (Reprinted from the August 1981 issue of *Venture, The Magazine For Entrepreneurs,* by special permission. © 1981 Venture Magazine, Inc., 35 West 45th Street, New York, NY 10036.)

Some final thoughts about pricing and valuation are the following: The entrepreneur's idea of valuation is nearly always too high and reflects his optimism, but not the possibility of the operating statement projections not being realized. One can always increase the price of the stock and the company's valuation in subsequent rounds of financing if the increases are warranted. However, achieving price or valuation reductions means that the company is in very difficult circumstances. Conditional prices that fall one way if the entrepreneur achieves a certain goal, or another way if the goal is not achieved, make opponents out of partners. It is best to agree on a single price and valuation and not conditional prices. If a price cannot be agreed to, at least you can leave the room as friends.

## TERMS OF INVESTMENT

When the venture capitalist completes his due diligence process, obtains approval for the investment in committee, and forms a syndicate with other venture capitalists to invest the full amount of money that is required, it is the duty of the lead venture capitalist to prepare a term sheet and submit it to the entrepreneur. The entrepreneur must approve all of the terms of investment listed on the term sheet, sometimes referred to as a "laundry list." When that occurs, the term sheet is presented by the venture capitalist to his attorney to draw up the closing documents.

### The Term Sheet

The laundry list is worked on by the entrepreneur and the lead venture capitalist. The deal can fall apart at this point if there is a misunderstanding about terms or a failure to agree on price. There are dozens of items that can kill an investment when it is in a contract stage, so it is better to hammer it out on the laundry list before the lawyers are involved, in order to save money. The most traditional subjects covered in the laundry list are summarized as follows:

1. *Amount of the investment.*

2. *Securities.* Generally convertible preferred stock, or common stock in the case of venture capital funds and subordinated convertible debentures in the case of SBICs.

3. *Conversion Price and Terms of the Preferred Stock (Debentures).* Valuation is established as well as the dividend (interest) rate, if any, and the date the money is repayable if the company has not done well enough to encourage conversion into common stock.

4. *Representations and Warranties.* These terms require the entrepreneur to prepare a list of documents, normally exhibits to the contracts, which prove various statements that he put into the business plan or made to the investors during the due diligence process. These include evidences of incorporation, trademarks, patents, indebtedness, leases, contracts, capital equipment, and other items, evidence of which might give the investors greater comfort. The entrepreneur, on the other hand, may ask the investors to represent and warrant that they are able to provide the time of their senior people, an additional round of financing if necessary, or other items that might give the entrepreneur greater comfort.

5. *Affirmative Covenants.* This is a listing of "do's"—a variety of actions that the entrepreneur agrees regularly to do so long as any of the preferred stock (debentures) is outstanding. These include making dividend (interest) and principal payments in a timely manner, tax payments when due and insurance payments, submission of financial statements, unaudited and audited. Vote enough of the entrepreneur's shares to elect the agreed-upon number of venture capitalists or their representatives to the board of directors, call board meetings regularly, maintain properties, books, and records in good order, and meet other reasonable requests.

6. *Negative Covenants.* These are a listing of "don'ts"—a variety of actions that the entrepreneur will not take or permit to occur without the consent of all or some of the preferred stockholders (debenture holders). This list can be relatively

long—more than 12 items—or relatively short, depending on several things, including the mutual trust of the parties, the financial health of the company, the number of investors in the syndicate, and the tautological desires of the investors' counsel. A standard listing to be elaborated upon below, consists of the following "don'ts":

a.  Change the type of business engaged in.

b.  Pay any common stock dividends.

c.  Incur liens on the company's assets.

d.  Make any loan or guarantee any loan to any person or entity above a minimum dollar amount; same for investment.

e.  Acquire or merge with any other company.

f.  Change the company's capital structure.

g.  Increase officers' salaries above agreed limits.

h.  Incur lease liabilities above certain minimums.

i.  Pay employees more than agreed amounts.

j.  Restrict dealings with insiders, such as an officer or director selling a service to the company.

7. *Default.* In the event that the company fails to comply with one or more affirmative or negative covenants, the company is in default and the amount invested by the venture capitalists becomes immediately due and payable. However, there is usually a "cure" period of 30–120 days, which can be extended by mutual agreement, to permit the company to take whatever steps are necessary to cure the default.

8. *Registration.* This section deals with the investors' right to have the company register its shares of common stock for an initial public offering when it registers the company's shares. If the company's founders do not choose to make the company public, the investors are able to seek their own underwriter. This would indicate considerable friction, and no underwriter would leap at the opportunity to make public the shares of a quarrelling company. Thus, though these terms and conditions appear harsh, they have never been enforced by a venture capitalist in recent memory.

9. *Co-Sale and "Take Me Along."* This section deals with offers by outsiders to buy the stock of management and how the entrepreneur must have the offer made to the investors as well. Should they receive a similar offer, they must take the entrepreneurial team along. This prevents either group bailing out without the other.

10. *Additional Provisions.* This section includes methods of modifying the agreements, means of notifying one another who will pay legal fees, and other primarily legal items.

The venture capitalist should take the time to review the term sheet with the entrepreneur very carefully until he fully understands the terms and the venture capitalist's reasons for the terms. In this manner, possible misunderstandings may be avoided.

### Preferred Stock

Venture capitalists should endeavor to own a security that is senior to common stock. Venture capitalists need to hold securities senior to those held by the entrepreneurial team in order to "monitor" the portfolio companies in a fiduciary manner. "Monitor" is a complex word. It means closely watch and influence the decisions of management. Without senior securities, it would be difficult for the investors to maintain their board seats or have other privileges not shared by common stockholders. And if venture capitalists were unable to exert leverage on their portfolio company managers, many of the advantages indigenous to venture capital investing would be eliminated. If a venture capitalist cannot make or influence management changes when things go wrong in his portfolio companies, then venture capital investing loses its leverage.

As G. Felda Hardymon, a partner in Bessemer Venture Partners, New York, says, "Venture capitalists put in all or most of the money and don't ask for a key to the company's offices. What other kind of investor would be so relaxed?"

Before resuming the analysis of typical terms and conditions that venture capitalists have their lawyers prepare for submission to the entrepreneur, it would be useful to review a sample laundry list, a Summary of Terms and Conditions with the laundry list items fully described (Exhibit 30). These terms and conditions ap-

*Summary of Terms*

1. **Amount**       $500,000

|  |  | Approximate<br>Purchase Price |
|---|---|---|
| 2. Investors | Lead Venture Capital Fund | $250,000 |
|  | Follower Venture Capital Co. | $250,000 |

3. **Instrument**     Series A Cumulative Convertible Preferred Stock (Perferred Stock or Shares), convertible on a share-for-share basis into the number of common shares that would represent 25% of the fully diluted equity shares of HTSU as of the closing of this private placement.

4. **Dividends**     Subsequent to October 31, 1987 (3 years hence), the annual dividend rate payable on Preferred Stock will be 10% of the liquidation value of the Preferred Shares, payable quarterly thereafter on June 30, September 30, December 31, and March 31 of each year. Dividends will be cumulative on Preferred Stock.

5. **Voting Rights**     Holders shall be entitled to receive notice of the shareholders' meetings and to vote for the election of directors. These rights exist as if each share of Preferred Stock had been converted into the number of shares of Common Stock into which it is then convertible.

6. **Preference in Liquidation**     The liquidation value (Liquidation Value) shall initially be the Holders' original cost per Preferred Share. The Liquidation Value of the Preferred Stock increases on each quarterly dividend date by the amount of any dividend not paid on such date (subject to reduction if thereafter paid). In case some Preferred Stock is redeemed, Liquidation Value of such Holders' remaining shares shall increase on the date of such redemption by the amount of any unpaid dividends transferred from shares redeemed.

In the event of liquidation or redemption, Liquidation Value also increases by an amount equal

EXHIBIT 30.  (continued)

to a dividend of 10% for each full year from date of issuance until liquidation. Preferred Shares, plus unpaid dividends, have preference over all Common Shares in liquidation. The Series A Preferred Shares shall rank on a parity with any other series of Preferred Stock subsequently issued and distributions will be made pro rata among the Holders of all series of Preferred Stock.

7. Conversion Privileges

A holder of shares may, at any time prior to the mandatory redemption dates, elect to convert, in whole or in part, into Common Shares. A Holder may convert, at any time, without notice to HTSU by (and upon) delivering to HTSU the shares which it intends to convert. The company shall reserve a sufficient number of Common Shares for the transaction and will promptly deliver the appropriate number of Common Shares to said Holder.

8. Mandatory Redemption

HTSU must redeem the Preferred Shares equally in years seven, eight, nine, and ten.

9. Voluntary Redemption Privileges

HTSU may make voluntary redemptions of the Preferred Shares at any time after March 31, 1987, provided:

a. HTSU gives the Holders 90-days written notice via registered or certified mail, return receipt requested, of its intent to redeem such Preferred Shares.

b. HTSU sends to the Holders, via registered or certified mail, return receipt requested, a certified or cashier's check at least 15 days prior to the date on which HTSU intends to redeem such Preferred Shares for an amount equal to all accrued dividends (to date of voluntary redemption), plus the Liquidation Value of the Preferred Shares which it intends to voluntarily redeem.

c. Voluntary redemptions are in multiples of $50,000 of Preferred Shares; and

d. Any optional redemptions must be offered

EXHIBIT 30. (continued)

pro rata to all Holders and will be applied in inverse order of the regular redemption schedule.

HTSU's ability to make voluntary redemptions will in no way abrogate any of the Holders' rights to convert into Common Shares prior to redemption. If, at any time, HTSU notifies the Holders that it intends to redeem, the Holders reserve the right, prior to the expiration of the 90-days notice, to convert any portion or all of their Preferred Stock into Common Shares.

10. Preconditions to Closing

All patent rights owned by the entrepreneur shall be transferred to HTSU. In exchange for the patents, the entrepreneur will own at least 70% of the fully diluted Common Stock of the company immediately prior to closing. In addition, the company must forego its Subchapter S status, converting to a conventional corporation.

11. Anti-Dilution Provisions

If HTSU sells any of its Common Shares at net prices less than the then existing underlying converson price per share (hereinafter called the existing conversion price), or if it sells or grants any options (convertible securities, warrants, etc.) to purchase Common Shares at less than the existing conversion price, then the lowest net price per share shall become the new price per share for which all of the Preferred Shares may be converted or exercised into Common Shares. In the case of a time sale of HTSU Common Shares, for the purpose of this Section, the price per share shall be determined by discounting the price to be paid over time (including interest based on a simple interest calculation) by the prime rate at the time the transaction is closed.

HTSU is encouraged to extend employee stock options, employee stock purchase plans, and similar compensation plans to key employees. Such plans, to be limited to an aggregate of 10% of the Common Stock of HTSU on a fully diluted basis immediately after the time of closing, will not

EXHIBIT 30. (continued)

affect these antidilution provisions. When granting such options, however, the minimum exercise price per share shall be the greater of (a) 90% of the market value of the Common Shares, or (b) one-half of the conversion price of the Preferred Shares.

12. Adjustment for Stock Splits and Dividends

In the event of stock splits and dividends, a pro rata adjustment in conversion price and number of Common Shares into which the Preferred Shares may be converted will be made.

13. Demand Registration Rights

At the earlier of 36 months from the date of closing, or any sale of Common Stock to the public, the Holders will have the right to demand *two* free registrations of their (to be converted) Common Shares; registration costs and filing fees for these demand registrations will be paid for by HTSU. Holders of 75% of the unregistered Common Shares of this private placement may elect to demand such registrations. HTSU will not be obligated to register its Common Shares for the Holders during any period within 6 months of a prior registration, offering, and sale of its primary or secondary Common Shares (other than a shelf registration). If the holders request, then HTSU, at its own expense, must keep a shelf registration active for 6 months after each demand registration prompted by the Holders. At the Holders' option, the shelf registration may be further extended at their expense.

In addition to the two free demand registrations, the Holders will be entitled to two additional demand registrations for which the Holders will pay their pro rata shares of all the registration expenses, such as employees, rent, telephone, etc. If a demand registration does not become effective, then such a demand registration will not be counted as a demand registration. The Holders shall have preference in any Holder-called-for demand registration. In the event that there may be other Holders who may exercise rights to de-

EXHIBIT 30.  (continued)

mand registration of their Common Shares simultaneously with the Holders exercising their rights to demand registrations, then all Holders wishing to register and sell Common Shares shall do so on a pro rata basis. HTSU shall bear the entire cost of such registrations under such circumstances, and such registrations shall only be counted as free provided that the Holders are able to register and sell at least 90% of those shares requested to be registered.

14. Rights to Choose Investment Bankers, Underwriters, Managers, and Co-Managers

The Holders reserve the right to select the investment banker(s), manager(s), and/or co-manager(s) for each of their demand registrations or for any shared demand registrations (those in which other institutions or persons participate). The Holders reserve the right to veto or approve of HTSU's selection of investment banker(s), manager(s), and/or co-manager(s) for all primary registrations and public sales of HTSU securities or private placement thereof; such approval by the Holders may not be unreasonably withheld.

15. "Piggyback" Rights

The Holders will have "piggyback" registration rights for their Common Shares and will not have to pay any registration expenses or filing fees so long as HTSU offers primary shares in connection with such registrations. If, however, the underwriters determine that a "piggyback" registration or a secondary sale may be detrimental to a primary. offering and selling primary shares, they must pay their pro rata expenses.

In case of underwriting limitation, HTSU will have registration and sale priorities for primary shares, and the Holder will have preference over the sale of any other secondary shares. HTSU will provide at least 90-days notice to the Holders of its intent to file a registration statement.

16. Affirmative Covenants

HTSU will furnish to the Holders the following:

(a) Monthly financial and operating statements (with comparisons to budgets and to corresponding periods of the preceding

EXHIBIT 30. (continued)

year) within 30 days after the end of the first 11 months of each fiscal year, prepared on a long-form, consolidated, and consolidating basis.

(b) Accompanying the monthly statements, certificates of compliance from HTSU's Chief Executive Officer stating it is or it is not in compliance with the Preferred Purchase Agreement and any other material agreements.

(c) Within 90 days after the end of each fiscal year, an unqualified certified audit report consisting of long-form, consolidated, and consolidating financial statements prepared by a nationally-recognized certified public accounting firm (also to be included with these reports are the CPA's management letter and their statement with reference to HTSU's compliance with all of its material agreements).

(d) Sixty days prior to the fiscal year-end, a detailed operating budget (prepared on a monthly basis) for the subsequent fiscal year. This budget should be prepared on a long-form, consolidated, and consolidating basis. The budget should also include detailed balance sheets, profit and loss statements, and cash flow statements.

(e) Within 10 days of issuance, duplicate copies of any general written communications with shareholders, directors, executive committee(s), or with the financial community, and any reports filed by HTSU with any security exchanges or with the SEC.

(f) Within 5 days after the discovery or notification that HTSU is not in compliance with the Purchase Agreement or any other material agreement, a detailed statement outlining such noncompliance(s) or default(s).

EXHIBIT 30. (continued)

| 17. | Negative Cove-<br>nants | HTSU may not do any of the following without the prior written consent of the Holders. |
|---|---|---|

(a) Pay any dividends except those related to the Preferred Shares for 3 years.

(b) Issue any security or note that has any equity-type feature, profit participation feature, or may be purchased as part of an investment unit if such security ranks superior to the Preferred Shares.

(c) Have any partially owned subsidiaries.

(d) Create any subsidiary outside of the United States or its territorial possessions.

(e) Cause any reverse splits in any of its equity securities.

(f) Change its fiscal year.

(g) HTSU will comply in all respects with, and will not amend without Holders' approval, the provisions in its Certificate of Incorporation and By-laws that affect, directly or indirectly, these Preferred Shares.

(h) Without the consent of the Holders, no merger, consolidation, or disposition of all or substantially all of HTSU's assets shall occur, except:

(i) A merger under which HTSU is the surviving corporation and its Common Stock is not changed; or

(ii) Other than in the normal course of business, a sale of assets which represent more than 10% of its total assets.

(i) Enter into or engage in businesses other than those presently engaged in or proposed to be engaged in.

(j) Repurchase any Common Shares.

(k) Create any other class of Common Stocks.

(l) Engage in any insider transactions.

212

EXHIBIT 30. (continued)

| | | |
|---|---|---|
| 18. | Inspection Rights | The Holders may inspect HTSU's properties, books, and other records (and make copies thereof and take extracts therefrom) and may interview HTSU's directors, officers, and any employees regarding HTSU's affairs, provided such interviews are held during any regular business hours and at such other times as may be reasonably requested. |
| 19. | Right to Attend Board of Directors' Meetings | Representatives of two venture capital funds may attend all board of directors' meetings and committee meetings of the board, and/or may be elected to the board of directors at their option. HTSU will pay all such Holders' representatives travel and out-of-pocket expenses for attending such board and committee meetings. There will be no less than four board of directors' meetings per year, at least 60 days apart. HTSU will give the Holders at least 10 business days notice of each meeting. |
| 20. | Life Insurance Policy | So long as any Preferred Shares are outstanding, HTSU will maintain insurance on the life of the entrepreneur, aggregating $500,000, and assign the proceeds of such insurance to the Holders. Such insurance will be obtained and the assignment made prior to the closing of this private placement. |
| | | The amount of this coverage may decline to coincide with Preferred Shares outstanding at HTSU's option. Any insurance proceeds payable by reason of death shall, at the option of the Holders, first be used to redeem any outstanding Preferred Shares. The balance of any insurance proceeds not used to redeem the Preferred Shares shall accrue to HTSU. The respective Holder must decide whether the insurance proceeds will be used to redeem its Preferred Shares within 60 days from time of receipt of such proceeds. |
| 21. | Ownership Retention | The entrepreneur shall not sell or transfer more than 20% of his Common Shares (as of the date of closing and as adjusted by any subsequent stock |

EXHIBIT 30.   (continued)

splits and stock dividends) until the Holders have recovered their cost either through the redemption of the Preferred Shares or sale of securities.

| 22. | Future Agreements That May Affect Dividend and Redemption Payments | After the closing, HTSU will not become a party to any agreement that by its terms may restrict HTSU's ability and obligation to pay dividends on the Preferred Shares or to make mandatory redemption payments on such Preferred Stock. |
| --- | --- | --- |
| 23. | Taxes and Debts | HTSU will pay all taxes and debts, unless contested in good faith. |
| 24. | Auditor | HTSU will retain a nationally known auditing firm. |
| 25. | Patents, Licenses, and Trademarks | HTSU will possess and maintain all necessary patents, trademarks, trade names, copyrights and licenses to conduct its business as now operated, without any known conflict with the valid patents, trademarks, trade names, copyrights, and licenses of others. |
| 26. | Amendments and Waivers | The Purchase Agreement may be amended or waived by unanimous consent of the Holders of the Preferred Shares. |
| 27. | Assignments | All of the terms, convenants, and undertakings contained in the Purchase Agreement will be binding upon and inure to the benefit of the Holder's respective successors and assigns and may be assigned by them at their discretion to any financial institutions and/or any corporations, trusts or individuals. In the event of any assignment, the new assignee must "legend" the transferred shares to comply with securities laws or regulations and obtain a letter of opinion from transferer's counsel that such transfer does not violate security laws or regulations. |
| 28. | Indemnification for Finder's Fees | HTSU will, at closing, give the Holders a letter listing any finder's or broker's fees that will be incurred in connection with this private place- |

EXHIBIT 30. (continued)

ment and agrees to promptly indemnify the Holders and their assigns against any claims (including legal, travel, and out-of-pocket expenses for defending such claims) that may arise for any such fees and expenses.

29. Attorneys' Fees

HTSU will pay, on the date of closing, all of the Holders' legal fees and expenses, as invoiced by its attorneys, in connection with its attorneys' efforts to prepare the Purchase Agreement, to a maximum of $10,000.

30. Other Terms and Severability

Other terms traditionally contained in purchase agreements of this type, including representations, warranties, etc., shall be contained in the Purchase Agreement. There will be a standard severability clause and the governing law of the Purchase Agreement for the Preferred Shares will be of the state in which HTSU is located.

31. Events of Non-compliance

An event of noncompliance by HTSU will occur if:

(a) HTSU breaches any of the covenants or fails to comply with other provisions of this Summary of Terms and Conditions.

(b) Any cumulative preferred dividend is unpaid or HTSU fails to make any mandatory redemption payment when due.

(c) All of HTSU's representatives and warranties are not substantially true as of the closing.

(d) Any current or future debt holder demands payment of a material debt prior to its stated maturity.

(e) HTSU files or fails to have dismissed within 90 days a bankruptcy or receivership proceeding, makes an assignment for the benefit of creditors, attempts to materially compromise debts with creditors, or suffers acceleration of a material third-party obligation.

EXHIBIT 30.   (continued)

| | | |
|---|---|---|
| 32. | Remedies for Events of Noncompliance | Immediately upon the occurrence of any non-compliance described in Section 31(c), (d), or (e), or after 15 days of continuous noncompliance described in Section 31(a) or (b): |

    (a)    The conversion price shall be decreased by 10% for each 6 weeks that HTSU is in continuous noncompliance. Notwithstanding the above, the conversion price shall not fall below 65% of the original conversion price, as adjusted by splits and antidilution provisions.

    (b)    At the option of the Holders, acceleration of the mandatory redemptions may be made.

    (c)    The foregoing remedies are not exclusive, and other available legal remedies may be pursued.

ply to a high technology, early-stage company whose revenues were approximately $20,000 per month at the time of the investment. The company, managed by a 27-year old entrepreneur and in search of a corporate achiever, needed the addition of a marketing plan and the people to implement it, especially in marketing and finance. The terms and conditions are typical for many high-technology start-up businesses.

Senior securities enable venture capitalists to demand that management remain in close contact with them after the investment. They also provide early warning signals, hooks, and handles that enable the investors to make changes in management or take other steps necessary to protect their investment when it begins to decline in value. There is on occasion an additional reason for using senior securities: as a measure of assurance of some income on the investment.

As the company grows and prospers, the senior securities may no longer be needed, or may be replaceable on more advantageous terms, for example, at a lower interest or preferred dividend rate. In recognition of this, it is customary for senior securities to be "callable" or "redeemable" at the option of the corporation. Sinking-fund provisions in senior securities, both debt and preferred stock, are in effect provisions for compulsory repayment at stated intervals.

The other side of the coin are provisions for the convertibility of senior securities into common stock, so that the venture capitalist willing to give up prior claims and hooks and handles necessary for proper monitoring may share in the growth and prosperity of the company through ownership of the common stock.

# 5

# MONITORING AND
# ADDING VALUE

## MONITORING

The purpose of close monitoring of portfolio companies is to avoid losses by seeing red flags in advance that warn of pending danger. The venture capitalist can take remedial action before serious trouble infects the company. The means of demanding monthly financial statements from portfolio companies is through the terms and conditions of the purchase agreement. If the investor does not demand prompt, accurate financial statement submittals at the end of each month, he will have no efficient means of monitoring the company. Then, if the portfolio company surprises him "out of the clear blue sky," with news of a product life cycle that is suddenly foreshortening itself, coupled with an inventory build-up and useless prepaid monthly marketing and advertising space, then the venture capitalist is going to lose his capital. Close monitoring is fundamental to preserving capital. If a venture capitalist does not avail himself of the privilege of close monitoring, then he is taking unusual risks with the capital entrusted to him.

This may seem like preaching. However, when the new issues market heats up, as it did in 1982, some venture capitalists believe that they can unload their problem investments on the public. During times like these, believe it or not, some venture capitalists *waive* the negative covenants in the terms and conditions of the closing documents. They are overcome with their own abilities to select good investments and the ability of the public market to bail them out by refinancing their portfolio companies at much higher prices even before the onset of possible trouble. One venture capitalist, who is currently managing a retail branch for his commercial bank, overlooked the warrant expiration date and his opportunity to buy the portfolio company's common stock expired. The company became a major software success. A well known Silicon Valley software company—spread-sheet packages for the Apple computers—began to go soggy when the members of the entrepreneurial team were permitted to sell some of their stock at a valuation of $100 million. What happened to the "take me along" clause? The entrepreneurial team should never be permitted to become liquid before the venture capitalists. Who is left with the drive in their gut to succeed when they have banked $5 million? Certainly not the entrepreneurial team.

### Tickler System

The most efficient method of close monitoring is to set up a tickler system. This can be done electronically on one's calendar or by using a tickler file. Let's discuss the tickler file.

This is an 8-inch by 5-inch accordian file with a slot for each month. An accordian file is purchased for each portfolio company. Into each month is put a piece of paper on which is written an obligation due on a day that month from the portfolio company. Exhibit 31 shows an example of one month's tickler for a portfolio company.

At its weekly staff meeting the venture capitalists should review the tickler file on each portfolio company, *before* going into the more interesting matters, such as new investment opportunities. Deficiencies in providing information to the venture capital fund can then be pointed out to the portfolio company on the day the deficiency is noted.

### Effecting a Focused Management Change

Among some of the more efficient hooks and handles are the negative covenants in the preferred stock or debenture agreement. These are the actions that the company cannot take without the

**EXHIBIT 31.   Example of Tickler for One Month**

Bacteria Diagnostics Corp.                                    May 1985
2320 Santa Monica Way
Collingsworth, Utah 80025


Board meeting:   Thursday, May 16, HQ

April financial statements due:   Wednesday, May 15

Officers & directors insurance due:   May 16

Dividend payment due:   Only if NPBT > $500K

Months remaining before PFD is converted:

Promises made by management at last board meeting:

Comments on 4/30/85 financial statements:

| WC _____ | LTD/NW _____ | EMP/SALES _____ |
| NW _____ | GPM _____ | PCTG Sales |
| Days A/R _____ | Days A/P _____ | CHANGE _____ |
| Days INV _____ | Mktg/Sales _____ | |


approval of a majority percentage of the preferred stockholders or debenture holders. If the action is taken without that prior approval, then the company is in default. The preferred remedy for default is that the preferred stockholders can elect a majority of the board of directors. In other words, the following scenario can be enacted:

1.   Portfolio company takes an action on its own initiative that requires preferred stockholder approval.
2.   Preferred stockholders indicate to portfolio company that it is in default.
3.   Portfolio company is unable to remedy its action during the cure period (30–90 days).

4.  Preferred stockholders elect majority of the board of 14 directors.

At the end of the fourth step, the venture capitalists are in the position to remove management and to bring in a new team. What actions might the entrepreneurial team have taken to cause the investors to devise a method of putting them in default for the purpose of firing them? Some of the following would suffice for most venture capitalists:

1.  Ethical conduct throughout the company, condoned by senior management, that is substantially beneath good business standards.
2.  A continual pattern of false statements to the board about the financial health and position in the marketplace of the company.
3.  Members of senior management operating another business on the side; or taking an opportunity that has come to the company for their own use.
4.  The regular payment of personal bills with company funds.
5.  Sustained chemical abuse by members of the management team.
6.  Felonious and fraudulent actions within or outside of the company, such as income tax evasion, bank kiting or malfeasance of other kinds.

A Southwestern venture capitalist was shocked one day to learn that an entrepreneur of a portfolio company 2000 miles away had shot and killed someone and was in jail. The venture capitalist had to run the company for several months until a new president could be found.

Therefore, it is possible to remove undesirable managements using the hooks and handles of the affirmative and negative covenants of the preferred stock agreement. It is not necessary in every portfolio company to step in and fire the entrepreneurial team that the venture capitalists originally put its capital behind. However, it is necessary to have the ability to do this in every portfolio company.

## Effecting a Voluntary Management Change

In the normal course of events, the original entrepreneurial team is unable to carry out the business plan that it and the venture capitalists believed was possible at the time the investment was made. The company begins to use up its capital on operating expenses, while the initial product dies in the marketplace. Another product must be gotten out with a revised marketing plan and an additional shot of venture capital. In this instance, the venture capitalists can withhold further investment until the entrepreneurial team agrees to permit a new chief executive officer to be hired. The entrepreneurial team could go elsewhere for capital, but interested potential investors will be dissuaded until the waters at the company are calmer. Thus, the threat of withholding capital can be an important catalyst to effecting a change in senior management.

Assume that the portfolio company enters a troubled period due to the failure of its first product to gain acceptance in the marketplace and it must introduce a new product with a new marketing plan. However, in this instance it has sufficient capital and bank support to carry out its plan. Yet, the venture capitalists would like to see the new plan worked on and implemented by a more seasoned manager whom they have identified and would like to bring into the company as President or Executive Vice President–Marketing. The entrepreneurial team is not pleased that they have lost the confidence of the venture capitalists. The venture capitalists have no means of forcing the new manager on the company because the company is not in default.

To accomplish the management change, the venture capitalists must use the leverage of their position as financial backer. The argument they can make is: "If you implement this new marketing plan on your own and fail, you will have lost our confidence to support you with more capital. If the new person comes in and his marketing plan fails, that is our error and we may still back you with more capital on a third product. Thus, the new person is your insurance policy. He takes the flak if this launch fails, but we all take credit if it succeeds."

In order for a venture capitalist to earn the respect of the entrepreneurial team to enable him to make voluntary management changes, he must have demonstrated his respect for the entrepreneurial team in at least three ways:

1.   Close monitoring of the company on a monthly basis.
2.   Daily contact to provide valuable services to the company.
3.   Attendance at all board meetings and major functions and willingness to assist the company every time assistance is sought: for bank loans, receivables financing, interviewing, references, and the like.

As in marriage, both parties must give 150% to make it work well.

## ADDING VALUE TO PORTFOLIO COMPANIES

Venture capitalists must become free, helpful employees of the companies they invest in. There is virtually no means by which early-stage companies can get through the well of the S-Curve as efficiently without the assistance of launch-experienced people as they can with such assistance. Whereas venture capitalists have been through many launches, entrepreneurs and their managers in all likelihood are new to the experience. An ounce of assistance by the venture capitalist is worth a pound of time saved in climbing the sales ramp.

Entrepreneurial teams are frequently relatively strong when the company is new and product-oriented. They generally know every aspect of the product or service that they have developed. They know all of the component suppliers, the cost of goods sold in various production runs, the cost of producing in-house or cottaging it out, how many people are required to make a number of units per day, per month, or per quarter.

Entrepreneurial teams generally know one or two possible customers where the product or service can be tested. They can negotiate a beta test with these customers and lose money or break-even on the test sales. They are skilled at demonstrating the product or service and making the solution seem exciting. In a product-driven stage, the entrepreneurial team cannot be aided particularly well by the venture capitalist. There are few things he can do or say to assist a company during the early stages of production where the capabilities of the product are being tested, explored, and examined.

At the next step up in professionalism, the product is debugged and some preliminary steps are being taken in marketing in order to generate sales, the venture capitalist can begin to be useful. He normally questions why advertising dollars are being spent prior to the marketplace being investigated. Perhaps, the venture capitalist might ask: "There may be several different market segments. Maybe we could benefit from the services of a marketing consultant who can measure the level of demand for the product among OEM's, corporate customers, international networks, individuals, and resellers." The venture capitalist does not share the boundless optimism of the entrepreneurial team for the product. He has seen many products fail. He has seen advertising dollars poured down the drain pipes of many media without sales returns. Those dollars are not retrievable.

The venture capitalist also knows the true outcome of the race between the tortoise and the hare. Wendy's was not Bobby McGee's. Neither was necessarily the first into the marketplace, but they offered a reliable steak and potato, or roast beef and fried zucchini. The customers deemed them valid and returned over and over again, frequently waiting in long lines. These restaurants are rarely franchised, and are almost always owner-operated, because "quality cannot be franchised."

And so it is with the full-menu, full-service computer and software retail chains, such as Businessland and Pathfinder. They are intent on capturing the business market with classrooms, instructors, technicians, and people to offer after-sale support. A segment of the market requires instruction, training, service, maintenance, and after-sale support. Neither of these two companies leapt into the market first, nor are they blanketing the globe as quickly as the limited- and fixed-menu chains.

Entrepreneurial teams are frequently not equipped to step back and look at the market they intend to address. Rather than a look-before-you-leap mentality, the entrepreneurs' axiom is more he-who-hesitates-is-lost. It is incumbent upon venture capitalists to assist the entrepreneurial team in taking the long view, identifying the market segments, counting the selling sites, and then locating the most outstanding people to design and implement a marketing plan to capture those market segments.

In addition to caution and research, the venture capitalist is required to assist the entrepreneurial team in locating, interviewing and hiring outstanding corporate achievers to professionalize the entrepreneur's company. The key hires are usually finance, marketing, and sales. It is frequently the case that venture capitalists are essential to hiring the best available corporate achievers to help the company grow from product-driven to market-driven. Venture capitalists are eager to back corporate achievers who know how to take an entrepreneurial product and sell it into a marketplace. However, they frequently invest at the start-up stage and then hire the corporate achievers. This lowers the valuation at the time of the first financing, but, by definition, makes the investment labor-intensive. Venture capitalists who do not wish to add value to their portfolio companies usually invest at a later stage, when the company is fully through the well of the S-Curve and infant mortality is no longer a consideration. Exhibit 32 points out the difference graphically.

Venture capitalists frequently involve themselves as if they were senior marketing personnel. With the entrepreneur's permission,

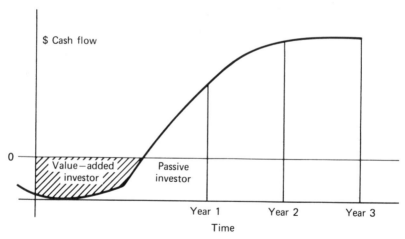

**EXHIBIT 32.   Investment Interests of Value-Added and Passive Venture Capitalists**

they call on large, key accounts to attempt to generate sales. Even when the company has a Vice President–Marketing who knows the sell-to and sell-through processes as well as he knows the back of his hand, he may never have negotiated an OEM contract or a licensing deal. The management team, including the venture capitalist, will frequently identify five or more valid market segments for a product. They also agree that the marketing team is up to its ears in adequately covering three of those markets. When they look around the room to see who is experienced to try to cover the remaining two market segments, all eyes rivet on the venture capitalist. For example, take the case of an early stage educational software company. It can identify nine valid markets, as follows:

Schools
Homes
Software retailers
Bookstores
Department stores
Book publishers
Computer manufacturers
Networks
Miscellaneous

Clearly, building a sales organization or a marketing representative organization to sell to schools and to sell into stores for sell-through to home users is a full-time job for the most capable of marketing managers. It is possible that they can hire and train sales managers to implement their marketing plans, but that does not diminish their involvement; it gives them more time to improve the marketing process and to make direct calls on major accounts, to oversee the advertising, to get involved in designing the packaging, and to produce new catalogs.

Although the marketing manager may be equipped to negotiate licenses with textbook publishers and to sell to computer manufacturers rights to market certain products under their label, he simply lacks the time to do it well. The entrepreneur has never done this type of chore, but he or she can learn. The task falls on the shoulders of the venture capitalist. Rather than wade into the licensing and OEM markets alone and add more experience to his bag, the venture capitalist takes a middle manager with him in advance to train him in the art of negotiating license deals. If the venture capitalist does not use these tasks to train middle managers, he may be adding value to the company's top line, but he is not building value. It is the duty of the venture capitalist to train the middle management of portfolio companies in areas that he can offer training.

This brings us to the financial aspects of the early stage company. Rarely does any person in the company know as much about raising money as the venture capitalist. The venture capitalist has dealt with more bankers, secured lenders, and investors than has the entrepreneur and his chief financial officer, in almost all instances. It is the duty of the venture capitalist to see that the portfolio company has proper and adequate commercial banking and receivables financing. All too frequently, commercial bankers look with disdain on early-stage companies because their financial statements are weak, even after venture capital is injected. Thus, the venture capitalist cannot be content to telephone a few commercial banks and hope for 80% receivables financing and a $1 million line of credit. It may take several visits to half a dozen banks by the venture capitalist and the chief financial officer in order to get proper banking for the company. The banker wants to see the venture capitalist's degree of commitment. He wants to ask the venture capitalist questions and see him answer them. Visiting commercial bankers hat in hand may seem demeaning, but it is a valid service to perform for portfolio companies. Venture capitalists must help their portfolio companies leverage others. In this area, venture capitalists understand financial leverage with extreme clarity.

Venture capitalists must be visible to the employees. Learning their names, complimenting them, asking them to demonstrate products, and having a beer with them after hours goes a long way in building loyalty and camaraderie. At board meetings, the venture capitalist should come early and stay late, become a part of the team and encourage personnel to increase the value of the company's stock.

Venture capitalists must take the lead in obtaining additional investors as needed, locating an investment bank to take the company public when appropriate, and building networks to potential acquirors who could step in when the company is in trouble or pay a premium for the company as it nears the top of the S-Curve.

Although this may seem like more than the venture capitalist is capable of doing for 6–8 portfolio companies in a 10–12 hour day, there is no such thing as a 10–12 hour day in the life of a venture capitalist. Much of the venture capitalist's time is invested in his portfolio companies. He can double and triple the prices that he paid to invest in them by becoming their free and highly efficient employee carrying out the duties, and training middle managers to carry on after him, that he is skilled at carrying out. To do less than the maximum that he can do for each portfolio company is to diminish their values. The only kind of venture capital that generates capital gains is value-added venture capital.

# 6

# SELLING, LIQUIDIFYING, AND PORTFOLIO MANAGEMENT

It is important that the venture capitalist make it crystal clear to the entrepreneur, at the time the investment is made, that the venture capitalist intends to sell his investment at the highest price within 5 years. The venture capitalist must gain a clear understanding with the entrepreneur that both parties share the same interest: to liquidify the investment at a substantial capital gain.

There have been instances in which the entrepreneur has determined, after running the company for a few years, that it is not going to become a very large enterprise, but it will make $1 million per annum for many years to come. However, a venture capital syndicate invested $3 million several years ago and they are a bit edgy about a no-growth situation that is paying a $250,000 annual dividend to them and $750,000 to the entrepreneur. They would like to be bought out. Yet, as minority stockholders, they have no rights. They cannot out-vote the entrepreneur and the company is not in default. In fact, the dividend is as regular as a Swiss watch, but there seems to be no hope for obtaining a multiple on the $3 million investment. Then, in the fourth year, the entrepreneur leaves for life on the Cote d'Azur and turns the business over to his 20-year old son. The venture capitalists are locked in, absolutely. The room has no doors or windows.

This situation can happen again, because randomness is the

only constant in the life of new companies. The best ideas for rapid growth can become no-growth cash cows that leave the venture capitalists locked in with a minority voice in a family-owned and managed business. Notwithstanding the verbal understanding at the time the investment was made, circumstances have changed and the entrepreneur prefers his $150,000 annual salary and $750,000 annual dividend, plus perks, to a capital gain. Clearly, more than a verbal understanding is required to prevent a lock-in from occurring.

In the term sheet presented to the entrepreneur, described in Chapter 4, there are certain sections that are inserted not so much to monitor the company, but to let the venture capitalist liquidify his investment. Let us examine these provisions to see how they are used.

### Conversion Privileges:

A holder of Series B Preferred Shares may, at any time prior to the mandatory redemption dates, elect to convert, in whole or in part, into Common Shares at a conversion price equal to $2.50 per Share.

The first and most important fact in this language is that the venture capitalist decides when and if he shall convert into the common stock of the company. The entrepreneur cannot fix the date. The conversion privilege is an election by the preferred stockholder to convert or not to convert. If the preferred stockholder converts, he gives up substantially all of his control features and his seniority over the common stock. Thus, conversion occurs after infant mortality is no longer an issue, when the company is profitable, and usually at the time of the company's initial public offering. In fact, if the underwriter is willing to permit the preferred stockholders to sell some of their common stock at the initial public offering, their conversion is an obvious and welcome step.

A second means of gaining liquidity is through redemption of the preferred stock.

### Mandatory Redemption:

The company must redeem the Preferred Shares equally in years seven, eight, nine, and ten.

The language clearly states that if the preferred stockholders have not converted by the seventh year, the company must buy them out. Thus, in a low-growth company, too unattractive for a public offering, the venture capitalists can remain in the preferred stock and anticipate a redemption in years seven through ten. There is no capital gain in a redemption arrangement, but at least the preferred stockholder earns a dividend and gets his bait back.

The company is able to force conversion under the terms of the next section of the Preferred Stock Agreement, known as Voluntary Redemption. The venture capitalist usually sets these terms so that voluntary redemption cannot begin for 3 or 4 years after the closing of the financing. This gives the company 36–48 months to get a product into the marketplace, market it hard, and either generate profits and rapid growth or slide by the wayside. If successful, the venture capitalist will have had time to gauge the interest of several underwriters in taking the company public. Note the formal steps required of the entrepreneur before he can attempt to buy out his backers at their cost, plus accrued dividends, or force conversion into his common stock.

*Voluntary Redemption Privileges:*

The company may make voluntary redemptions of the Preferred Shares at any time after June 30, 1988, provided:

(a)   The company gives the Holders 90-days written notice, via registered or certified mail, return receipt requested, of its intent to redeem such Preferred Shares;

(b)   The company sends to the Holders, via registered or certified mail, return receipt requested, a certified or cashier's check at least 15 days prior to the date on which the company intends to redeem such Preferred Shares for an amount equal to all accrued dividends (to date of voluntary redemption), plus the Liquidation Value of the Preferred Shares upon which it intends to voluntarily redeem.

(c)   Voluntary redemptions are in multiples of $50,000 of Preferred Shares; and

(d)   Any optional redemptions must be offered pro rata to all Holders and will be applied in inverse order of the regular redemption schedule.

The company's ability to make voluntary redemptions will in no way abrogate any of the Holders' rights to convert into Common Shares prior to redemption. If, at any time, the company notifies the Holders that it intends to redeem, the Holders reserve the right, prior to the expiration of the 90-days notice, to convert any portion or all of their Preferred Stock into Common Shares.

Demand registration rights are an important part of every preferred stock agreement and speak directly to the issue of liquidation. As you will see when you read this language carefully, the venture capitalist says to the entrepreneur, "If you have not located an underwriter within 36 months of the closing of this financing and if that underwriter has not arranged an initial public offering of the company's common stock, then *we* have the right to find an underwriter to arrange an initial *and* a secondary public offering of the company's common stock, and you will pay for it." That will normally get the attention of the entrepreneur to determine if he wants to have the company publicly-held or if he wants to repurchase the preferred stock held by its venture capitalists. Note that the 36-month demand registration should occur just before the voluntary redemption date. In this manner, the venture capitalist has the advantage of getting liquid at a capital gain, rather than being forced to convert into the common stock and losing the control features of the preferred stock.

### Demand Registration Rights:

At the earlier of 36 months from the date of closing, or any sale of Common Stock to the public, the Holder will have the right to demand two free registrations of its (to be converted) Common Shares; registration costs and filing fees for these demand registrations will be paid for by the company. Holders of 75% of the unregistered Common Shares of this private placement may elect to demand such registrations. The company will not be obligated to register its Common Shares for the Holders during any period within 6 months of a prior registration, offering, and sale of its primary or secondary Common Shares (other than a shelf registration). If the Holders request, then the company, at its own expense, must keep a shelf registration active for 6 months after each demand registration prompted by the Holders. At the Holders option, the shelf registration may be further extended at their expense.

In addition to the two free demand registrations, the Holders will be entitled to two additional demand registrations for which the Holders will pay their pro rata shares of all of the registration expenses other than the company's normal expenses, such as employees, rent, telephone, etc. If a demand registration does not become effective, then such a demand registration will not be counted as a demand registration. The Holders shall have preference in any Holder-called-for demand registration. In the event that there may be other Holders who may exercise rights to demand registration of their Common Shares simultaneously with the Holders exercising their rights to demand registrations, then all Holders wishing to register and sell Common Shares shall do so on a pro rata basis. The company shall bear the entire cost of such registrations under such circumstances, and such registrations shall only be counted as free provided that the Holders are able to register and sell at least 90% of those shares requested to be registered.

In the second part of the demand registration language, you will notice that the venture capitalist has the right to additional registrations and sales of its common stock, paid for by the company. It can make the demand for registration several times until all or most of its stock has been liquidified. These requests are known as "knocks," meaning that the venture capitalist may knock on the company's door several times—the number to be determined by the venture capitalist—and, if the market conditions are in accord, the venture capitalist can have his stock registered and sold. However, in these subsequent registrations, the venture capitalists must pay their pro rata share of expenses.

There is an important rule governing investors' and entrepreneurs' bail-outs. This rule, promulgated by the Securities & Exchange Commission, is known as Rule 144. Occasionally, it is amended and altered; thus it is important that the venture capitalist reviews the latest version of Rule 144 with counsel. The essence of Rule 144 is that the founders and private investors may not sell any of their stock, except if it is registered in a public offering, unless they have held it for 2 years and then they can only dribble out the stock. The dribble-out rule fixes the number of shares that the insiders can sell to the public in any 6-month period. For example, assume that a company is formed with 2,000,000 shares issued to founders and 1,000,000 shares issued to the venture capitalists on December 31, 1983. On December 31, 1985, it registers and sells 2,000,000 shares to the public, but insiders' shares are neither registered nor sold at the initial public offering. The underwriter, in fact, restricts sales by insiders for a period of 9 months after the underwriting, notwithstanding that Rule 144 would permit some dribbling out before then. Nine months later insiders, can begin selling, but Rule 144 prohibits the sale in any 6-month period of an aggregate of more than 1% of total float from all insiders. The total float is 2,000,000 shares; thus, the founders and venture capitalists must squeeze their sales into an aggregate of 20,000 shares. At the dribble-out rate, complete liquidification will come fairly slowly.

To speed up the process of getting liquid, the venture capitalist should strive to have some of his shares registered in the initial public offering. If the company has done well and the stock market is "hot," many underwriters will permit up to 20% of the initial public offering to include insiders' shares. Any more than 20% could give the appearance to public investors of a loss of faith and bail-out by insiders. If the company is not yet profitable, but the stock market is "hot," some underwriters can be persuaded to permit perhaps 10% liquidification by insiders. However, it is probably bad judgment on the part of the underwriter to permit the entrepreneurs to fatten their billfolds before their companies have become profitable. Nonetheless, the persuasive powers of entrepreneurs and venture capitalist have been known to make reasonable people commit unreasonable acts.

The initial public offering of Businessland Inc., a chain of retail computer and software stores, is a case in point. Computer and software distribution through conventional retail outlets was a relatively new industry when Businessland was launched in late 1982 with $23.5 million in venture capital from some of the better known venture capital funds. The company opened 9 stores and acquired 4 more, and had aggregate sales of approximately $10 million at the time that Businessland management and its pride of venture capitalists induced two large, well-known underwriters to manage an initial public offering in December 1983. A small number of computer and software retail chains had achieved their initial public offerings earlier in 1983 and in late 1982, but with smaller, less well-known underwriters, and for much less money than the amount raised by Businessland. The industry as a whole was unprofitable in 1983, because most of the costs of new store openings must be written off. Yet, there was a common denominator among the publicly-held computer and software retailers: their market values were approximately $1.8\times$–$2.0\times$ revenues. The initial public offering for Businessland valued its common stock at $20.6\times$ its revenues. The company raised $50 million in its initial public offering, more than twice the amount that the total industry had raised publicly. Naturally, the price of Businessland common stock fell immediately after the offering.

Notwithstanding the lack of profitability and the weak stock market at the time of its initial public offering, Businessland insiders were permitted to dribble out stock 6 months after the initial public offering. The bottom line of this example is not a value judgment on the worth of Businessland's common stock. Rather, it is that a syndicate of well-known venture capitalists convinced two prestigious underwriters to raise $50 million from the public at an inflated price. The larger, more prestigious underwriters have responded to the requests of venture capitalists to sell overpriced stocks to the public on many occasions throughout the last decade, but no more frequently than in 1983. The Businessland example, summarized in Exhibit 33, is only one of many such instances.

The public market is not an infinitely large sponge that is content to soak up the pricing deals flung on them by usually reliable underwriters. The smaller underwriters appear to protect their customers, whereas the large underwriters seem to protect their relationships with venture capitalists.

According to a study conducted by *Venture* magazine, if you had purchased the initial public offerings of the 10 largest underwriters in 1983, you would have lost 2.3% of your investment. The *Venture* study is summarized in Exhibit 34.

These underwriters raised over $5 billion from the public in

EXHIBIT 33.   Comparison of Businessland with Other Computer
Retailers Whose IPO's Were Managed by Smaller Underwriters

| Name of Chain | Date of IPO | Amount Raised | IPO Valuation | Latest 12 Months Revenues | Market Value Revenues | Number of Stores |
|---|---|---|---|---|---|---|
| Businessland | 12/83 | $50MM | $209MM | $10MM | 20.6x | 13 |
| CompuShop | 4/83 | 10MM | 28MM | 19MM | 1.5x | 21 |
| Computer craft | 12/82 | 7MM | 37MM | 21MM | 1.8x | 26 |
| Computer factory | 5/83 | 5MM | 26MM | 13MM | 2.0x | 6 |
| Inacomp | 1/84 | 9MM | 56MM | 37MM | 1.5x | 24 |

1983 for relatively new and untested companies. The $5.5 billion
they raised was worth $200 million less by year's end. The public,
after awhile, finds losing money discouraging and turns its back
on initial public offerings. This clogs up the system and denies
even worthy companies in venture capitalists' portfolios from
gaining access to the public market. The absence of an ability to

EXHIBIT 34.   Performance of the Initial Public Offerings of the 10 Largest
Underwriters in 1983[a]

| Underwritten | Number of IPO's Under-written | Average Offering Size | Total Amount Raised | Average IPO's % Change in Offering Price to 12/30/83 |
|---|---|---|---|---|
| 1. L.F. Rothschild | 29 | $37.6MM | $1,090.4MM | (2.1)% |
| 2. Prudential Bache | 29 | 26.9MM | 780.0MM | (7.9) |
| 3. Merrill Lynch | 19 | 36.7MM | 697.3MM | (9.0) |
| 4. Morgan Stanley | 12 | 50.8MM | 609.6MM | (3.1) |
| 5. Goldman Sachs | 10 | 60.3MM | 603.0MM | (6.8) |
| 6. Shearson/American Express | 9 | 45.1MM | 405.9MM | (12.5) |
| 7. Salomon Bros. | 7 | 53.7MM | 375.9MM | 5.7 |
| 8. Drexel Burnham | 13 | 26.9MM | 350.0MM | 12.5 |
| 9. Kidder Peabody | 10 | 31.9MM | 319.0MM | (2.6) |
| 10. Lehman Bros., Kuhn Loeb | 13 | 21.8MM | 283.4MM | 3.3 |
| Average | 15 | $39.2MM | $ 551.4MM | (2.3)% |

[a]Source: *Venture*, April 1984, p. 59.

liquidify its portfolios causes venture capital funds to suffer from lack of fresh cash. Its portfolio companies begin to strain their credit lines and the ability of the venture capital community to provide new cash. Some of them must be sold at cheap prices and some go out of business, because they run out of cash. If there is someone's ox to gore, it is the avaricious venture capitalists and large underwriters who discourage the public from initial public offerings by raising too much money from them at inflated prices.

The smaller underwriters, according to the same *Venture* article—where the average initial public offering size was less than $10 million—greatly outperformed the larger underwriters. The price performance of the initial public offerings of the most active small underwriters in 1983 is summarized in Exhibit 35.

The smaller underwriters raised less than $10 million for each new issue, but the average change in price was a positive 12%. The $654 million raised by the 10 most active small underwriters in 1983 grew to $732 million by year end. The public was better served and one could say that the new companies and their in-

EXHIBIT 35.    Performance of the Initial Public Offerings of the 10 Most Active Small Underwriters in 1983[a]

| Underwriter | Number of IPO's Under-written | Average Offering Size | Total Amount Raised | Average IPO's % Change in Offering Price to 12/30/83 |
|---|---|---|---|---|
| 1. D. H. Blair | 34 | $4.5MM | $153MM | 10.6% |
| 2. Rooney Pace | 13 | 7.9MM | 103MM | 1.1 |
| 3. Ladenburg Thalman | 8 | 7.8MM | 62MM | 6.4 |
| 4. William Blair | 6 | 9.5MM | 57MM | 53.3 |
| 5. Mosely Hallgarten | 6 | 9.5MM | 57MM | 16.5 |
| 6. Laidlaw Adams & Peck | 8 | 6.0MM | 48MM | (17.0) |
| 7. Boetcher | 5 | 5.0MM | 46MM | (19.0) |
| 8. Muller | 12 | 3.8MM | 46MM | 34.9 |
| 9. Dain Bosworth | 7 | 6.1MM | 43MM | 18.6 |
| 10. Advest | 6 | 6.5MM | 39MM | 14.8 |
| Average | 10.5 | $6.7MM | $65.4MM | 12.0% |

[a]Source: *Venture*, April 1984, p. 59.

vestors were, as well. However, the clients of the larger underwriters raised more money at higher stock prices than did the clients of the smaller firms.

Do venture capitalists do the best thing for their clients by introducing them to the large underwriters for richer initial public offerings? Or should the new issues be spread among the smaller underwriters, whose prices are much lower, in order to satisfy their customers? The debate is probably not resolvable. However, when initial public offerings are continually over-priced by the larger firms, as they were in 1983, the effect is to kill the new issues market. When that happens, the venture capital industry begins to suffer from lack of liquidity.

Because greed cannot be contained, every new issues market that begins to boil like an unattended teapot, very quickly comes to a screeching halt. In 1983, the boiling new issues market ended in about 7 months. In 1969, it lasted more than 18 months, and in 1972 it lasted about 12 months. There appears to be a trend toward shorter and shorter periods of time when greed overtakes reason on Wall Street. The next boiling new issues market may only last 6 months or 3 months.

In any event, venture capitalists must learn other means of achieving liquidity in their portfolios. This includes knowing who the buyers of rapidly-growing venture capital-backed companies are and their acquisition criteria. They must learn how to acquire publicly-held companies as a means of achieving public markets for their companies via the back door or shell route. Selling portfolio companies back to the entrepreneurs is another exit route. The purchase price may be lower than desired and possibly via an installment payment plan, but liquidification in a cashless world can be the most important achievement of a venture capitalist for the entire year.

One large venture capital firm in Chicago acquired an interest in a small underwriter in 1983 to achieve greater leverage in getting its portfolio companies public in the next few years. If others follow this lead, the venture capital funds of today may begin to resemble the British merchant banks of the late 19th Century. They would buy the companies, fatten them up and then sell them, but control each of the three processes. When liquidification becomes difficult to achieve, the venture capitalists will have to become more creative with regard to how they will sell their deals.

## PORTFOLIO MANAGEMENT

The subject of portfolio management is enigmatic in some respects to venture capital investing. It implies that the companies selected for inclusion in the portfolio fail to meet their projections, for some inexplicable reason, and defy their business plans, thus falling off their S curves. Certainly, these would be accidental occurrences, few in relative number, and caused by once in a century exogenous variables, like tidal waves or earthquakes. Indeed, some venture capitalists have selected one or two companies for their portfolios that have produced such unusually high returns that the other 18 companies in the portfolio were practically forgotten. When that occurs—selecting a Holiday Inn, McDonalds, ActMedia, Digital Equipment—the need for portfolio management diminishes. The customers have been furnished with yachts.

Venture capitalists have been overheard from time to time, while thumping their backs, telling one and all that theirs is the only business where to be "right" half the time will generate great wealth. If being right means selecting companies that produce returns of 20 to 1, then doing that with 10 investments out of 20, if each investment is the same size, will indeed produce huge fortunes. Assume, for example, a $20 million fund, where $10 million increases in value by 20 times and $10 million is written off. The return in $200 million, or 10 times overall. The venture capitalist who has done this well, who has batted .500, is rare. If one thinks of venture capitalists as major league baseball players, a lifetime batting average of .300, that is, 6 winners in 20 times at bat, year after year, fund after fund, would rate inclusion in the venture capital hall of fame.

Peculiar as it may seem, particularly if one practices the fundamentals of venture capital investing, most investments fail to produce rates of return in excess of 5 to 1 in 3 years or 10 to 1 in 5 years, the typical target ROI in the venture capital business. Financial statement projections are rarely met. Revenue projections are generally sooner and greater than actual revenues. Expense projections are generally later and smaller than actual expenses. The need for greater amounts of venture capital, frequently not cited in the business plan, occurs sooner than expected. Because the Murphy's Law affliction attacks most venture capital portfolios, there arises a serious need for portfolio management.

Three axioms should be followed for a venture capitalist to succeed at portfolio management. These axioms are the following:

1.  Only invest in companies in which you know something about the industry.
2.  When you invest in a company, price the investment on the basis that you will be investing a like amount in the same company within the year in order to protect your initial investment.
3.  Save 25% of the fund's capital at all costs and against all temptations, as a bail-out reserve for the portfolio.

The first axiom of portfolio management seems obvious, but it is frequently violated. Venture capital investing, it was said at the outset, is an active business. Investors' become actively involved with entrepreneurs to create value. To benefit entrepreneurs, however, it helps if the venture capitalist knows a great deal about the entrepreneur's business. This does not mean the kind of information one turns up in the process of due diligence; rather, it signifies the kind of knowledge, contacts, and "feel" that one accumulates by being a member of an industry for a number of years. For example, defense contractors are different in dozens of respects from bakeries; they have few things in common. However, if a venture capital fund has two managers with backgrounds in defense and bakeries, it would be appropriate for the fund to have investments in electronics, capital equipment, and computer systems companies because of their relationship and kinship with defense contractors, and in food beverage distributors and restaurants because of their similarities with the bakery field.

When young, rapidly-growing companies get into trouble, it is imperative that the venture capitalist become actively involved in the affairs of the troubled companies to rescue them from possible failure. A venture capitalist who does not know the industry in which his troubled company operates will have precious little ability to construct a work-out plan.

A work-out frequently involves asking the principal suppliers of goods and services to a company to accept a slow-pay arrangement or less than dollar for dollar of the amounts owed to them. Although work-outs are duck soup to Eastern liquidators and secured lenders with the scars of several recessions across their backs, pitifully few venture capitalists know the difference between a creditor's committee and a sheriff's padlock—a critical distinction if ever there was one. Thus, knowing the key people in an industry in order to negotiate a work-out plan is very useful, because there is an element of mutual trust that the venture capitalist can rely on, which will give him the time to structure a stretch-out.

For example, if a computer retail chain has been floor-planned by ITT Financial Corp. for 3 years and has never been late on a payment, the venture capitalist who helps rescue the now troubled chain will garner considerably more sympathy if he knows the lender at ITT over a period of time and through industry contacts. A cold call to the ITT lender, seeking a 90-day grace period, could result in rapid foreclosure. When there has been a prior working relationship, a visit to a contact person at ITT, with the entrepreneur in tow, to discuss a work-out plan, is more likely to result in obtaining the desired grace period.

All too frequently, venture capitalists do not know the principle vendors and lenders to their portfolio companies. It is relatively easy to obtain their names during the due diligence period while checking references, and then to contact them occasionally to monitor the portfolio company via external checkings. In that way, the venture capitalist can maintain close ties in the industry, which can be utilized to gain leverage during work-outs and stretch-outs. If one invests with the foreknowledge that he is likely to be managing a rescue operation for the portfolio company within 2 years, it becomes clear that investing in those industries where the venture capitalist has experience and contacts become an important axiom. Andrew Carnegie said it first and best: "If you're going to put all your eggs in one basket, you'd better watch the basket closely."

The second axiom in portfolio management is to assume that each dollar invested will require another dollar to protect it. Very few entrepreneurial companies are successfully launched with one round of venture capital. A variety of uncontrollable events conspire to knock small companies off their S curves. Recessions have a way of turning linear sales projections into sine waves. The best laid plans of mice and men . . . and all that. As a result, entrepreneurial companies return to their venture capitalists with hat in hand when they are least expected to do so.

To protect the capital of the fund from this form of erosion, the fund managers should take the following preventive steps. First, invest approximately one-half the amount that you expect to invest in total; or conversely, reserve an amount for second-round investment equal to the amount initially invested. Second, invest at a price significantly less than the entrepreneur has suggested and pegged at one-half the anticipated price of the second-round investment. Third, aggressively seek co-investors for the first round; and, a corollary, choose venture capital funds with more capital than your own as syndicate partners. Fourth, actively begin raising second-round capital from non-venture capital sources, such as underwriters, international licenses, and R&D limited partnership packages immediately after investing the first-round capital.

If these four preventive steps read "Invest cautiously, pay little, find well-heeled partners, and look for additional capital from others sources," they are meant to. Unless caution is exercised at all times, the fund will be illiquid and the portfolio companies will be starved and left to die.

The third axiom is to save 25% of the fund's capital in reserve. No matter how great the temptation to invest in a deal that looks like it absolutely cannot miss, or to add additional capital to a portfolio company that is beginning to cross break-even, the fund must maintain a 25% reserve.

Successful fund managers operate as if they have only 75% of their capital to invest, rather than 100%. As they approach full investment with the 75%, they begin planning their next venture capital fund. To do so, of course, means that the first fund must necessarily have some successful investments in it. Without higher valuations, it is difficult to convince financial institutions to invest in a second fund.

The 25% maintained in reserve should be used for absolute, optionless emergencies. For example, assume that a portfolio company in which the fund has a 200% gain begins to suffer serious reversals and appears headed into bankruptcy without a rescue plan. The fund's reserve capital could be used to keep the company alive, by carefully dripping in capital on a monthly basis to meet payroll and other vital payments, while a work-out plan is implemented. The advances could be in the form of notes that accumulate interest, so that the fund can recoup its principal plus interest if the rescue plan succeeds.

As in many aspects of venture capital investing, portfolio management requires the discipline of looking ahead at how one gets out of his deals. Getting in is simple: getting out is complex. It is useful to think of the portfolio as 15–20 bonds, each with redemption dates 3 years after the date of investment. For example, assume that a fund begins investing $20 million on January 1, 1985 and invests $750,000 in one deal every other month until $15 million is invested, with the balance held in reserve. The yield curve of projected redemption dates is illustrated in Exhibit 36.

The yield curve is a hypothetical projection of the 20 investments growing and developing evenly and continuously, with the first investment crossing above the target return on investment line ahead of the second, the second ahead of the third, the third ahead of the fourth and so on. This kind of perfection in investing is not likely to happen, but it is important to plan in this manner. When the first several investments fall off the yield curve and give no evidence of crossing the ROI line in the third year, that will increase the liquidity of his portfolio. The yield curve diagram acts like a graphic tickler file.

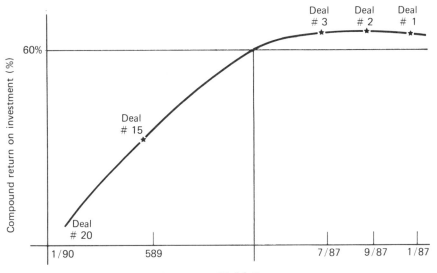

EXHIBIT 36.   Yield Curve

A money management firm that invests in publicly-held companies can sell its investments when they fail to perform as expected or when they increase substantially in value. The sale can be made instantaneously. Liquidity is a given.

A venture capitalist cannot sell on demand his investments when they fail to perform or when they increase substantially in value. A venture capitalist is locked into his portfolio. He can effect change to correct mistakes in several positive ways, none of which have immediate effects.

The venture capitalist can declare his troubled deals to be in default and move quickly to change management, acquire control through additional shares and change the company's direction, bring in additional capital or sell the company. If the venture capitalist fails to build these hooks and handles into the terms and conditions of his investment, then he will have a portfolio over which he has no control. If he fails to gain the confidence of his entrepreneurial teams, it will be difficult to recommend to them major changes or cost-savings programs. An investor must have either liquidity in his portfolio or the power to control and change the companies in his portfolio. The absence of both factors will produce portfolio losses in large numbers. The venture capitalist will soon run out of funds to manage and will lose institutional sponsorship.

The leverage or advantage that a venture capitalist has over any other kind of investor is that the venture capitalist can change materially the nature of the entity in which he invests. Capital can be protected by having the company spending and liquidate, selling out for cash, selling stock to the public, or acquiring another company in an unrelated field. The venture capitalist can put the company in default and take control of the company's assets, sell them, and get his cash back. The venture capitalist can also add value to his portfolio companies to assist them in growing and developing more rapidly.

Although these remedial actions are possible, it is impossible for a venture capital fund to service a portfolio of critically ill companies in a competent manner. If a $20 million venture capital fund invests in 24 companies serviced by 3 partners, and each of the companies needs close monitoring or bail-out assistance on a round-the-clock basis, very few of the 24 will be rescued. How might all of the portfolio companies become critically ill simultaneously? How can a venture capital fund get into a liquidity problem in all of its investments? Given a strong deal flow, careful due diligence, experienced management, and tightly drawn terms and conditions, is a total liquidity crisis possible?

Venture capital funds get into trouble when they focus intensively on their portfolio companies and lose sight of their overall business plan. Trouble comes primarily from over-committing funds in the same industry, in one period of time, and in companies in the same stage of development.

The venture capital funds launched in 1970–1971 in which the bulk of capital was invested during those two years, for example, did relatively poorly, because their portfolio companies were not ready for the boiling new issues market of 1972 and the next decent new issues market did not begin to show signs of life until 1979. In the interim, the companies were starved for lack of cash. If the venture capital funds of that era spread their investments over 4 years, through 1974–1975, they very likely got into the Federal Express investment, which returned over 100 times cost (if the investor did all three rounds) and compensated its backers for many losers. The depression of 1974–1975 was disastrous for most of the SBICs and for the handful of venture capital funds; but the survivors of that period are cycle-tested and probably know more about rescuing cash-starved companies than do venture capitalists who came into the industry later. Syndicating deals with these experienced venture capitalists can be helpful to the newer venture capital funds.

Overloading a portfolio in one or two industries can be detrimental as well. An excessive number of oil deals made in 1980–1981 have been an anchor on the portfolios of several venture capital funds who doubtless thought that oil prices would keep climbing. Their costs exceed market values in many of their investments. An excessive number of investments in the computer industry can be detrimental if a giant force, such as IBM or AT&T, enters the market and begins to standardize software or other key factors around their systems. The cost of retooling and reprogramming for the rest of the companies, many of them venture-backed, could be devastating. Several of the entertainment and education software companies that developed packages for

Atari, Commodore, and Coleco home computers are mere memories today.

Finally, investing in companies at the same stage of development and addressing the same risks (e.g., production and marketing) is poor portfolio management. If a fund puts 80% of its capital into 1985 start-ups, and if the new issues market is very quiet from 1987 to 1989, and if the economy is in recession, the fund will likely run out of cash trying to salvage its investments. Although they may be rescued, there may be no means of liquidification; thus, the fund's capital could become exhausted.

However, if the capital is spread between start-ups, first-stage deals, and second-stage deals, achieving liquidification is not as time-sensitive. The venture capitalist can achieve liquidity for more mature companies fairly early and for start-ups fairly late. Also, later stage companies require considerably less monitoring time. They are less labor-intensive. Therefore, the venture capitalist has more time and capital to invest in his start-ups and in his troubled deals.

Efficient portfolio management means investing over a 2- to 3-year period, investing in companies in several stages of development and in a variety of industries, and investing with tight controls to enable the venture capitalist to effect changes in his portfolio companies as required.

## FINAL THOUGHTS

There is only one way to keep the ball in play in the venture capital business and that is to continuously, unrelentingly, and intelligently attempt to create value. When people enter the venture capital business to get rich quickly, they generally leave the business much poorer, sadder, and wiser than when they entered it. As the gifted *Forbes* columnist Thomas P. Murphy continually reminds us, the primary requirement of a venture capitalist is *patience*. Second, venture capital investing is a craft, practiced fairly locally or regionally, in order to be near one's investments. When they get into serious trouble and must be baby-sat, it is advantageous if they are nearby.

Venture capital investing is a process—a dynamic rather than a static business. It changes constantly. It renews itself daily. Innovation is continually judged by venture capitalists to determine its validity, and somehow the judge changes as well with new insights. There are no firm rules for venture capital investing, merely road signs.

The first road sign is to form a venture capital fund and to choose complimentary partners. Investors generally prefer to see a team that includes a venture capitalist—or private investor/ monitor of start-up companies—an operating person, and a source of technical expertise in the person of a third manager, advisory group, or consultants. The management group must specify clearly its investment objectives, region of concentration, and industries of interest.

Generating a deal flow is the second step in the process. Although other venture capitalists and successful entrepreneurs provide many good deals, it is critical that the venture capital fund develop the underpinnings in its region that will lead to an entrepreneurial community. The task is not simple. It requires cloning Silicon Valley.

This means helping to form an incubator and a seed capital fund to help would-be entrepreneurs test their new ideas. Is there a problem in search of a solution? Is it aware of the problem? Will it buy the solution? What should the solution look like? How should it be priced? What are the maintenance, training, and service features? The incubator and seed capital fund concepts can nurture 50 development stage deals per annum, and when the development and production risks are mitigated and the entrepreneur needs $1 million to begin marketing, the venture capital fund is ready to provide funding and assistance.

The venture capital fund should also shoulder the responsibility of generating entrepreneurial enthusiasm in its region by forming a venture capital club, a forum for entrepreneurs, investors, and fellow travelers to come together socially one evening per month. Other important catalysts to generate a quality deal flow include a newsletter of entrepreneurial happenings with local and national stories, plus announcements and seminars several times a year in which national speakers visit the area to discuss topics of importance to entrepreneurs, such as managing the small business, the SBIC grant program, and launching the high-technology company.

It is important, as well, that the venture capitalist actively involve the region's universities, laboratories, and technical corporations. They can provide funds for seed capital. They can be sources of technology transfers and they can provide entrepreneurs and managers for the companies in the venture capital fund. The universities, to the extent that they have the appropriate departments, can provide students and faculty to assist the entrepreneurs in the incubator. The corporations can provide lab space, used furniture and equipment, and other services to the entrepreneurs.

Therefore, in addition to forming the venture capital fund and managing it, the venture capitalist must generate a system that will continuously supply quality deals to the fund. If that sounds like pioneering and building, it is. But that kind of effort built Silicon Valley. It didn't happen by luck and accident there and it will not happen by luck and accident elsewhere.

The process of investigating, structuring, monitoring, adding value, and selling venture capital investments is essentially one of thoroughness and discipline. The objective is to protect capital and turn over the investments at higher prices than the fund pays. Venture capitalists get better at this process every time their investments run into serious trouble, but the objective is to avoid the trouble. The purpose of problems is to teach. The venture capital business is, consequently, one of continual learning.

# APPENDIX

Utah Innovation Center
417 Wakara Way
Research Park
Salt Lake City, Utah 84108
Don A. Stringham, Director
801-583-4600

The Enterprise Corporation of Pittsburgh
Mellon Institute
4400 Fifth Avenue
Pittsburgh, Pennsylvania 15213
John R. Thorne, Chairman and CEO
412-578-3481

Advanced Technology Development Center
Georgia Institute of Technology
Atlanta, Georgia 30332
Leaman Scott, Director
404-894-3575

University City Science Center
3624 Market Street
Philadelphia, Pennsylvania 19104
Randall Whaley, Director
215-387-2255

Massachusetts Institute of Technology
Innovation Center
77 Massachusetts Avenue
Cambridge, Massachusetts 02139
617-253-1000

Rensselaer Polytechnic Institute
Incubator Space Project
110 Eighth Street
Troy, New York 12144
Michael Wackolder, Coordinator
518-266-6000

Lehigh University Small Business Development Center
Murray H. Goodman Campus
Bethlehem, Pennsylvania 18015
John Tate, President
216-861-3119

Indiana Institute for New Business Ventures, Inc.
One North Capital Street
Indianapolis, Indiana 46204
Robert V. Cummins, President
317-634-8418

# INDEX

*Italicized* numbers refer to information in a table or figure.

ActMedia, 241
Adding value, 2–3, 17
  arranging financings, XI1, 228
  free help, 224
  high visibility to employees, 228
  hiring managers, XII, 226
  identify customers, 227
  networking, XII, 224–225
  teach middle managers, 228
Advanced Technology Ventures, *35*
  Welsch, Carson, Anderson & Stowe, *35*
Advent V, 21
Advest, *239*
Agrigenetics Corporation, 105, 174
Airborne Freight, 99
AIDS, 95
Albany, New York, 51
Albuquerque, New Mexico, 35
Allen & Co., 79
Amdahl Corp., 22
American Cancer Society, 97
American Dream, 104, 157
American Express, 16
American Research & Development Corp.,
  17, 124
American Society of Radiologists, 117
Ann Arbor, Michigan, 51
Apple Computer, 112, 116, 124, 141–142,
  180, 220
Arco, 26
Arcoa, 104
Atari, 9–10, 247
Atlanta, Georgia, *35*, *44*, 51, *72*

AT&T, 131, 171, 247
Atlanta Technology Development Center,
  62
Austin, Texas, *35*, 66
Automatic Data Processing, 112

Bankruptcy, 184
Battelle Memorial Laboratory, 91
Baxter Travenol Corp., 135
Beta-Test, 224
Beginning Library, 55
Bellevue, Washington, 47
Benton & Bowles, 161
Benton, William, 161–162
Bessemer Venture Partners, 205
Biogen, 97
Blair, D. H., *239*
Blair, William, *239*
Board of Science Advisors, 102
Bobby McGee's Conglomeration, Inc., 163,
  225
Boetcher, *239*
Boulder, Colorado, *35*, 49
Brentwood Associates III, 21, 29
Brown, John Y., 104
Broxodent, 129
Business Development Partners, *35*
  Kleiner, Perkins, Caufield & Byers, *35*
  Brentwood, Rothschild, *35*
Businessland, Inc., 23, 225, 236–237, *238*
Business plan, 100
Buy-out, 184
*Byte*, 70

Cable Howse Partners, 135
CAD/CAM, 129, 197
Cambridge, Massachusetts, 36
Capital management, 10
Capital Publishing Corp., 18
Carlson, Chester, 91, 105
Carnegie, Andrew, 243
"Catch Entrepreneurs," 50, 52, 77
    Pyramid method, 50
Centennial Fund, 39
    Daniels & Co., 39
Cetus, 97, 113
"Characteristics of Successful New
    Businesses," 87
Champaign, Illinois, 51
Chase Manhattan, 97
Chun King Corporation, 160
CIGNA Corp., 43
Citicorp, 11
    Chairman, Walter Wriston, 11
Citicorp Employees Retirement Fund, 43
Civil Aeronautics Board (CAB), 136
Coleco, 248
Columbus, Ohio, 66
Combined Insurance, 159
Commodore, 248
Competere, 123
CompuShop, 238
ComputerCraft, 238
Computer Factory, 238
Conflict of interest, 12, 14
Conversion privileges, 232
Cookie-cutter, 126
Coppola, Francis, 160
Crossroads Capital, 35
    Pathfinder Venture Capital Co., 35
Crossroads Partners, 43
Cupertino, California, 10

Dain Bosworth, 239
Daisy Systems, 197–198
Dallas, Texas, 36, 72
Dalton School, 79
Daniels & Co., 39
Davis & Rock, 4
Davis, Tommy J., 10, 17, 39
    Stanford University, Department of
        Engineering, 39
Deal Generation, 2, 17
    destination sources of capital, 48

consultants, 75–77
incubators, 52–61, 249
laboratories, 74, 250
methods of, VIII, 47–78, 249
newsletters, 61–68, 249
pyramid methods, 50
seminars, 71–73
university participation, 73–75, 250
venture capital clubs, 68–71, 249
DEJ, 150
Demand Registration Rights, 234–235
Demonstrable Economic Justification, 121
    eight factors of, 121–151
    existence of qualified buyers, 122–123
    existence of qualified sellers, 123–125
    homogeneity of buyers, 125–128
    invisibility of new company, 149
    lack of institutional barriers, 132–137
    large number of buyers, 128–132
    optimum price/cost relationship,
        140–149
Detroit, Michigan, 133
Development Risk, The, 89, 90
Dewey, John, 138, 140
Digital Equipment Corp., 17–18, 108, 241
Disclosure, 118
Discover, 70
Doriot, General Georges, 17–18, 124
Drexel, Burnham, 238
Drucker, Peter, 107
Due diligence process:
    adequacy of, 30
    audit of P, 116
    business plan audit, X, 191–193
    cause of failures, IX, 114
    contracts, review of, 193
    Deal Log, 81–85
    Deal Log Summary, 87
    financial, X, 183–193
    five audits, 114–194
    market size audit, X, 116–153
    legal audit, X, 193–194
    people audit, X, 102, 153–182
    reference checking, X, 192
    surprises in, 187
    turn-downs, 85
Dun & Bradstreet (D&B), 149, 170

Eastman Kodak, 165
Eaton Corporation, 8

Electronic Data Systems Corp., 108, 150, 152, 159
Emery, 99
*Encyclopedia of Associations, The,* 132, 170
*Encyclopedia Brittanica,* 162
Endorsements, 32, 39, 42
Entrepreneurs:
  absent father, 104, 156, 161--162
  age, appearance and outward signs, 102
  characteristics of, 102–108, 153
  communications skills, 107–108, 156, 173–174
  competence, 124
  courage, 105, 156, 172–173
  creative, 106, 156, 167–170
  deprivation, 104, 156, 159–161
  dissatisfaction, 164
  energy, 164
  guilt, 104–156, 162, 164
  happiness, 107, 156, 174
  honesty, 170–172
  insights, 107, 156, 164
  intense focus, 105, 156, 164
  middle-class backgrounds, 103, 156–159
Eugene, Oregon, 51
Exxon, 6, 9
Exxon Alumni, 9
Exxon Enterprises, Inc., 9, 11
  George Kokkinakis, 11
Exxon Office Systems, 9

Fairchild Semiconductor Corp., 109, 152
Federal Express, 8, 18, 49, 92, 98–99, 116, 136–137, 159, 161, 173, 247
Federal Government, 74
  federal funding, 74–75
Fialkov, Herman, 4
Five risks of a start-up company, 89–92
  development risk, 90–91
  manufacturing risk, 91–92
  marketing risk, 89
  management risk, 89
  growth risk, 92
Florence, South Carolina, 34
Food and Drug Administration (FDA), 134
Footnotes, 186, 191
*Forbes,* 27, 66, 248
  Allan Sloan, 27
  Thomas P. Murphy, 248
Ford, Henry, 125

Ford Foundation, 43
*Fortune,* 197
Fort Wayne, Indiana, 51
Franchises, 225
Friedman, Milton, 35, 134, 136, 137
Fund, raising $20,000,000, 31, 44
Fund of Funds, 15–17, 50
Funds, investment banking sponsored, 10
Funds, regional, 29, 34–35

*Gamesman, The,* 177
Gates, Bill, 47
Geffen, David, 162
Geiger, Richard, 4
Geiger & Fialkov, 4
Genentech, 97, 113
General Electric Employees Retirement Fund, *43*
General Instruments Corp., 4
General Motors, 152
Genentechian, 36
Genex, 97
Geritol, 140
Goldman, Sachs & Co., 11, *238*
Grove, Andrew, 109, 152
Growth Risk, The, *89*, 92
Gulf Oil Corp., 26

Haloid Corp., 91
Hambrecht, Bill, 17
Hambrecht & Quist (H&Q), 4, 12
  H&Q-Arizona, 12
  H&Q-Larry Mohr, 12–13
  H&Q Ventures, I, II, III, IV, 12–13
Hamilton, Scott, 105
Hardymon, G. Felda, 205
Harvard College, 163
Heinz, H. J., 99
Heinze, Walter, 163
Heizer Corp., 22
Held, Raymond L., 16
Hewlett-Packard, 49, 108
*High Technology,* 70
Hill Partnership, The, 35
  Mayfield Fund, 35
Hockey stick method, 199, 201
Holiday Inns, 159, 162, 241
Holography, 125

IBM, 23, 58, 92, 128, 141–142, 144, 220, 247

Inacomp, *238*
*Inc.*, 70
Intel, 108–109, 152, 196
Interwest Partners, 44
Investment Advisors, Inc., *43*
Investment Banking Sponsored Funds, 10
Itek Corporation, 165
ITT Industrial Credit, 243
Inventory, 11, 85

Japanese venture capital firms, 8
   Japanese-American venture capital
      firms, 8
Jobs, Stephen, 112

Kelly, Tom, 174
Kentucky Fried Chicken, 104
Kidder Peabody, *238*
Kidder, Tracy, 177
Kleiner and Perkins, 4, 19–20, 29
   Business Development Partners, *35*
Kleiner, Perkins, Caulfield & Byers, III, 19,
   21
Kohlberg, Kravis, Roberts & Co., 26
Kokkinakis, George, 11
Kroc, Ray, 162
Kuhn, Loeb, 11

Ladenburg, Thalman, *239*
Laidlaw, Adams & Peck, 239
Land, Edwin H., 104–105, 145, 163
Lauren, Ralph, 125
Lautenberg, Frank, 112
Laws of Venture Capital:
   invest in big-P companies, 88, 96,
      112–113
   laws of portfolio management, 242
   minimize risks, 86, 89–94
   $V = P \times S \times E$, 88, 94
LBOs, 27–28
Legal audit, 188
Lehman Brothers, 11, *238*
Limited, chain, The, 162
Liquidification:
   agreement with entrepreneurs, 231
   initial public offering, XII, 235–239
   plan, 32, 40, 235–240
   redemption, 232–233
   sale to founders, 40, 240
   sale to larger company, XII, 234

Listerine, 140
Little, Royal, 17
Lotus Development Corp., 36
   Genetechian, 36
   Lotus 1-2-3 package, 36
   Supercalc, 36
   Visicald, 36
LTX, 165

MacArthur, General Douglas, 162
Maccoby, 176–177
McCowen, Charles, 108
McDonalds, 241
McKinsey & Co., 8
Madison, Wisconsin, 51
Management Risk, The, *89*
Mandatory Redemption, 232
Managers:
   age, appearance and outward signs, 110,
      175
   capacity for work, 112
   characteristics of, 110, 112
   creating wealth, 108
   corporate achiever, 110, 176
   dissatisfaction, 110
   energy, 110
   harnessing the vision, 109
   heart, 111
   practicality, 112
   terms of employment, 178
   thoroughness, 112
Mayfield Fund, 9–10, 17, 29, 39
   Hill partnership, *35*
   Mayfield II, 43
   Stanford University, Department of
      Engineering, 39
MCI Communications, 108, 131
Mead Data Corp., 118
Megafunds, 21
   sweepers for, 29
   take-down rate of, 27
*Megatrends*, 95
Memphis, Tennessee, 49, 99
Menlo Park, California, 47
Merrill Lynch Pierce Fenner & Smith, 11
Merrill Lynch Venture Capital Ltd., 11, *238*
Mesa Petroleum, 159, 162
Microsoft Corporation, 47
Middle Eastern, 70
Midwest, 34

Mitsubishi, 8
Molecular Genetics, 97
Monitoring, 2–3, 17
    attendance at all meetings, 224
    changing management, involuntary, 220
    changing management, voluntary, 223
    daily contact, 224
    information requirement, 219
    objective of, XI, 219–229
    surprise avoidance, 219
    tickler system, 229
Monsanto Co., 15
Moore, Gordon, 109, 152
Morgan, Stanley & Co., 8, 10, 238
Mosely Hallgarten, 239
Moses, Edwin, 105
Mostek, Inc., 36
MRP, 130
Muller, 239
Multiplier, 126
Murdoch, Rupert, 79
Murphy, Thomas P., 248
Murphy's Law affliction, 241
Muzak, 162

Naisbitt, John, 95
National American Bank, 186
National Science Foundation, 62
Navratilova, Martina, 105
Neditch, Jean, 99
New England, 33
New Farm Implements Corp., 133
New York State Employees Retirement
    System, 43
New York, New York, 34, 68, 75
New York Times, The, 95, 97
New York Venture Capital Forum, 68
New York Venture Capitalists, 5
Nexus, 118
Nicklaus, Jack, 105
Nixon, Richard M., 8
Noro-Moseley Venture Capital Partners, 44
    Noro Group, 44
North Carolina, 33
Northern California, 33
Noyce, Robert E., 108–109, 152

Oak Investment Partners III, 21
OEM sales, 182, 225, 227–228

Olson, Kenneth E., 108
Osborne Computer, 141–142, 144–145

Packard, David, 108
Padwa, David J., 105, 174
Palo Alto, California, 73
Paolucci, Gino, 160
Patent applications, 193
Pathfinder Venture Capital Co., 35, 225
    Crossroads Capital, 35
    Security Pacific Capital, 35
Performance, 32–33, 36, 41
Perot, H. Ross, 108, 145, 150, 159
PERT, 145–146
Philadelphia, Pennsylvania, 59, 63
Phoenix, Arizona, 35
Pickens, T. Boone, 159, 162, 165
Pittsburgh, Pennsylvania, 51
Polaroid, 105, 163
Portfolio management, 2
    batting average, 241
    comparison with money management,
        246
    economic cycles, XII, 247
    flexibility, 246
    industry considerations, XIII
    laws of, 242
    leverage, 246
    market conditions, XII, 240
    reserve funds, 242
    yield curve, 245
Portland, Oregon, 35
Pratt, Stanley L., 33
Princeton University, 163
Promoter, 32
Promotion, 32
Protection from loss, 32, 39
Provisions, 232
    conversion privileges, 232
    demand registration rights, 234–235
    mandatory redemption, 232
    voluntary redemption, 233
Prudential Bache, 238
Prudential Insurance Co., 16, 43
Purchase Agreement, 101
Purolator, 99
Pyramid method, 50

Qume, 180

Racine, Wisconsin, 44
Raising $20,000,000 Fund, 31, 44
Raleigh, North Carolina, 35
RCA, 105, 160
Regional Funds, 29, 34–35
Reliance, 109
Research Triangle, 35, 60
Revlon, Inc., 160
Revson, Charles, 160
Rock, Arthur, 124
Rocky Mountains, 34
Rolm Corp., 23, 26
Rooney Pace, 239
Rosen, Benjamin, 36
Rothschild, L. F., 29, 238
Rule 144, 235–236

Salazar, Alberto, 105
Salt Lake City, Utah, 51, 59
Salomon Bros., 238
San Francisco, California, 44, 68, 75, 178
San José, 49
Santa Barbara, 133
Saran Wrap, 149
Sarnoff, David, 105, 160
SBIC, 36, 40–41, 195, 203, 247, 250
Schoen, Dr. Leonard H., 104
S. C. Johnson & Sons, 39, 44
Schuman, Stanley, 79
Science Digest, 70
Scientific-Atlanta, 116
SDS, 124
Sears, 16
Securities & Exchange Commission, 9, 235
Security Pacific Capital, 35
    Pathfinder Venture Capital Co., 35
Selling, 2, 17
Sevin, L. J., 36
Sevin-Rosen Management Co., 36
Shearson/American Express, 238
Shewmaker, Bruce, 11
Shockley Transistor Corp., 152
Sikora, Robert, 163
Silicon Valley, 5, 49, 66, 73–77, 249, 250
Singer Co., The, 10
Singleton, Dr. Henry E., 109
Sloan, Allan, 27
Small Business Investment Co., 3, 36, 41,
    195
Smith, Fred, 99, 105, 159, 161, 173

Smith, Dr. Lyman, 135
Smith Laboratories, Inc., 134
Socal, 26
Solution awareness, 138
Soul of a New Machine, 177
Southeast, 34
Southwest, 34
Specialty Shop Venture Capital Fund, 14
Sports Illustrated Racquetball Clubs, Inc., 9
Stamford, Connecticut, 49
Standard Oil, 9
Stanford University, Department of
    Engineering, 39, 43, 73
    Davis, Tommy J., 39
    Mayfield Fund, 39, 43
Start-Up companies:
    demographic changes create, 130
    five risks of, 90
    measure market size for, 120
    value-added investor needs, 226
    well of S-curve, 224
Steinberg, Saul, 109
Stone, W. Clement, 159, 161, 162
STP corporation, 163
Structuring, 2, 17
Summary of terms and conditions,
    High-Tech Start-Up Corporation
    (HTSU), 206–216
Sunnyvale, California, 10, 45
SVP, 118
Syndicates:
    criteria for selecting, X
    formation, X
    lack of experience of some members, 31
    megafunds, relation to, 28
Syndicating, 2, 17
Systems Technology, 49
Swedish, 44
Sweepers for megafunds, 29

Tandem Computer Corp., 49
Tandy, 109, 141–142
Tandy, Charles , V., 109
Taub, Henry, 112
Technology factor, 101
Technology venture investors, 47
Telecomputing Corporation of America,
    174
Teledyne, 109, 124, 129
    "Water Pik", 129

Terman, Dean, 73
Terms and conditions:
    affirmative covenants, 203
    anti-dilution, 208
    attorneys fees, 215
    board of directors, 213
    conditions precedent, 208
    conversion price, 203
    co-sale, 205
    default, 204, 215
        remedies for, 216
    life insurance, 213
    negative covenants, 203
    piggyback rights, 210
    preferred stock, 205
    registration, 204
    representations and warranties, 203
    voting rights, 206
*Thomas Register of Manufacturers*, 170
TIE/communications, Inc, 49, 131, 174
Time, Inc., 9–10
    Bruce Shewmaker, 11
Track record, 32, 37, 41, 112
Troy, New York, 51
TVI, 48

U-Haul, 104
Underwriters, 239
U.S. banks, 8
United States Football League, (USFL), 124
U.S. postal service, 99
United Technologies Corp., 36
University of California, *43*
University of Chicago, *43*

Valuation:
    application of V = P x S x E, 197
    hockey stick method, 199, 201
    logarithmic scale, 200
    methods, 195
    target rates of return, 93
    term sheet, 202
*Venture*, 66, 70, 176, 201, 237, *238*, 239
Venture capital funds:
    abilities of partners, X
    compensation, VIII, 6–7
    corporate sponsored, 6, 36

    fees, 19
    formation of, 18, 249
    management team, VIII
    optimal size of, 18, 243
    regional, 29, 34–35
    raising $20 million fund, 31, 144
    special limited partners, 43
    specialty shop venture capital fund, 14
Venture capital investing:
    eight functions of, 2–4
    learning, 250
    patience, 248
    portfolio management, 241–248
    process, VIII, 249
    profession of, 35
Venture capitalists:
    active investor, VII
    aprenticeship requirements, 36
    complimentary partners, 249
    passive investors, IX
*Venture Capital Journal*, 33
Voluntary redemption privileges, 223
von Meister, Bill, 174
Vulcan Engineering, 6

Wall Street, 11, 16, 89
    Main Street, 16
Wang, Dr. Ansu, 104, 109, 163
Wang Laboratories, 104, 109, 163
Warburg, Pincus Capital Partners, 21
Warburg, Pincus & Co., 4, 21
*Washington Post, The*, 95
Wendy's, 225
Wexner, Leslie, 162
Wilson, Kemmons, 159, 162
World Football League, 124
Weight Watchers International, 99–100, 122
Welsh, Carson, Anderson, Stowe, *35*
    Advanced Technology Ventures, *35*
Wind Point Partners, 39
Wriston, Walter, 11

Xerography, 91
Xerox Corp., 91, 165

Yellow Pages, 138, 170